S.V. *parijñā' nupalambho'tra hānirakhyānamiṣyate /*
upalambhanimittā prāptiḥ sākṣātkriyāpi sā //

Eng. The above explained comprehension is to be known as non-perception (of the duality, i.e., the imaginary aspect), the rejection is to be known as non-manifestation (of the appearance i.e. the conditional aspect), the realization is that attainment of knowledge which may be regarded as direct apprehension.

gñi-ga-la-mi-dmigs-pas /
gñis-kyis rnam-par-rtogs-par-'gyur /
yoṅs-grub-de-yi-rnam-rtogs-phyir /
gñis-ni-med-par-rtogs-par-'gyor // 35

gñi-ga-la-ni (=ubhayam) mi-dmigs-pas (=anupalaṁbhena) / gñis-kyis-rnam-par (=dvayākāra) rtogs-par-' gyur (=vigachati) / yoṅs-grub (=niṣpanna) de-yi (=tasya) rnam-rtogs-phyir (=vigamā) / gñis-ni-med-par (=dvayābhāva) rtogs-par'gyur (=adhigamyate) //

Skt. ubhayamanupalambhena dvayākāro vigachati, tasya vigamā niṣpanne dvayābhāvo adhigamyate.

S.V. *ubhayamanupalambhena dvayākāro vigachati /*
vigamā tasya niṣpanne dvayābhavo' dhigamyate //

Eng. Through the non-perception of duality (i.e. imaginary aspect), the semblance of duality (i.e. the Relative aspect) vanishes; when it has passed away, the absolute i.e. the non-existence of duality is realized.

glaṅ-po-che-ri-mi-dmigs-daṅ /
de-yi-rnam-pa't-rnam-rtogs-ste /
śiṅ-dag-la-ni-dmigs-pa-ni /
dug-gcig-sgyu-ma-la-bshin-du // 36

glaṅ-po-che-ni (=hastin) mi-dmigs-daṅ (=anupalaṁbhaḥ ca) / de-yi-rnam-pai (=tadākṛteḥ) rnam-rtogs-ste (=vigama) /

śin-dag-la-ni (=kāṣṭha) dmigs-pa-ni (=upalambha) / dus-gcig (=yugapad) sgyur-ma-la-bshin-du (=māyāyam yathā) //

Skt. hastinaḥ anupalaṁbhaśca tadākṛteḥ vigamśca, kāṣtha (sya)
upalambhaśca māyāyām yathā yugapad.

S.V. *hastino' nupalaṁbhaśca vigamaśca tadākṛteḥ /*
upalambhas' ca kāṣṭhasya māyāyām yugapadyathā //

Eng. The non-perception of the elephant, the vanishing of the form of the elephant and the realization of the wooden elephant, happen simultaneously on the case of an illusion (of elephant).

gñen-po-blo-ni-sgyun-phyir-daṅ /
blo-yis-bdag-med-mthoṅ-ba'i-phyir /
ye-śes gsum-la-rjes' jug-phyir /
*'baṅ-pa-med-par-thar-pa-thob //*37

gñen-po (=pratipakśaḥ) blo-ni (=jñānam/dhī) sgyun-phyir-daṅ (=nivṛtya/vāraṇatvāt) / blo-yis (=jñānena/buddhyā) bdag-med (=nairātmya/vaiyarthya) mthoṅ-ba'i-phyir (=darśanatvāt) / ye-śes-gsum-la (=jñānatrayam) rjes-'jug-phyir (=anuvṛtteḥ) / 'baṅ-pa-med-par (=ayattnam) thar-pa (mokṣa/mukti) thob (=prāptiḥ) //

Skt. pratipakṣajñānam vāraṇatvād, nairātmya darśanatvād, jñānatra-yam anuvṛtteḥ mokṣa prāptiḥ ayattnatah //

S.V. *Viruddha dhīvāraṇatvād buddhyā vaiyarthadarśanāt/*
jñānatrayānuvṛtteśca mokṣāpattirayattnataḥ //

Eng. By restraining the opposite thought, seeing the vanity of things through the intellect and by following the three types of knowledge (*śruta, cintā* and *bhāvanā*), salvation is achieved without any effort.

sems-tsam la-ni-dmigs-pa-yis /
śes-bya'i-don-ni-mi-d' migs ñid /
śes-bya'i-don-la-dmigs med pas /
sems-ni-mi-dmigs ñid-dui-'gyur // 38

sems-tsam-la-ni (=cittamātra) dmig pa-yis (=upalambhena) / śes-bya'i-don-ni (=jñeyārtha) mi-dmigs-ñid (=anupalambhatā) / śes-bya'i-don-la (=jñeyārtha) dmigs-med-pas (=anupalambhena) / sems-ni (=cittam) mi-dmigs-ñid-du (=anupalambhatā)'gyur (=syāt) //

Skt. Cittamatra upalambhena jñeyārthānupalambhatā, jñeyarthānupalam-bhena cittam anupalambhatā syāt //

S.V. *cittamātropalambhena jñeyārthānupalambhatā / jñeyarthānupalambhena syaccittānupalambhatā* //

Eng. Through the attainment of the condition of the pure-consciousness, there is the non-preception of the perceivable; and though the non-perception of the perceivable there is the non-acquisition of the mind (citta).

gñi-ga-la-ni-mi-dmigs-pas /
chos-kyi-dbyiṅs-la-dmigs-pa-ñid /
chos-kyi-dbyins-la-dmigs pa-yis /
'byor pa ñid la-dmigs-par-'gyur //39

gñi-ga-la-ni (=ubhayam) mi-dmigs-pas (=anupalam-bhena)/ chos-kyi-dbyiṅs-la (=dharmadhātu) dmigs-pa-ñid (=upalambhatā) / chos-kyi-dbyiṅs-la (=dharmadhātu) dmigs-pa-yis (=upalambhena) / byor-pa-ṅid-la (=vibhutra) drigs-pa (=upalambhatā)'gyur (=syāt) //

Skt. ubhayam anupalambhena dharmadhātu upalambhatā, dharmadhātu upalambhena vibhutva (sya) upalambhatā syāt //

S.V. *ubhayamanupalambhena dharmadhātūpalambhatā / dharmadhātūpalambhena syādvibhutvopalambhatā //*

Eng. Through the non-perception of these two, there arises the realization of the essence of reality (*dharmadhātu*) and through the realization of the essence of reality, there occurs the acquisition of 'the supernatural power of destroying ignorance and attaining prosperity, (*vibhutva*).

> *'byor-pa-ñid-ni-thob-'gyur-na /*
> *raṅ-daṅ-bshan-gyi-don-'jvg-phyir /*
> *sku-gsum-bdag-ñid-byaṅ-chub-ni /*
> *bla-med-blo-daṅ-ldan-pas-thob-ces-bya'o* //40

'byor-pa-ñid-ni (=vibhutva) thob'gyur-na (=upalabdha)/ raṅ-daṅ-gshan-gyi-don (=sva-parārtha) jug-phyir (=parveśataṭḥ) / sku-gsuṃ-bdag-ñid (=kāyatrayātmika) byaṅ-chub-ni (=bodhi) / bla-med (=anuttara) blo-daṅ-ldan-pas (=dhṛmatyā) thob-ces-bya'o (=prāpnoti) //

Skt. vibhutva upalabdha (śca) svaparārtha-prāveśataḥ, kāyatrayāt-mikā (m) anuttarā-bodhia(m) dhrmatyā prāptiḥ (bhavati) /

S.V. *upalabdhavibhutvaśea svaparārthapraveśataḥ / prāpnoti anuttarām bodhim dhīmān kāyatrayātmikām/*

Eng. After obtaining *vibhutva* and having a clear knowledge about oneself and others, a wise person realizes that supreme wisdom (*bodhi*) which is embodied with three essential forms (*svabhāvika*, *sāmbhogika* and *nairmāṇika*).

mtshan-ñid-gsum-la-'jug-pa / slob-dpon-chen-po 'phags-pa-klu-sgrub-kyi-shal-mṅa-nas-mdsad-pa-rdsogs-so //

mtshan-ñid-gsum-la'jug-pa (=lakṣaṇa-traya-praveśaḥ) slob-dponchen-po (=māhāguru), phags-pa (=ārya) klugrubkyi-shal-mna-nas (=nāgāarjunasya mukhāt) mdsad-palrdsogs-so (=kṛtiḥ sampuraṇā)

Skt. Mahāguru ārya Nāgārjunasya (iyam) kṛitḥ sampurṇā/

Eng. This work of Ārya Nagarjuna ends (here).

kha-che'-i-paṇḍita-dge-sloṅ-zla-ba-grags-pas-bsgyur-ba'o //

kha-che'i-paṇḍita (=kashmira (deśasya paṅḍita) dhe-slon (=bhikṣu) zla-ba-grajs-pas (=candrakirttṭinā) bsgyur-ba'o (=anuditaḥ) /

Skt. kāshmirades'asya paṇḍita-bhiksu Candrakīrttinā anuditah //

Eng. This work has been translated by the Bhikshu Cnandrakirtti, hailed from Kashmir.

Contributors

Biswanath Banerjee : Professor Biswanath Banerjee is an eminent scholar on Sanskrit and Pali. He has been awarded by the President of India for his outstanding contributions in the field of Indological studies in general and Sanskrit language and literature in particular.

Arpita Chatterjee : Dr. Arpita Chatterjee is an emerging young scholar. Presently she is working on a project sponsored by the Deptt. of Culture, Ministry of HRD, Govt of India being attached to the Deptt. of Indo-Tibetan Studies, Visva Bharati.

Suniti Kumar Pathak : Prof. Suniti Kumar Pathak is a well known Tibetologist in India. After his retirement from Visva-Bharati, Prof. Pathak worked as a Research Professor in the Asiatic Society, Calcutta for some years.

Pranabananda Jash: Professor Pranabananda Jash is a renowned scholar in Ancient Indian History and Culture. He teaches Buddhist religion at Visva-Bharati since last 30 years. He is credited with a good number of articles and books. Presently he is the Dean of the Faculty of Humanities and Social Sciences, Visva-Bharati, Santiniketan.

Lama Chimpa: Professor Lama Chimpa, Mongolian by birth, completed his studies on Tibetan language and literature and on Buddhist Philosophy from the famous monastic University of Drepung at Tibet. He was a senior faculty of the Deptt. of Indo-Tibetan Studies of Visva-Bharati. He is living at Kalimpong after his final retirement.

Kalpika Mukherjee: Dr. Kalpika Mukherjee is the Professor of Sanskrit at Visva-Bharati. She has done wonderful work on Dandin with her profound knowledge of Sanskrit and Tibetan.

Dechen D. Dorjee: Dr. Dechen D. Dorjee has retired from the post of Principal in "Sheda, Gangtok". Presently Dr. Dorjee is working at Visva-Bharati as a Visiting Professor. Dr. Dorjee is a traditional Tibetan scholar with profound knowledge in Buddhist Philosophy.

Anandamayee Ghosh: Smt. Anandamayee Ghosh has completed her studies on Chinese and Tibetan from Visva-Bharati. She is a good scholar having a good number of research papers to her credit.

Malavika Bandyopadhyay: Dr. Malavika Bandyopadhyaya combines her knowledge of Sanskrit and Tibetan. She is also credited with many research papers.

Jampel Kalden: Sri Jampel Kalden teaches Tibetan at Kalimpong for last 25 years.

Bela Bhattacharya: Dr. Bela Bhattacharya is a renowned scholar on Pali and Buddhism. Presently Dr. Bhattacharya is working in the University of Calcutta as the head of the Pali Department.

Chittaranjan Patra: Dr. Chittaranjan Patra, a scholar on Pali and Buddhism, is presently working at the Indian Museum, Calcutta.

Barbara Gerke: Barbara Gerke, born in Germany, first came to India in 1988, with interest in Ayurveda and went on subsequently to Dharamsala and studied the Tibetan language and Tibetan medicine, first with D Barry Clark, later with

Dr. Lama Trogawa Rinpoche at the Chakpori Medical Institute in Darjeeling. She was associated with the Germany Society for Tibetan Medicine as one of its founder members till 1993 during which time she accompanied Trogawa Rinpoche twice, assisting with consultations and lectures during his European tours. Thereafter she left the Society and pursued her studies on Tibetan at Visva-Bharati and North Bengal University from where she obtained a Diploma and Degree in Tibetan Language and Literature. Since 1995 she has been mainly living in Kalimpong where she founded the International Trust for Traditional Medicine. Presently she is co-ordinating ITTM research projects through the International Research Circles (IRC) of ITTM, and pursuing her own research on Tibetan Medicine. She is also editor of the bi-annual periodical on Indo-Tibetan medicine, *Ayur Vijnana*, published by ITTM, Kalimpong.

Heramba Chatterjee Shastri : Prof. Heramba Chatterjee was an eminent scholar on Sanskrit and Pali. He was the Principal of Government Sanskrit College, Calcutta, Prof. Shastri passed away from this world this year.

Narendra Kumar Dash: Dr. Dash teaches Tibetan Language and Literature at Visva-Bharti. He is also a sound scholar of Sanskrit and Prakrit languages.

Biplab Kumar Mondal: Sri Biplab Kumar Mondal is presently working on Indo-Tibetan relations for his P.hd Degree at Visva-Bharti.

Prakriti Chakraborty: Smt. Prakriti Chakraborty is a Scholar on Chinese and Tibetan. She is attached to the Dept. of Indo-Tibetan Studies at Visva-Bharti.

Lalita Chakraborty: Dr. Lalita Chakraborty teaches Sanskrit at M.U.C. Women's College, Burdwan. She is also a sound scholar of Tibetan language. Presently she is working on the *Dharmadharmata Vibhaṅga-kārikā*.

Index

Second World War
AS CATALYST FOR
Social Changes in India

S.B. SINGH

PRAGATI PUBLICATIONS
DELHI

First Published 1998

ISBN 81-7307-053-9

Published by Vinod Kapoor for Pragati Publications
9926 Library Road, Azad Market, Delhi 110 006

Lasertypeset and Printed by Vikas Print Communication Services,
New Delhi 110 026

On the fiftieth year of India's independence
this book is dedicated to sacred memories of those
who sacrificed their lives for freedom
of the country

Contents

Preface

The Second World War was really global in its scope and significance. It affected social conditions all over the world. It caused unprecedented scientific and technological innovations which opened possibilities for enormous social changes all over the world.

Realising its historical importance, an International Committee with Prof. Henri Michael as president was set up in Paris in May 1967 to promote historical research on various aspects of the Second World War. India was represented at the conference. The ICHR encouraged research on impact of the Second World War on India's economy, society, polity and international relations. Consequently, some good works have come out on the subject. My first research project entitled "Impact of the Second World War on Indian Government and Administration" was sponsored by the ICHR in 1984–85. It resulted in publication of the book entitled "Imperial Retreat" in 1992. Subsequently, my second research project "Second World War as catalyst for social changes in India" was also sponsored by ICHR. It traces in broad outlines the main trends of social changes in India as a consequence of the War. It has particularly spotlighted on changes in tribal society in North-East India. The War uprooted them from their traditional moorings and gave birth to powerful political and ethnic ambition which later on developed into insurgency. From bows and arrows the tribals in North-East India took to sophisticated modern fire-arms. The War affected agriculture, industry, transport and communications, science and technology and public health services enormously.

I am extremely thankful to ICHR for sponsoring my two research projects concerning India and the Second World War. I am also indebted to the Nehru Memorial Museum and Library and the Gokhale Institute of Politics and Economics, Pune, for providing facilities for research.

The main credit for completion of my two research projects goes to my daughter Dr (Mrs) Abha Singh and her husband Shri Bhagawan Singh for providing me with warm and affectionate hospitality in Delhi during the period of my research. I am sincerely indebted to Mrs Malti Singh and Mr R.P. Singh for lavish hospitality at Kakrapar (Surat) where I finally drafted this project. Similarly, I am also grateful to Dr (Mrs) Kanti Singh and Mrs Krishna Bagachi for affectionate hospitality at Bodh-Gaya and Calcutta respectively. Moreover, I am thankful to Prof. R.S. Sharma for making some valuable suggestions. Principal K.K. Gupta of Anumala (Surat) was kind enough to go through the manuscript very carefully. I also owe my sincere gratitude to Prof. Girish Mishra and Shri Vinod Kapoor for taking interest in its publication.

D-31, College Lane
New Delhi-110001

S.B. SINGH

Abbreviations

ACTE	All India Council for Technical Education
BCW	Bombay Chronical Weekly
CABE	Central Advisory Board of Education
CBSE	Central Board of Secondary Education
CLA	Central Legislative Assembly
CS	Council of State
CSIR	Council of Scientific and Industrial Research
CTPB	Central Technical Power Board
HMG	His Majesty's Government
IAF	Indian Air Force
IASSI	Indian Association for Social Science Institutions
ICAR	Indian Council of Agricultural Research
ICHR	Indian Council of Historical Research
ICO	Indian Commissioned Officer
IPTA	Indian Peoples Theatre Association
IVRI	Indian Veterinary Research Institute
KCO	King Commissioned Officer
MIT	Massachusetts Institute of Technology
NISTADA	National Institute of Science and Technology and Development Studies
NPC	National Planning Committee
OWI	Overseas War Intelligence
PPH	Peoples Publishing House
Progs	Proceedings
RAF	Royal Air Force
RTC	Round Table Conference
TVA	Tennessee Valley Authority
WAC(I)	Women Auxiliary Corps (India)

CHAPTER 1

The Army and the Social Changes in India

From the point of view of social mobility the Second World War proved a blessing in disguise. It had broken some of the old social barriers and prejudices and accelerated the pace of modernity in India. To meet the challenges of the war the British took up the modernization programme of the Indian army on a war footing. They started recruitment of soldiers vigorously and the number of Indian soldiers increased from nearly two lakhs to more than twenty lakhs during the war. Never before in history had such a huge expansion of the army taken place in India. To meet the situation a new recruitment policy had to be adopted. Since 1892 the British had divided the Indian population into martial and non-martial people and preferred the martial people for recruitment in the army. In fact the composition of the British Indian army kept on changing with the variation in the recruitment basis and flexibility of the policy, keeping in mind only the loyalty of the army to the crown. With the adoption of the concept of martial races the principle of 'pick and choose' from caste and classes was introduced in recruiting ideology. Accordingly, many classes were excluded from recruitment in the army. Madrasis, Bengalis and many classes of Brahmins, Ahirs, Gujars, Mahars and Hindustani Muslims were denied entry into army. They became victims of the theory of martial races. Thus, the British encouraged certain caste groups to join the army while the other caste groups were declared unfit for recruitment. At the beginning of the British rule in India members of the depressed classes were recruited in the British Indian army. The old Bombay army almost entirely consisted of Mahars, Chamars and others of equally humble origin.[1] They had to their credit many deeds of unchallengeable valour and courage. But after the mutiny the low castes like Mahars, Chamars and others were altogether debarred from recruitment in the army. The Mahars had helped the British to give a death blow to the Maratha power in Western India in the famous battle of Koregaon near Poona in 1818. There still stands a monument in the memory of the Mahar soldier who died fighting for the British.[2] Dr B.R. Ambedkar accused the British of ingratitude towards the Mahars who had been denied recruitment to the army since 1892.[3] This had been done only to please the Mahrattas and the Brahmins who had joined the British Indian army later on and were not willing to mix with Mahars and other depressed classes or to serve under them.[4] The Mahars regarded the dropping of their recruitment in the army as loss of their status in the society. In 1910 they represented to the British government against this and even offered to serve in segregated regiments or in Muslim regiments if the high caste Hindus objected to their presence in the army. They offered to serve in any capacity in the military – even as menial servants or as mule drivers.[5] Thus, before 1939 the recruitment in the British Indian army was confined to martial races of Bombay and the Punjab provinces only. The British turned more and more to the higher strata of Indian society for recruitment of soldiers. Even in the Punjab the Balmikis and the Chamars and the many other lower castes were not recruited in the army before 1941. If they were converted as Mazhabi Sikhs, they were recruited in the army but not as Balmikis and Chamars. Thus, the Government indirectly helped conversion of the depressed classes to Sikhism.

Sir Philip Chetwode, the Ex C-in-C of the Indian army exploded the myth of the theory of martial races. He took pains to explain that the recruitment of a large proportion of Indian army from the Punjab did not mean that the people of the Indian peninsula were without martial qualities. He recalled that it was with the help of soldiers of South India that the British had to fight for a footing in India and it was among them that the hero of Waterloo, Col. Arthur Wellesley, first learnt his lesson in military strategy.[6] The martial races theory was the handiwork of vested interests, bogus caste prejudices and parochial minded British officers and VCOs who were trying to maintain a narrow class composition of the British Indian army. It was only when the Axis powers began their march towards India that the government came to senses and decided to give up the theory of martial races. Public opinion too favoured a new recruitment policy of soldiers which would include all regions and classes fit for military services. Even the governors of Madras and Bengal asked for resumption of recruitment of soldiers in their provinces. The Bengal Legislative Assembly too passed a resolution to this end.[7] Dr B.R. Ambedkar was also pleading for resumption of recruitment of Mahar and other depressed classes in the armed forces. Dr G.V. Desmukh too demanded resumption of recruitment of Maharastrian Brahmins in the army. Ultimately, public opinion and the need for expansion in recruitment of soldiers forced the government to change the policy and distinction between the martial and non-martial races was done away with. General Auchnileck, the C-in-C widely extended the class composition of the Indian army. The depressed classes were recruited in the army and five separate regiments were formed for them. Even the tribals of north-east India were recruited in the Assam rifles and Assam regiments. This was really a new experience for them. The war affected their outlook of life and broadened it. In place of bow and arrow now they learnt to use modern weapons effectively. The Assam regiment represented the composite culture of North-Eastern India because it consisted of Lushais, Nagas, Garos, Kukis, Assamese and men of other tribes. To their credit and achievement, almost all of the regiments had learnt how to read and write.[8] The war had shown that all men could become martial under training and discipline. Mechanization of the army had put a premium on men with brain over men with mere brawn.

Military service plays an important role in the improvement of the army personnel. It carries with it social prestige and gives them an important place in the society. The army encourages socialization among its members to generate a sense of national unity. In the process of socialization great emphasis is laid on discipline in all activities. Education of the army personnel is a continuous process. Drill, physical training and sports go a long way to develop a healthy disciplined personality among members of the army community. Literacy is a must for them. Both officers and troops have to keep on improving their standard of knowledge throughout their service career. This makes for a direct impact on the outlook of their families. Every soldier virtually becomes a teacher. His outlook is completely changed. Rigorous military training imparts soldierly qualities as well as infuses the qualities of citizenship and patriotism and makes him a responsible and useful member of the society. He develops the qualities of brotherhood, discipline and loyalty in the army and after demobilization he displays the same qualities in civilian jobs. The army may be called the most modernized group with greater sense of integration, with a non-parochial non-sectarian outlook. The army as an organization has to be modern as far as the professional aspect is concerned. As a matter of fact modernization of defence forces cannot be achieved piecemeal. It has to be a continuous process. Modernization in the army is necessarily accompanied by modernization in the social affairs. The two are interlinked and cannot be separated.[9]

By 1939 war had become a highly technical business and the soldier had to be able to handle complicated scientific equipment. Hence, he had to have some education. The army deliberately set about educating him. Sooner or later he was bound to be acquainted with the newspapers and to open his mind to a variety of influences.[10] Fundamentally, the soldier was the same stout-hearted peasant as he was forty years ago, but the war had changed and he had also changed with it. On the whole he was adapting himself with an astonishing speed to mechanization, driving, maintenance and all other elaborate systems of inter-communications that modern war required. The Second World War was a highly mechanized war and the Indian soldier had to move with time. The War had broadened his mind on two lines. Firstly, the war was a great leveller. All social distinctions were swept away. In the hours of greatest peril privileged and unprivileged both stood on the same plane. A sense of unity prevailed all over the country. The war brought the best out of him. Secondly, the war created in an Indian soldier a sense of toleration and sympathy with people whose religious beliefs were different from his own. Indian soldiers went abroad and saw how women and children were treated. If they remembered even a small fraction of what they saw on their foreign travels, it was to be of tremendous help in building a new India.[11]

In 1942 the recruitment of soldiers in India was in the following order:

Punjab	–	50%
UP	–	15%
Madras	–	10%
Bombay	–	10%
NWFP	–	5%
Bengal	–	2%
CP	–	between 1 and 2%
Assam, Bihar and Orissa	–	less than 1%[12]

Roughly, the composition of the Indian army during the War caste-wise was Hindu 41 per cent, Muslim 35 per cent, Sikh 10 per cent, Gurkha 8½ per cent, and others 5½ per cent. The Punjab supplied roughly 50 per cent of the whole.[13]

During the early period of the British rule in India, Indian units of the army were generally commanded by Indian officers. But the situation changed soon after the revolt of 1857. The number of native officers was reduced drastically. Soon it became impossible for a native to become an officer. Till the end of the First World War the officer cadre of the British Indian army was almost the monopoly of the British people. Pressure from the British and Indian public opinion forced the government to start Indianization of the officer-cadre of the army in 1918. It was decided that 10 seats in Sandhurst would be reserved for the training of Indians as officers every year. They were to be selected through an entrance examination. Between 1918 and 1926, 83 Indian boys passed the Sandhurst entrance examination. Of these, 35 were from Punjab, 12 from Bombay, 9 each from UP and Bengal, 5 from NWFP, 6 each from Rajputana and Hyderabad, 2 each from Burma and Coorg and one each from Bihar, Assam and Central Indian Agency.[14] Collectively, they were most reliable, apolitical, aristocratic and conservative group of Indian officers. They were commissioned in the army as KCOs. Most of them had an aptitude for sports and a few were strong academically. They had joined the army for prestige or honour and came from an aristocratic background. As KCOs they had a unique status. They could command even British units of the army. They tried to live up to the status of their rank.

In 1920s articulate nationalist public opinion was quite dissatisfied with the pace of Indianization in the Indian army. Ultimately, a committee was appointed to enquire into the matter. It recommended the setting up of a military academy of Sandhurst type in India. This led to the establishment of the Indian Military Academy at Dehradun in 1932. This academy turned out Indian military officers known as ICO. They were mostly the sons of elite urban classes including many Bengalis, Madrasis and non-Kshatriya castes. They were no less heroic in the field than the officers from the martial or Punjabi background. They held the less prestigious position than the KCO. By 1939 there had been only 396 Indians in a total of 4429 army officers in India. As the war progressed, the expansion of the army increased ten-fold. Requirements of officers in the army increased in almost the same proportion. To meet the situation emergency commissioned officers (ECO) were recruited both in Britain and India. More than one thousand ex-students of the Aligarh Muslim University were recruited as officers in the Indian armed forces on an emergency basis.[15] Perhaps this was the only university in India which contributed so much to the official cadre of Indian army. Previously there was not much social contact between the Indian and British army officers. But the war did help to end the isolation of the Indian officers with the arrival of a large number of young British officials who did not share the old Anglo-Indian prejudices.[16] Consequently mixing between the two increased. Many British officers who got war-time emergency commission came from a variety of social backgrounds. As meritocratic criteria were uppermost in the war office selection boards in the UK, class or education did not always count for everything and there was also a new feeling in the British armed forces that the officer corps was no longer a snobbish elite. These young British officers of the Indian army came with a new outlook. They were quite indifferent to the glorious heritage of the Raj. Many of them were friendly to the idea that India should be independent. They were a different breed from pre-1939 type. Instead of spending an evening in the club, they would very often try to meet the officers on equal terms to discover as much as they could about the customs, languages and culture of the Indian people. This new outlook bred a new way of thinking and a new belief that British should get out of India once the War was over. They argued that if they were fighting for the rights of the nations to be free, then the same privilege should be accorded to India. As a matter of fact the war time emergency officers brought a new breath of fresh air in army messes where politics had once been taboo. Previously, the Indian officers of the army lived in a social ghetto. The British officers loved their men in a way that they could not love British troops but they had no love for Indian society or Indians in general. But the war brought about a great change. Thousands of young Englishmen both soldiers and officers who came to India during the war did not care a damn what they were. They were friendly and mingled with the Indian society if they could.[17] By the end of the war there were 8390 Indians in a total of 42930 officers in the Indian army. The ratio of British officers to Indian officers decreased from 10.1:1 to 4.4:1.[18] It was really a great gain to India from the war. Soon they proved to be a valuable asset to the country.

During the war the recruitment of soldiers in the Indian army was extremely uneven. Over a large tract of the country there was hardly a man in service. At the same time there were a number of comparatively small areas which had been practically stripped of their man power and these were bound to be severely affected by demobilization after the war. All these men had become accustomed to a far higher standard of living than they had previously enjoyed. They had acquired a considerable amount of education as well as skill in use of modern weapons and modern machinery. Many of them had been abroad and their outlook had been broadened. Moreover, they had learnt to take pride in themselves and had been encouraged to hope for better things after demobilization. Their demands on life were likely to be much higher than before. Unless they were satisfied with the condition to which they could return, they were likely to form a formidable haven of discontent instead of becoming a stable and progressive element of the community. They were likely to usher in a new wave of social change in the countryside. They could easily assume leadership in the reconstruction of the country.

The Punjab contributed well over a third of the entire army. By the end of the war its contribution amounted to more than 6 lakh men. A high proportion of them had been drawn from the northern districts which were generally poor and underdeveloped. A majority of them were agriculturists, probably 80 per cent, though not more than 30 to 40 per cent owned land. The remainder were landless tenants and labourers or village artisians of various kinds with rural background. Many of them had learnt some trades, while in the army. Of them, 64,000 had been enlisted as motor transport drivers and 14,000 as fitters.[19] These skills proved assets to them when the country witnessed transport revolution after the war.

The NWF province had been heavily recruited from considering its areas and population and had over 70,000 men in the army. 80 per cent of them had an agricultural background and on demobilization they were to return to village life as farmers, tenants, labourers and menials. Of these over 8,000 had been enlisted as motor transport drivers and a large number had acquired proficiency in a variety of mechanical trades. The UP contributed over 2 lakh men but no district had been as heavily recruited as from Garhwal and Kumaon. The districts of the UP were very large with populations of the size of 2 to 4 millions and a few of them were to absorb more than 3000 to 4000 men after demobilization. In Garhwal and Kumaon the problem of re-settlement was comparable to that of the northern districts of Punjab. The vast majority of soldiers from the UP came from an agricultural background.

Bengal had nearly 1,00,000 men in the army. One-third of them were technical men. A high proportion of them had come from towns rather than from villages. Bengal had supplied a large proportion of technical needs of the army. A considerable number of them were serving with Royal Indian Navy as officers and ratings. In the RIN 14 per cent of the ratings were Bengalis. A large number of Bengali merchant seamen, chiefly from East Bengal had been serving in the HMI ships since the outbreak of the war. Bengali ratings recruited in the normal way were well represented in the communication branch. They had practically served in every area of operations to which HMI ships had been ordered. A considerable number of them were serving in the IAF as pilots, mechanics and radio-technicians. Bengal could well be proud of pioneers of the calibre of Wing Commander S. Mukherjee and Squadron Leader Hem Choudhari who were among the first officers from Bengal to be commissioned in the IAF. Wing Commander S. Mukherjee was the first Indian to command a station at Kohat in NWFP and ultimately, he became the first Indian Chief of the IAF. In the squadrons that operated in Burma were some Bengali pilots who acquitted themselves with great credit including Wing Commander Majumdar who was the first officer in the IAF to win the coveted DFC.[20] Moreover, there were roughly 25,000 Bengalis in the Auxiliary Pioneers Corps working on roads, building aerodromes and loading and unloading supplies at wharves and road sidings; a fair number of them had been recruited to the Indian coastal artillery in which they formed a complete battery. Large proportion of them were however in those branches of service where skilled technicians were required. Some Bengalis were also recruited as ECOs in the army, where they acquitted themselves with credit.

Madras supplied more men to the army than any other province except the Punjab – over 2,00,000. A majority of them came from villages and belonged to the working classes. Bombay had nearly 1,00,000 men serving in the army but the Mahratta districts were heavily recruited from more or less homogeneous population such as farmers, agricultural tenants and labourers. Bombay had contributed fewer technical troops and tradesmen than other provinces and also fewer menials. The Bombay government had promised that the recruiting areas would be provided with all round development in the post-War period.[21]

Orissa, Assam, Bihar and CP presented almost the same picture. Recruitment to the army was not heavy in these provinces. Most of the recruited were in ancillary units and trades of all kinds. Generally speaking most of the recruits came from villages rather than from towns. Only a small proportion owned land. In the Punjab, UP and NWF Provinces the number of land owners was considerable but not elsewhere. The bulk of the army came from all over India, but a few districts were heavily recruited. A considerable number of recruits came from artisan and working classes.[22] Moreover, the Central Labour Department had trained 80,000 artisans as technicians. Most of them were absorbed in the army. On demobilization they proved a valuable asset to the society.

A great deal of vocational training was carried out within the various battalions through lectures regularly on matters connected with health, hygiene, sanitation, better seeds, manure pits and animal husbandry. There were 110 army training centres throughout British India and a great many of them contained a number of agricultural demonstration plots. Every army training centre had an institute which imparted education to the soldier while he was still in the army. These demonstration farms served as depots for seeds. They could also be extended to grow vegetable seeds which could be distributed through soldier boards to demobilized soldiers in the villages. These training centres had also dairy farming and poultry farms and kept good herds of cattle which could be distributed among demobilized soldiers on easy terms.[23] In order to give sepoys knowledge of better farming methods and improved system of crop husbandry, arrangements were made to take batches of them around the central farms, dairy and implement sheds and workshops of the agricultural college, Coimbatore. A course of lectures on agricultural topics was also arranged for the troops stationed nearby. Special schemes of supply of vegetables to army were started in Madras, Chingleput, Trichinopoly and Coimbatore districts in addition to those already working in Nilgiri hills, Salem, Chittoor and Vizagapatam districts.

Dr Sam Higginbothom, Principal of the Naini Agricultural

Institute, offered to train army men in agricultural science. He took in thirty or forty NCOs of various regiments and gave them a fairely long training so that they could go back and teach agriculture to sepoys in their own regiments, just as they taught them to use a brengun and other weapons of war. Another centre was at Government Agriculture College, Cawnpore, where similar work was being done. The work of agricultural education was being done in regiments and units in various cantonments which were raising large quantities of chickens, rabbits and other foodstuffs to supplement the army diet. This became useful to the soldiers and served them well on demobilization. Some of the soldiers were also trained in cottage industries. Some were taken to see the rural development work being done in the villages of UP. A good many soldiers went to spend two or three weeks in such villages so that they could see what could be done. Endeavours were also being made to provide training at other agricultural institutes where soldiers could get further training particularly in mechanized agriculture.[24]

About one and a half million men from the army were to be rehabilitated in civilian life on demobilization in 1945. It was really a very tough job from social and economic point of view. About half a million wanted to return to land, a quarter of a million were to be absorbed in technical jobs, a quarter million wanted higher administrative jobs or clerical employment and bulk of the remainder requiring assistance were unskilled. A large number of men who had been trained for various trades in services were skilled technicians, many of whom desired employment of a similar nature in civic life.[25] A considerable number of men had been trained in the army as motor transport drivers. They wanted their expertise to be utilized by the society. There was also the problem of demobilized labour force which had been sent to various parts of India to help in building aerodromes and other projects of the kind. After the war they also needed assistance for employment. About 40,000 of the men had been disabled during the war. To rehabilitate them the responsibility was shared both by the war department and the labour department of the Central Government. To help them the government constituted a post-war-reconstruction fund which amounted to about 9,750,000 pounds at the end of the war.[26]

As a matter of fact there had been a complete metamorphosis of Indian soldiers during the war. From agriculturists they had become technicians. They were taught not only to handle the most modern mechanical weapons of war but also to maintain them. They had learnt to use mechanical weapons of all types. As this was a highly mechanized war, they had to be acquainted with different types of machines. Their whole outlook in life had changed. They began to use note-books and writing pads because they were now better educated. Imitating the Europeans they began to buy shaving soaps and razor blades to shave. They began to demand modern brand of hair cream instead of perfumed coconut hair oil. They had become time-conscious as never before and now everyone wanted to have a watch. All these changes were to continue as part of their life even before demobilization. They had now become conscious of their changed status in the society. They were sure now to become an agency for social change in the society.

The arrival of the British conscript army in India added a new dimension to the British social history. Previously, local contacts of the British troops had been frowned upon. But during this war they were encouraged to learn as much as possible about the countries in which they were stationed. Whenever military duties permitted they were allowed to identify themselves with local enterprises which introduced them to civilian population. The effects of such contacts with British soldiers in many cases were most marked and beneficial. It had its effect on local population too. In the middle east both British and Indian troops had built up a lasting edifice of goodwill for Great Britain which diplomats, traders and financiers had failed to build in the past.[27] The imperial gulf between ruler and ruled could not be bridged by generations of officers and commanders whose roots were in the system that was rapidly passing away. Such Europeans in India were not capable of understanding the new and revolutionary psychology prevailing both in India and Great Britain. They were not even in rapport with the Indian intelligentsia and in some cases they were even more out of touch with current British thought. They did not realize that the British conscript army during the war was perhaps as representative of British opinion as the House of Commons or any of the British institutions.[28] Britain's first national citizen army was a powerful accumulator of the forces of change. In the British army in those days the social revolution and the scientific and technological revolution formed the two most important themes of discussion. Even *The Times* considered it a duty to prepare the nation for the social change after the War.[29] Beveridge was able to capture and reflect, almost perfectly the spirit of the time. The Report was a landmark in the advance of British democracy and a striking evidence of the stimulating power of War. The radicalism of the home front and of the armed forces found a common cause. The old garments no longer fitted. A new one was being designed. Even Louis Fischer told Mahatma Gandhi in June 1942 that a vast, popular ferment was going on in England. People were resolved not to be ruled after the War by the sort of people who ruled them before and brought on the War. There was much genuine goodwill towards India in England.[30] Even Pt Nehru viewed the Second World War obviously only as part of a great revolution taking place throughout the world.[31] So the English people also hated the old order and a strong wave of egalitarianism was sweeping the country during the War. Hence, it was not surprising that a great many British soldiers who came to India were sympathetic to Indian aspirations. The Indians wanted a new India and the British soldiers too wanted a better Britain. Consequently, there was a common ground for friendship.

When the British army arrived in Bengal during the War, there was an extraordinary transformation in public opinion. It could be called the conquest of Bengal. The behaviour and thoroughness of British troops had charmed the people of Bengal. Largely through the zeal and efforts of Mrs Milford, the East and West fraternity club was organized in India. It was a meeting place for those interested in exchange of ideas and cultures. At first meetings were arranged in private houses. But later on, the gathering was shifted to a local club. To the visitors from abroad the fraternity club had much to offer. Informal talks were arranged on many aspects of life. Concerts and exhibition of art were held. Discussion on current and international interests were organized. Such fraternity clubs were started in different parts of India. It became an all-India movement.[32] It went a long way in establishing cordial relations between British troops and Indians. Indian ladies proved themselves lively and kindly hostesses.

The arrival of American troops in India added a new dimension to the Indo-American social relations. The first thing notable about them was their informality which made them so unlike the British. As individuals, they were friendly and informal, anxious to start conversations and eager to be invited to Indian homes. They established a rapport with the local population wherever they went. They made the Chowringhee of Calcutta a more colourful place than it used to be. Their informal behaviour was an eye-opener to the people who began to love them. There was no imperial hangover in their behaviour. Rickshawalla's loved them because they were paid liberally. Hotel waiters and servants loved them and so did the Indian families who received them. When visiting a family home they made friends with children and treated the older people like their own parents back home.[33] They were quite shocked at what they saw in India. They did not conceal their opinion that the British had done their job in India very badly. They even criticized them openly for poverty, illiteracy, poor communications and general inefficiency. American officers and soldiers moved about similarly dressed and were indistinguishable in language and demeanour, while British officers and men patently belonged to different worlds. The British generally disapproved of American opinions and thought them brash and ignorant. Generosity of the Americans caused favourable reaction among the people. They did not understand the value of rupee and generally paid more than what was due. Coins, less than a rupee, they usually gave away as they did not count part of a cent. In Calcutta the Anglo-Indian girls had a wonderful time with the Americans. They preferred Americans to the British who had more money and better goods in their canteens. Moreover, the Americans were genuinely warm and generous and displayed no sign of embarrassment when taking them out. On the other hand the British officers did not like to be seen in public with Anglo-Indian girls. The girls sensed this. But they were quite at home with the Americans who were very open and cordial.[34] Some of the Anglo-Indian girls got emotionally involved with American soldiers but the authorities did not allow them to get married. They came partly from European stock, always spoke English and dressed in Western clothes, which made for ready familiarity. Yet their relationship seemed to remain generally at the simple level of having a good time. They were used to this from the British with whom affairs had seldom matured. This was in contrast to the American attitude in other theatres of the War. In 1945–46 at least one lakh British girls married ex-servicemen from the USA and Canada.[35] Dr Margaret Mead, the sociologist, was sent to England by the OWI to clear up a cultural misunderstanding about the American idea of a date.[36]

The American officers seemed very diffrent from their British counterparts. They gave the impression that military life to them was more of an adventure and an outlet for an excess of spirit than a deadly serious profession.[37] Moreover, the American military police was found to be very cooperative in doing justice than the Indian civil courts. They saw to it too that punishment fitted the crime. They got on quite well with the Indian civil administration. They took care to see that the civil population was not unnecessarily harassed by the American forces.[38] They were so humane and warm. It was a new experience for the Indian people.

Another factor in changing Indian attitude was the presence of American Airmen of the 10th US Airforce on the Burma front. Whenever the RAF or IAF lads came into contact with them, they were astonished at the prodigality of equipments and luxury items which the Americans took to War with them. Within hours of setting up camps they had refrigerators and ice-cream machines working. Their stores were well stocked. Moreover, they were in stark contrast to the hardpressed British squadrons. The Indians were much impressed by their behaviour and efficiency. They seemed to be better equipped and better off than their British Allies. Not only that, most of them were in favour of Indian independence and had no time for imperial trappings. A British airman in the forward base in Assam was astonished to hear an American pilot telling his Indian ground crew that they had to think in terms of Bunker Hill if they really wanted to be free from the British.[39]

Notes

1. M.K. Singh, *The Indian Army: A Sociological Study* (Poona University, 1985), p. 150.
2. *Asiatic Review*, April 1944, p. 147.
3. M.S. Gore, *Ambedkar's Social and Political Thought* (New Delhi, 1993), p. 85.
4. Progs. CLA, 19 November 1943, p. 572.
5. P. Stephen Cohen, *The Indian Army* (Oxford, Delhi, 1992), p. 60.
6. ISR, January 1948, p. 258.
7. Progs. CLA, 19 November 1943, p. 570.
8. Bishnu Ram Medhi, *Towards A Welfare State* (Shillong, 1969).
9. M.K. Singh, op.cit., p. 79.
10. Philip Mason, *A Matter of Honour* (London, 1974), p. 512.
11. *Asiatic Review*, October 1944, p. 384.
12. Progs. C.S., 26 February 1942, p. 142.
13. N. Mansergh, *Transfer of Power*, Vol. I, p. 328.
14. P. Stephen Cohn, op.cit., p. 122.
15. *Indian Information*, 1 April 1944, p. 300.
16. Zareer Masani, *Indian Tales of the Raj*, p. 27.
17. Trevor Royale, *The Last Days of the Raj* (London, 1989), p. 101.
18. P. Stephen Cohen, op.cit., p. 143.
19. *Indian Information*, 1 April 1944, pp. 302–3.
20. *Indian Information*, 15 October 1943, p. 206.
21. ISR, 23 September 1944, p. 10.
22. *Indian Information*, 1 April 1944, pp. 302–3.
23. Ibid., p. 305.
24. *Asiatic Review*, Vol. XLII, April 1946, p. 149.
25. Ibid., p. 146.
26. Ibid.
27. Ibid., Vol. XLI, 1945, p. 57.
28. Ibid., January 1945, p. 60.
29. Harry Hopkins, *The New Outlook* (London, 1963), p. 32.
30. Louis Fischer, *A Week with Gandhi* (Bombay, 1944).
31. BCW, 23 August 1942, p. 4.

32. *Indian Information*, 1 December 1944, p. 731.
33. Prakash Tandon, *Punjab Saga (1857–1987)* (New Delhi, 1987), p. 369.
34. Ibid.
35. BCW, 32 September 1945, p. 5.
36. Jane Howard, *Margaret Mead: A Life*, (Harwell Press, UK, 1983), p. 238.
37. Badruddin Tyabji, *Memoirs of An Egoist* (New Delhi, 1982), pp. 154–55.
38. Nari Rustomji, *Enchanted Frontiers* (Oxford, 1971), p. 46.
39. Trevor Royale, op.cit., p. 101.

CHAPTER 2

North-East India in the Eye of a Storm

Prior to the Second World War North-East India was comparatively little known and cared for by the distant Central Government in Delhi. Assam was known as the Cinderella of the provinces, and was so remote and neglected by the Centre that many people did not even realize that it was a part of India. It was thought more often as an adjunct of Burma or Siam. It was when the Japanese threatened to invade India through Assam that our Cinderella began at last to receive the attention due to her.[1]

The Japanese conquest of Burma in March 1942 and the subsequent retreat of the British army and the Indian refugees' trek from Burma to India through the Naga and Manipur hills brought ripples in the placid social life of the people of North-East India. Never had anything like this happened before. They saw the coming of a modern war at their door steps. The Japanese and the INA made heart-rending appeal to the Nagas for cooperation. Only a few went to their side on the promise that after victory Nagaland would be recognized as an independent state. But the Nagas, as a whole, supported the Allied forces. Many of the Naga villages were destroyed as a result of fighting, bombardments and other military operations. Thousands of houses containing paddy stocks were set afire to prevent them from falling into the hands of the Japanese. Such houses numbered 2780 in the Naga hills and 9103 in Manipur. Many of the Nagas flew into nearby jungles and many went to Imphal. But the personal and material damage suffered by them was greater as a result of the British military operations against the Japanese than what they suffered at the hands of the Japanese. The Nagas put in extraordinary labour and showed spontaneous loyalty to the British and helped them in different ways in the hope that the British would do something for them. Many Nagas and Kukis were recruited as regular soldiers in the Assam Rifles and in Assam Regiment and many more acted as faithful spies and rescued stragglers and brought important military information on the movement of the Japanese troops and supply lines which enabled the Allied forces to ambush and destroy or capture the Japanese patrol parties and even misled the Japanese by giving wrong information. They removed dead bodies and carried the wounded from the battle fields. They killed some of the Japanese, arrested some others and brought them to the Allied troops. At one time they had the distinction of having captured more Japanese prisoners than the whole of the 14th army. They refused food supplies to Japanese. As a matter of fact the loyalty of the Nagas did much to bring the Japanese invader overlooking the plains of Assam to a halt.[2]

The British Government raised forced labour from the Naga villages for widening the Dimapur-Imphal Road and a number of other road-building works for the smooth mobility of Allied troops. Accordingly, thousands of Nagas were employed as forced workers along with labourers from other parts of India. In the beginning, many of the Naga road workers suffered and died of different diseases arising from the unhygienic conditions prevailing there. F.M. Slim rightly testified that in the most depressing time of the invasion the Nagas never faltered in their loyalty to the British. Despite floggings, torture, executions and burning of their villages, they refused to aid the Japanese in any way or to betray the British troops. Their active help to the British was beyond value or praise. Many a British or Indian officer owed his life to the naked head-hunting Nagas and no soldier of the 14th Army who met them would ever think of them but with admiration and affection.[3] The Nagas has seen a modern war. They had watched the Japanese and the Allies fighting in the jungles. Unknowingly, they had trained themselves for jungle warfare. The Second World War widened their horizon and brought them into a new world of modern warfare. The war had an unsettling effect on them. It gave them new ideas. As a matter of fact the war swept the Naga hills like a tidal wave and swept away most of the neolithic ways and sowed the seeds of modernity. The large-scale contact with British, Indian and Japanese soldiers touched off a revolution in the minds of the Nagas. A window was opened to the outside world and through it blew in the winds of change that disturbed their placid life and brought in new ideas and concepts. It kindled a new awakening among them. It brought them new ideas of living and new concepts of freedom. Their social outlook underwent a change. A mental ferment was generated among them.[4] To their surprise they found that the armies of the British Government were not always invincible. They were beginning to feel their strength and to think in terms of helping themselves for a change. The Japanese invasion had brought them into the forefront and given them an opportunity of knowing more of what the outside world thought of them. They began to conceive of themselves as part of a larger whole. One effect of the Japanese invasion had been apparently to give the Nagas a sense of partnership with all the enemies of the Japanese. It was reported to have been very much noticeable in many places and in a manner not anticipated by officers well acquainted with them. They could not avoid considering their position in regard to external affairs which hitherto had affected them but very remotely.[5] They now began to assess their sacrifices in life and property for the British in this war. They were no longer ready to be lorded over by anybody else. The prospect of British withdrawal from India fired them with ideas of their own independence. They would like to run their own affairs and if there was to be a link with India, they would prefer it should be with Delhi. Delhi was far away and there was less likelihood of interference in their internal affairs from Delhi than from irredentist Assam. So ran the thinking in the minds of the Nagas.[6] The Naga Club founded in 1918 in Kohima had presented a memorandum before the Simon Commission in January 1929 and had demanded a direct administration of Nagaland from Delhi. They said: "You conquered us. When you go we should be left as we were."[7] They even asked for separation from India in the event of India getting independence, to avoid being ruled over by the Assamese or the Bengalis. In 1947 they pleaded that they were independent and their country was not subjugated even by the Ahom kings of the Assam valley. Nagaland never formed part of Assam or India at any time of recorded history before the advent of the British. Little was known of Nagaland, when the British obtained suzerainty over the Assam valley by the treaty of Yandabo.[8]

The Japanese, at the time of withdrawal, left behind huge arms dumps, to which the Nagas avidly helped themselves. They also dispossessed the stragglers and the dead of both sides of their weapons. Apart from those who joined the Assam Rifles and the Assam Regiments, the Nagas were also recruited in the special forces raised during the War which meant training in the art of guerilla warfare and the use of modern weapons. These lent an edge to the Nagas post-war aspirations which were further sharpened by the impending independence of India as a whole.

Towards the end of the war some British officials toyed with the idea of a 'Crown colony' consisting of all contiguous hill areas of Burma and Assam to be governed by the British Government after its withdrawal from India. Initiative was taken in forming the district level political bodies in which the tribal elite could participate. This succeeded in kindling an urge for autonomy and political participation and even nursed the seeds of suspicion in tribal minds against their more advanced neighbours in the plains.

The opening up and improvement in communications by road, railway and air linking them with parts of India and Burma for the military needs, transformed tremendously the economic, political, social, moral and cultural life of the Nagas. As a matter of fact the war detached them from their traditional moorings. Their traditional customs, culture and social values were challenged and thrown into a welter of confusion and uncertainty. Modern dress and modern ideas both took hold of them. Socialization among the Nagas speeded up. They gave up the traditional head-hunting and feuds. They began to talk in terms of unity and nation. The standard of living of the

Nagas went up in contrast to that of other tribes of Assam as they received higher wages. Their earnings rose thanks to the purchase of indigenous products by the Japanese and British troops in cash and payment of compensation for their War services. The result was that a tiny bourgeois class who made profits out of the War had arisen among the Nagas.[9] After the War the Nagas demanded more educational facilities because they began to realize that education was the key to progress, power, influence, and other benefits of civilization. This demand for expansion of educational facilities was a definite sign of social change after the War. The War had also propelled psychological cataclysm far beyond its confines than anything that had taken place during the British rule for about seventy years. Moreover, it had also set off powerful political ferment among the educated middle class Nagas, particularly those of the areas affected by the War.[10] Educated Nagas who had influence over the masses considered themselves different from Indians. Western education and other civilizing processes led to a spiritual and cultural isolation of the Nagas from the mainstream of Indian society. Thus, the educated Nagas with political ambitions fanned and propagated the idea that the Nagas had never been a part and parcel of the mainstream of the Indian society, that the Naga country was never a part of India, but an independent territory between Burma and India and after the withdrawal of the British the Nagas had *ipso facto* become independent. The Christian missionaries and the British policy were responsible for this development.

Rani Guidallo, Queen of the Naga hills, had revolted against the British with her followers. But she was defeated and put behind prison bars. In 1946 she was released from the British prison. Referring to the problems of Assam hills, more particularly of the Nagas, she had said: "We, the Nagas, form part and parcel of the Indian nation. Our hill has already made a glorious record in the contribution to the struggle for Indian independence. We shall stand shoulder to shoulder with our country men – in our great trial for emancipating ourselves from political slavery". She complained that very little had been done by the plains people and there was immense need and possibility of social uplift. She feelingly said: "These woods and hills cry out for help and their cry is yet unheard". Further the Rani made it quite clear: "We do not like much interference by outside authority. We love freedom and we must live as lords in these hills and forests in a free and united India. Any overzealous compulsion and interference will mean bloody revolt. A bullying authority will fail as it failed in the past. Service, love, tolerance and sympathy alone can conquer our hearts. Will the people of the plains respond to this cry of the wilderness"?[11]

After coming out of the prison she found three most distinct and significant movements agitating the Assam hills. They were the rise of a genuine sense of national self-consciousness even in the remotest parts of the hills, the growing need of and immense opportunity for improving the economic well-being of the neglected tribal people and re-moulding of the cultural religious, social and economic aspects of this tremendous awakening so as to meet the challenge of the time.[12]

Under the inspiration of the British Deputy commissioner of the Naga hills the Naga Club was organized in 1918 in Kohima. This was the seed of political consciousness sown among the Nagas. In April 1945 C.L. Pawsey, the D.C. of Naga hill district, replaced the Naga Club with the Naga Hills District Tribunal Council with a view to uniting the Nagas on modern lines. It proved a harbinger of future political agitation and upheaval in Nagaland. It aimed at achieving local autonomy for the Naga Hill district within the state of Assam. At the end of the Second World War, Phizo took advantage of the situation and rallied a dozen desperate and feuding tribes to the cause of Naga independence and set up a parallel underground government. This was the beginning of insurgency in north-east India.[13]

The Lushai chief of Mizoram declared war against Japan on 3 April 1942. They promised the British to offer total resistance to the enemy. From north Lushai hill alone more than 300 young men worked along with the British soldiers. They also set up a "village protecting force" whose duty was to defend the villages. This force was set up in every village of the Lushai hills. The government supplied them with guns.[14]

Earlier, when the British had come to the Lushai hills, they had recognized the chiefs as true spokesmen of the villages and established a chief council of 23 chiefs. The British generally favoured the chiefs in contrast to the common people. As this was an excluded area, the British generally did not allow any political activity in Lushai hills. So the people had no political experience nor the opportunity to have it. But the closeness of Japanese troops in Burma and the political enslavement of the Mizo people at the hands of the British and the chiefs generated a lot of political consciousness among the educated Mizo youths, who never relished the handing over of power to the chiefs by the British. In December 1940, when Robert Reid, the Governor of Assam, visited Lushai Hills, the people asserted that they would be better off if they were attached to the Hills of Burma.[15] In 1942–43 McCall, the District Officer, tried to initiate the Mizos into active politics and administration. He tried to induce them into accepting his plan of re-grouping Mizo areas of India and Burma into one composite state under the trusteeship of UN. His successor Macdonald tried to sell the idea of Mizo state remaining as a protectorate of the British Government. The first district conference of Mizos was held in January 1946 on a parity formula of chiefs and commoners. The Mizo Union opposed the idea of giving 300 chiefs and 15 lakh people the same number of seats in the District Conference, i.e. 20 each. It debated three options: either (a) to join Burma, or (b) to join India and (c) to remain independent. Finally, it decided to remain with India on the condition that after ten years, Mizos would review this position. In the event of Mizo remaining with India their customary laws would be retained. As a matter of fact the Lushais had a keen desire for education and had high degree of intelligence. The missionaries had really helped them to develop educationally which in turn made them keep up with the plains people in culture, education and literacy. Particularly in literacy, the Lushai hill people were better off than a good number of the plain areas. In 1971 about 87 per cent of the people in Mizoram were Christians. The literacy rate at Aizawl was 66 per cent and about 50.9 per cent in general.[16] On the other hand Assam's literacy rate was 28 per cent.

Kohima and Imphal were the two world famous battlefields in north-east India during the Second World War. The

Japanese remained entrenched in these two places for more than two years before they withdrew. This was a turning point in the history of the Second World War in Asia. Nagaland and Manipur both faced the worst fury of the War in the Asian sector. Imphal, the capital of Manipur, had been encircled on all sides by Japanese soldiers. War had put Manipur on the communication map of the world. It had brought in Allied troops with their war machines and equipments in this land-locked country. The battle for Imphal became one of the most decisive battles of the War in South-east Asia. Modern amenities, mechanized transport, aeroplanes, all types of vehicles, had come to Manipur. The Japanese and the INA forces started the operation on 4 March 1944 and the INA forces set foot on Indian soil on 18 March 1944 amidst scenes of jubilation. But the fact is that only a small insignificant minority of Manipuris had joined the INA movement. On the whole the people in general were indifferent to the movement. The INA was able to liberate Moirang, a small town about 38 km south of Imphal in April 1944, where Major General Malik of the INA set up his intelligence headquarters. The INA raised its flag at Maibram Lokpaching about 20 km from Imphal on the Imphal-Tedium road.[17] When the battle of Imphal was raging, some tribals joined the INA and went to jail with the Meiteis. In 1973, twelve *tamrapatras* were awarded to freedom fighters in Manipur. The people in general in Manipur supported the Allies in the battle for Imphal and did whatever they could for their success. Manipur made profits from War contracts as from no other business before. The congregation of a huge army in the valley was a new experience for the Manipuris. By the end of March 1944 the Japanese succeeded in cutting the road to Dimapur and began to press hard on the fringes of Imphal plains from three sides. Kohima also faced a similar situation. The 5th Indian division had to be flown to Dimapur. On 22 June 1944 the 2nd and 5th divisions met at a point 29 miles north of Imphal and the road to the plains was opened. On the same day the convoys of the Allies began to roll in. The Allied forces comprised of 11,89,000 ground troops and 73,000 airforce men for fighting against the Japanese.[18] The Allied forces, operating from Assam had constructed a 478 mile supply road called the

Stilwell Road which was finally connected with Burma Road. A lot of Chinese labour was employed in construction of this road link with Burma. They continued to stay on in Upper Assam till many of them were deported during the Sino-Indian border trouble of 1962. The Chinese brought in a new element in Upper Assam frontier society.[19]

The failure of the Japanese Airforce to reinforce its army on Kohima and Imphal fronts ultimately led to their withdrawal from India. Their loss in men and material had been tremendous and that was the beginning of their end.

Manipur state consists of hill tracts and the valley. The hill areas of Manipur are inhabited by tribals who are either Christians or animists. In 1907 the administration of the hill tribes was taken out of the control of the Maharaja of Manipur and was entrusted to the vice-president of the Darbar who belonged to the ICS. But the right of the Maharaja to be consulted in all matters concerning the hill tribes was recognized by the British Government. Thus, from 1907 onwards the hill tribes of Manipur were treated in a different manner than the Maharaja's Manipuri subjects, being only dependent on the Manipur state but not incorporated in it and excluded from the jurisdiction of the State Darbar. This policy generated contradictions in socio-political life of Manipur. It was a deliberate policy of the British to keep the hill tribes away from the mainstream of Manipur's life and develop in them an isolationist psychology. Thus, till 1947 the hills of Manipur were excluded from the benefits associated with the introduction of self-government. Under the Act of 1935 the president of the Manipur State Darbar used to directly administer the hill tribes nominally on behalf of the Maharaja, who was, of course, consulted on all matters of importance. But the political agent, in consultation with the president of the State Darbar, used to give effect to the Maharaja's wishes so far as they were consistent with the orders of the Governor of Assam. The Maharaja advocated the transfer of the administration of hill tribes to the exclusive management of the political agent. The hill tribals of Manipur were apprehensive of domination of the Hindu Meiteis of central Imphal valley. Hence, their demand was for merger with the contiguous hill areas of Assam and separation from the Imphal valley. Their attitude to the Meiteis of the valley was somewhat similar to that of the hill tribals of Assam to the Assamese plainsmen.

The Japanese invasion and the counter-offensive of the Allies brought both the valley and hill people of Manipur face to face with a huge modern army in their midst. The War tore the curtain behind which Manipur was living so far. They found in the Allied soldiers a new world with which they were altogether unfamiliar. The vehicles that the Allied army brought in helped people appreciate the role of machines in life. Later on they proved second to none in India in repairing the machines of daily use. Motor mechanics in Manipur are today some of the best one can find anywhere in India. Today Imphal is choked with bicycles. There is no one, man or woman, who does not know cycling. It was the Allied soldiers who introduced bicycles into the town in a big way. Before the War, a man on a bicycle was almost a unique sight. The War ushered in a period of emotional integration of the valley and the hills of Manipur. Social and religious differences were relegated to the background. These were positive gains of the War. The common political experience created similarity of outlook. The hill tribes outlived the helot role assigned to them by the feudal and social order of the valley. The valley recognized this and conceded the tribals rightful place in the scheme of things in Manipur. In social sphere also the relationship between the hills and valley registered some progress. The plains society turned inward-looking under the influence of Vaishnavism and showed remarkable accommodation with the hill people. Many tribals were absorbed into the valley society without disabilities. Plainspeople continued to have tribal wives in keeping with the old custom. But the process in the reverse is yet to be the norm. A few valley wives have already been found in the hill areas. But marriage of a valley girl with a hill man is still considered a taboo in the valley. As a matter of fact the Manipur bowl is a chip of India. Nothing that came to Manipur valley, be it man or religion, retained his or its foreign identity for long.[20] This process took place in the case of tribals also. They lost much of the tribals about them as soon as they came down to the valley. The War forced the hill and valley people to come closer to one another to work out a common destiny. The War had some adverse effects too on Manipuri society. When Imphal and most of Manipur were swamped by Allied soldiers, there was a distinct caving in of sexual morality. But then, let us not forget, these were abnormal times.

The main impact of the War had fallen on the frontier areas lying between Assam and Burma. Except for Manipur, all these areas were under the Excluded Area Act of 1935 and were administered directly by the Governor of Assam. The fall of Rangoon in March 1942 into the hands of the Japanese led to the evacuation of the British army as well as the civilians both Indian and European from Burma to India. These refugees were to enter Assam by the Manipur road. Half a million Indians came from Burma to India between December 1941 and July 1942 through four different routes. From Imphal to Dimapur, the rail head in Upper Assam, there was a single track metalled road. Down this one route something like 2,00,000 refugees passed into India. India had to face a first rate communication problem in April 1942. Major-General Wood was sent to Assam to deal with the problem of communication on the North-East frontier. Thousands of coolies were engaged in widening the existing road and constructing new ones. The Indian Tea Association was asked to place their resources at the disposal of the Government in this hour of national peril. The Tea industry did wonderful work in connection with the construction and improvement of roads on the frontier at the time of evacuation from Burma. 90 per cent of young assistants on tea gardens had been called upon to join the forces. The ITA also provided thousands of labourers from its own work force and under its own supervisors helped build the strategic roads and air-strips all over Assam. Before 1941 not a single aerodrome existed in Assam but in 1943 there were about 20.[21] Men and women of the tea planting community established camps for refugees and opened canteens on Railway platforms and at steamer ghats to provide food, drink, and clothing to the refugees. Later on, they turned to troops and ran canteens for them. The women of Assam, especially those in the hills, came forward to work as nurses. They joined the auxiliary nursing service. They were among the first to go overseas. People came in large numbers to do the ARP work, especially those in the women's voluntary service. A large number of Khasi girls came forward to serve as nurses in military hospitals. Due to high prices and shortage of food, the Khasis, the Garos and the Mikirs – all came in large numbers to work as labourers or porters. The exodus from Burma in the summer of 1942 produced the first of emergency calls on the tea industry for labour. In view of defence projects in Assam the labour population in Assam tea gardens rose from 11,55,147 in 1941–42 to 11,75,431 in 1942–43.[22] The Tea industry workers rendered valuable service to the stream of refugees from Burma. They acted as porters and stretcher bearers under the most appalling conditions when all other forms of labour had broken down. There were a few casualties among the tea garden labourers but there was no sign of panic and no attempt to leave the garden. Some 250,000 tea garden workers had been engaged in improving the road from Dimapur to Imphal and beyond to Tamu. The Ledo road employed another 70,000 coolies.[23] As a matter of fact the CPWD had the biggest share in the construction of airfields in eastern India and in other parts of the country. They employed no less than 600,000 Indian labourers at the peak period. Labourers were also brought to Assam from Cochin and Travancore, Patiala and Nabha. Oriyas and Santhals and labourers from Gorakhpur also joined. Local labour from tea-gardens and Nagas from the hills was also utilized in large numbers. It was no uncommon sight to see some of these primitive people putting one of their men to watch over a small heap of their belongings, including bows and arrows, while they turned to work on airfield construction, using such modern appliances as were available. Labour, not mechanical equipment, made these airfields and made them in record time. Despite the invasion panic of April 1942 a jungle was turned into runways in sixty working days and without the assistance of any mechanical equipment except some steam rollers and concrete mixtures. At the peak period the CPWD had under construction at one and the same time a large number of airfields in five different provinces and two states and completed in all 83 airfields.

For the first time the Central Government was faced with a

grave communication problem in North-Eastern India. The Japanese were standing with a huge modern army on the borders of India. This threat had to be faced with all resources of the country. Roads and aerodromes had to be built in record time to carry arms, ammunitions and soldiers to the front. To meet the situation the South-East India Command with Lord Mountbatten as Supreme Commander was created and the resources of the Allied Powers were at his disposal. It was no longer the business of the Government of India to face the situation but the Allied Powers owned the responsibility. Besides the construction of roads and airfields the railways were also placed in operational control of the American Army Engineers for speeding up efficiency. More than a million soldiers were rushed to the front to meet the situation. The American planes were also engaged in carrying war-materials from Upper Assam to Chungking across a mountain hump of 23,000 ft. It was a gigantic task supplying war-materials to the Chungking Government in China from India. The area had never seen such a huge congregation of soldiers, war equipment, aeroplanes, and army vehicles of all kinds before. The whole area was converted into a big battlefield. Previously, there was only one small garrison of army in Shillong, but now units of army of different nationalities could be seen everywhere in the area. They spent a lot of money on local purchases. Hence, there was plenty of loose money floating around. The American soldiers were well known for their extravagances.

The presence of such a huge army (more than a million) created a demand for fresh vegetables in the area. It was quite a novelty in the province. It had an important repercussion on the agricultural economy of the province. The few who could foresee the development earned good money. The others also quickly responded to the need for increased production of more vegetables, potatoes and foodgrains. The Khasis, specially, did very well and tons of potatoes and fresh vegetables were being sent from Shillong every day for military stations all over Assam. This was also stimulated by the purchase of table potatoes for the civil population of the Lakhimpur district, where potatoes and fresh vegetables were in great demand.

Large demands and enquiries also poured in from other parts of India for seed potatoes produced in Khasi and Jaintia hills.[25]

The army recruited *mali* units for growing vegetables for its own use. The *malis* (gardeners) who were mostly Christians from Ranchi and Chotanagpur areas were formed into units, each of about 800 strong. They got free rations and clothing besides pay and they served on a six-month contract. In charge of every ten men was a trained mali with considerable local experience. Manure for the garden was made locally by preparing compost from tank weeds, jungle growth, grass scrappings, cattle manure and lime. Just 50 miles behind the fighting line several thousand acres of paddy land were converted into vegetable plots for the supply of fresh vegetables to the 14th Army.

During the War years the panic-stricken immigrant shopkeepers and petty traders left the hills. This compelled some local hillmen to take up these lucrative professions as well as petty war contracts. Thus, there emerged a small stratum of middle class people of local origin, which was not in existence there earlier except in the Khasi-Jaintia hills. Besides, war-time contacts with soldiers of different provinces and from many nations exposed the hillmen to the world outside and allowed them to be politicised. Moreover, the partition of the country largely disrupted the hill economy, since some parts of Garo, Mizo, Khasi and Jaintia hills had long been economically more integrated with Eastern Bengal than with the plains of Assam. People in these areas had to suffer great hardships because of the disruption of their normal trade channels. This experience, too, further strengthened their urge for local autonomy.[27]

The withdrawal of the Japanese from Indian borders and the subsequent decision of the British to hand over power to the Indians created a situation which called for a high degree of political experience and statesmanship. But there was none among the Indian leaders who could comprehend the problem fully and try to find out a solution. It was really unfortunate that during the crucial period when far-reaching decisions were to be taken regarding the future of the hill areas, there were as many as five changes in the office of the Secretary responsible to the Assam Government for the administration of hill districts. There was a tendency to allow things to drift in the fond hope that they would solve themselves than risk taking any radical decision.[28] The attitude of the Assamese people and their representatives in Government was highly regrettable because they considered tribal areas as their patrimony.

The distinguishing feature of the Assam hills and the frontier tracts was that they were divided into fairly large districts inhabited by simple tribes of fairly homogeneous groups with highly democratic and mutually exclusive tribal organisations. Another feature was that there were greater potentialities in the hill districts of Assam like the Lushai hills and the Khasi hills for faster development than in the tribal areas in other provinces. Moreover, the tribes in places other than Assam were more or less hinduised and assimilated into the culture and civilisation of the people among whom they lived. But this was not the case in regard to Assam. They had roots in their own culture and civilisation. They did not adopt the mode of life and manners of the people surrounding them. Their laws of inheritance and marriage and their customs were different from their neighbours'. It was sheer arrogance on the part of the Assamese to consider these hill areas as an integral part of Assam. The hill people of the area never relished this attitude of the Assamese. Hence, there developed animosity between the two.

The whole tribal society in North-East was metamorphosed by the War. It uprooted the tribal people from their traditional moorings. Their traditional customs, culture and social values were challenged and thrown into a whirl of confusion and uncertainty. Their centuries-old isolation was broken and they began to think of themselves as part of a larger world. The War brought in a psychological storm. It gave birth to powerful political ambition, nursed by the British during the War. Later on, there developed insurgency in the area which posed a great problem for the Indian Government.

NOTES

1. N. Rustomji, *Enchanted Frontiers* (Oxford, 1971), p. 116.
2. Yonuo Asoso, *The Rising Nagas* (Delhi, 1974), p. 142.
3. Ramunny Marcot, *The World of Nagas* (New Delhi, 1988), p. 29.
4. D.R. Mankekar, *On the Slippery Slope in Nagaland* (Bombay, 1967), p. 21.
5. *Man in India*, Vol. XXVI, June 1946, pp. 97–109.
6. N. Rustomji, op.cit., p. 86.
7. D.R. Mankekar, op.cit., p. 24.
8. Yonuo Asoso, op.cit., p. 154.
9. Ibid., p. 142.
10. Ibid.
11. ISR, 21 December 1946, p. 126.
12. Ibid.
13. D.R. Mankekar, op.cit., p. 26.
14. *Proceedings of North-East India History Association*, 10th session 1989, p. 444.
15. Bhawani Singh, *Politics of Alienation in Assam* (Ajanata, New Delhi, 1984), p. 33.
16. Bimal J. Dev and Dilip K. Lahiri, *Manipur—Culture and Politics* (Mittal Publishers, New Delhi), p. 268.
17. R. Constantine, *Manipur—Maid of the Mountains* (New Delhi, 1981). p. 10.
18. Yonuo Asoso, op.cit. p. 142.
19. M.L. Bose, *A Social History of Assam* (Concept Publishers, New Delhi, 1989), p. 68.
20. R. Constantine, op.cit., p. 32.
21. *Asiatic Review*, January 1944.
22. *Indian Information*, 15 January 1945, p. 60.
23. John Rawntree, *A Chota Sahib: Memior of a Forest Officer* (Cornwall, UK, 1981), p. 95.
24. *Indian Information*, 15 September 1945, p. 258.
25. *Indian Farming*, December 1942, p. 652.
26. *Indian Information*, 15 July 1944, p. 68.
27. A. Guha, *Planter's Raj to Swaraj* (ICHR, New Delhi), p. 322.
28. N. Rustomji, op.cit., p. 86.

CHAPTER 3

The War Necessitated New Agricultural Policy

Between 1900 and 1945 the population of India increased by 37.9 per cent, the average acreage under cultivation by 18.4 per cent, food output remained stationary and the output of commercial crops went up by 59.3 per cent resulting in the increase of 12.6 per cent in agricultural output.

There was surplus of foodstuffs to the extent of 5 million tons in 1880, but there was a deficit of 10 million tons in 1945. By 1945 nearly 30 per cent of India's population was suffering from chronic malnutrition.[1] About 85 per cent of the population was dependent directly or indirectly on land.[2]

Over years this tragic situation was developing in India before the Second World War and the Government did not pay adequate attention to it. The colonial Government in India was mainly guided by the idea of preserving law and order, and leaving the people alone to shape their economic destinies. It contented itself with the duty of preventing deaths from starvation and had concerned itself mainly with the supply of the minimum quantities of cereal grains needed to sustain the population at a low level of nutrition. In normal times, protective works were constructed with a view to increasing the powers of resistance of the people to face a famine. It was generally guided by the idea of *laissez faire* in economic matters, although it had unlimited powers with limited outlook. The famine policy developed in the nineteenth century was intended to relieve distress and to prevent the occurrence of famines as far as possible. Few attempts were made to increase the material welfare of the people in real sense of the term. Consequent upon the recommendations of the Famine Commission of 1901 and the Irrigation Commission of 1903 a forward policy in the matter of agricultural research and improvement was embarked upon by the colonial Government in India. With a handsome donation from a Chicago philanthropist the Imperial Agricultural Research Institute was established at Pusa in Bihar in 1903. Subsequently, the Government set apart Rs 20 lakh per year for agricultural research, experiment, demonstration and education in the provinces. Accordingly, agricultural colleges were established at Coimbatore, Poona, Nagpur, Kanpur and Sabour and Lyallpur. In 1904 the Board of Agriculture was constituted to advise the Government on agriculture matters generally and to bring agriculture experts working in various parts of the country into touch with one another. Thus, the infrastructure for agricultural-education was set up in India in the first decade of this century but its progress was very tardy. To help the agriculturists the Departments of Agriculture and Cooperation were created in the provinces but they were charged merely with the duties of information, advice, demonstration and research.[3] Leaders of public opinion in the country were crying for state action to improve agriculture but the colonial Government was very slow in realizing the realities of the situation.

The limited outlook of the colonial Government had been changed by the force of circumstances during the period 1921 to 1937. The functions of the state in economic life had undergone revolutionary changes in the West. Even in England *laissez faire* was dead and state intervention in economic activities had come to stay in the first two decades of the twentieth century. It was not possible to stop the extension of this conception of the state in economic life in India. Still it took a long time for this new idea to take root in India. Between 1921 and 1937 the state in British India was altered to some extent in structure. Ultimately, the colonial administration in India accepted its duty to take some positive steps for improving the condition of the people in addition to the maintenance of security. By that time the central and provincial legislatures had begun to voice the grievances of the people. As such, the public opinion for improvement of agriculture had its effects in the corridor of power. Consequently, the Government accepted the proposal for the appointment of the Royal Commission on agriculture in 1926 for suggesting ways and means for improving agriculture in India. The Commission was directed to concentrate its enquiry on improvement of agriculture only and not on restructuring the agrarian structure. Among its various recommendations the one that was very important was the proposal for the establishment of a Central Council of Agricultural Research with the primary function of promoting, guiding and coordinating agricultural and animal husbandry research and education throughout India. In pursuance of this the Imperial Council of Agricultural Research was set up in 1929 in Delhi. It marked a new era in the history of the development of agricultural research in India. Within a period of less than twenty years its activities had spread far and wide and left its vitalizing influence on every branch of agriculture in India. It had become a model showing how science could be introduced in agriculture. It provided leadership in initiating and coordinating research in various aspects of agricultural science. As a matter of fact the application of scientific method to agriculture having a deep or lasting effect could only be achieved by planned, coordinated schemes in which all aspects of rural development were considered together.[4] There was also the need for real rapport between scientific workers on an agricultural research station and the cultivators to understand their problems and the ways of solving them. All these were handled effectively by the ICAR. It could justly claim its credit for great success in its activities in connection with the production and utilization of sugar canes. Since it began its work the area under sugar cane increased considerably and the old indigenous varieties were largely supplanted by newer ones. From its beginning the ICAR gave a prominent place in its programme to research in sugar cane and thus, it was able to provide technical information necessary for implementing the Government's decision to foster the production of white sugar in India.[5] Sir T.S. Venkataraman made a commendable contribution to the technique of plant breeding and forged some powerful instruments for the breeders. He had caused more money to circulate in the countryside than anyone else. He doubled the yield of sugar. Thus, he deserved a lasting place in the gratitude of his countrymen.[6]

During the Second World War the ICAR took up the challenge of the 'freedom from want' on war-footing and undertook agricultural research on a coordinated basis on problems of immediate economic importance to the cultivator both on cash and food crops. The exigencies of the War and the Bengal famine brought home to the Government the necessity of paying greater attention to agricultural production and research than had been done before. Dr William Burns wrote a monograph on "Technological possibilities of agricultural development in India".[7] He estimated that the yield of rice could be increased by 20 per cent to 30 per cent by manures, 5 per cent by improved varieties and 5 per cent by protecting from pests and diseases. He was very hopeful that the yield of rice could be increased by 40 to 50 per cent by these means. Moreover, he stressed on the breeding of better varieties of seeds which should be made available to the cultivators.[8] As a matter of fact the genetic improvement of major foodcrops needed special attention. Hence, there was an urgent need of scientific plant breeders. They held the keys of increased foodcrops in their hands. Consequently, India needed a long range agricultural policy even during the War period. Whatever the War did, it surely focused attention on the absolute necessity for national agricultural policy as a basis for every other action. A well considered policy in reference to food production was therefore an integral part of successful war efforts. Hence, the first conference on food production held in April 1942 inaugurated the "Grow More Food" campaign in India. "As an army marches on its stomach, the morale of a nation in War depends upon its food supplies".[9] Even the Indian Science Congress in 1943 recommended organized planning as regards food production and its conservation, transport and marketing with minimum price guarantee to the producer with the help of subsidies, if required.[10]

The UN Conference on Food and Agriculture in May 1943 at Hot Springs (Virginia, USA) was convened to consider the world problems regarding food and agriculture. Its objective was to achieve 'freedom from want' for all people of the world. It focused on the primary responsibility of each nation to see that its own people got the food needed for health and well-being. Hence it recommended that each nation should adopt a policy for rural education and rural adult education and promotion of research in all the branches of science including economics relating to food and agriculture, training of scientific workers and rural leaders.[11] Never before had food and agriculture received such recognition in the world. Never before had it been so clearly and widely established that better diets and improved agriculture were so fundamental to the well being of all people and never before had the problem of world distribution of food been internationally explored so critically and on such a scale.[12] Even President Roosevelt in his special message to the Congress in November, 1943 stressed that food was as important as any other weapon in the successful prosecution of the War. The major objective of the food programme should be to raise in the most efficient manner enough food and the right kind of food to meet the needs of the people. Food was to win the War and write the peace.[13]

Governments and authorities represented at the Hot Springs Conference undertook to do their best to implement its resolutions. India was also represented at the Conference and was morally bound to implement its resolutions concerning food and agriculture. Thus, the Hot Springs resolutions marked an important landmark in the social and economic history of the world as well as of India. Sir John Russel rightly pointed out that implementation of the Hot Springs resolutions necessitated considerable planning in Indian agriculture both by nutrition and agricultural experts. Economic organization was also needed. The resolutions held out the possibility of a better life not only for the towns people but also for the rural people engaged in food production. Their implementation also envisaged change in social outlook and habit. He further pointed out that food of a considerable proportion of population in India was lacking in first class protein, in vitamins and in mineral substances. These deficiencies could not be made up by increasing the quantity of grain consumed but could be met partly by consuming more vegetables and fruit and also by more milk. They could also be best met by consuming all these and, in addition, eggs, meat and fish. This meant a change in the dietary habit of the people. It was a slow process but the War might accelerate it. The soldiers returning home after the War with new ideas might induce the people to adopt new dietary habits. One of the best ways of popularizing the idea was to feed the children at school. They would take home the ideas and persuade their parents to follow them. Previously, nutrition experts did not come sufficiently into the picture because nutrition science was a new one. But during this War nutrition experts were in great demand and were able to say much more definitely as to what vegetables were better for growth. To meet the requirement of a wholesome diet Sir John Russel suggested that animal husbandry mixed with growing crops was the best form of agriculture for a country like India.[14] He particularly emphasized the need for increased production of vegetables, fruits, milk, eggs and fish in order to improve nutritional value of food in India. In all these matters a new era had already opened up with recommendations of the Royal Commission on agriculture. They were still to be implemented in full. War forced the Government to look at these problems afresh and to adopt a new agricultural policy in India. There was a big gap between what appeared on the experimental farms and what happened on the cultivator's land. A great wealth of scientific knowledge was gathering dust in the agricultural and scientific research journals, but not enough was being done to publicize this knowledge so as to lead to its application to agriculture. A kind of total war was needed against the ignorance and apathy of Indian cultivators. Agricultural demonstrations backed by service organizations were urgently needed to dissipate the normal scepticism of the peasant about the benefits of scientific agriculture.[15] Educating the peasant was the dire need of the time. All this implied rural reconstruction and called for a lot of social change in the countryside.

Implementing the Hot Springs resolutions on food and agriculture and the "Grow-More Food" programme posed a great challenge to the agricultural scientists and administrators of India during the War. Among the principal measures of improvement in agricultural production were increased irrigation, development of manurial resources, multiplication and distribution of improved seeds and control of pests. Agricultural improvement also involved revising the land tenures and taking measures to deal with excessive fragmentation of holdings. These measures, however, affected the social and economic interests of the people and required very careful handling. According to Prof. A.V. Hill, secretary to the Royal Society, London, the main problems of India were biological, namely, the problems of agriculture, health and population. They all acted and re-acted on one another and with other scientific and technical problems of industrialization, transportation, communications and not the least education.[16]

To meet the challenge of 'freedom from want' the ICAR had much expanded particularly in the area of genetic improvement, hybridization and multiplication on the farmers' field. A new breed of administrators like Sardar Datar Singh assumed position of leadership. A movement for establishing district agricultural farms with new tasks began. Some of the agricultural scientists tried various breeds of rust resistant wheat, hybrid maize and Tanjore rice in research stations and demonstration farms which proved successful. As a matter of fact the agricultural scientists had to telescope two centuries in two decades.[17] In June 1944, the ICAR prepared a plan for doubling India's agricultural production within a period of 15 years at an estimated cost of Rs 1000 crores.[18] The plan was practicable within the combined powers of the authorities in India and of her rural population. It was to increase seed production by 15 per cent and to arrange for its multiplication, storage and distribution. It was to secure the active interest of the landlords and the cultivators for its successful prosecution. The problem was by no means one of employing force. It was one of explanation and persuasion; that is, of real leadership. Thus, the problem of increased food production was essentially to speed up the work on the plant. Once this was done, there would be more for the population to eat and for the cattle which provided the much needed supplies of milk and milk products. The ICAR had been initiating and guiding research in most of the problems which confronted the agriculturists in India during the War. Agriculture and animal husbandry went hand in hand and were complementary to each other. Development of better cattle breeds helped to grow more cereals and also helped produce more protective foods like milk, milk products and poultry which were essential supplements to the normal cereal diet of a majority of the people. The Royal Commission on agriculture had warned against the fallacy that the Indian milk problem could be solved by import of foreign bulls of heavy milking breeds. For all such matters they had urged the Government to engage the services of an expert adviser in animal husbandry. This was accepted and Sir Arthur Olver, one of the foremost experts in the world, was appointed.[19] His outstanding achievements were a survey of Indian cattle breed and their possibilities. His survey revealed that there were various herds of Indian cattle producing milk in greater quantity and substantially richer in butter than the good commercial herds in Europe. He concluded that by proper feeding and management Indian milk cattle could be raised to the highest standard. The annual cattle show in Delhi since 1938 was an object lesson in all this and was inviting great attention. It was a regular annual social event of great importance in Delhi even during the War. It afforded a meeting ground for various breeders scattered in different parts of the country. It enabled them to exchange ideas, to discuss common problems and to learn and unlearn many things.[20]

As a matter of fact social and economic prosperity of India was intimately bound up with the health of Indian agriculture, which in turn was primarily dependent upon the security and fertility of soil. The agronomical method of soil conservation involving the scientific and planned utilization of crops, grass and trees in checking soil erosion and in building up soil fertility was emphasized.[21] In order to accelerate breeding more economic livestock, to increase crop production and to make better 'land use' and more balanced system of agriculture in India, the establishment of a rural dairy industry was of prime necessity.[22] It was also highlighted that in the post-war planning for rural reconstruction and agricultural development, plant breedings needed enormous expansion and special attention had to be given to the genetic improvement of major food crops in India. The need for producing grains of higher dietic value and the possibility of associating food chemists and nutrition experts with plant breeders were also highlighted. Thus, there was the necessity of scientific plant breedings and an organization for multiplication and distribution of seeds of improved varieties of crops among the cultivators.[23] The main drawbacks were the ineffectiveness of the extension staff, the means to multiply the seed, the means to show its value, the means to place the seed with the cultivator and the means to make him grow this.

As a matter of fact all planning for permanent agricultural prosperity must include the establishment of a sound balance between food, fodder, fertility and cash crop on the farm. Agriculture should be so organized as to make the maximum contributions to the well-being of the nation. It must provide food for the people and must help in the social problems concerning national health, population, unemployment and also must be ready to expand in times of emergency. The War and the Bengal famine made the Government realize this changed situation. Ultimately, the colonial Government in India had to change its old bureaucratic outlook and accepted it as its first and foremost duty to provide an adequate quantity of good and nourishing food for all the people of this country. Lord Wavell, the Viceroy, held the view that agriculture was India's main industry and it must take a high place, perhaps the highest in the planning for post-War development. He further observed: "Unless we succeed in raising substantially the standard of living in our villages, not only for the small farmer but for all who make living on land, India cannot become a wealthier or a healthier, or a better educated country".[24] He particularly focused on the fruits of many years of research available to this country and the need to translate this knowledge into action. The crux of the problem was the lack of personnel who could carry fruits of research to the tiller of the soil. He appealed to the ardent young men who believed in India's destiny, having the country background and upbringing with University education to come forward to qualify themselves with a course of training to assist the Government in their plan for the agricultural development of India.[25] The need for extension workers was greatly felt by the Government. Like the "Bevins' boys" in industry, there was an urgent need for the "Wavell's boys" in agriculture.[26]

The Famine Inquiry Commission 1944 made a series of recommendations which defined the broad lines of an agricultural and food policy designed to prevent any future threat of famine and to improve the diet of the people. A broad principle was enunciated that the state should recognize its ultimate responsibility to provide enough food for all and all the resources of Government must be brought to bear in order to achieve this end in view.[27] The principle of state responsibility in the feeding of the people was in line with the Hot Springs resolutions of the UN. During the last one hundred years of British rule in India the Government had only accepted the duty of preventing widespread starvation death from famine but took no steps to improve nutrition and to create a healthy and vigorous population. Hence, the Commission recommended a new food production policy to meet the situation. The main objective was to be to achieve self-sufficiency in cereals as the basic food of the country. To balance cereals it was essential to increase the production of pulse, fish, vegetable oils, vegetables, fruits, milk and eggs. A well organized urban milk industry was to be urgently speeded up. This had to be supplemented by the development of poultry farming in the neighbourhood of urban centres. The production of eggs as a subsidiary village occupation might form a part of the programme of rural development. Among the 'protected group of foods, prominent place should be given to production of fish. The Central Government should undertake the responsibility of stimulating and coordinating the development of the fishing industry.'[28] Extensive research should be fully investigated to increase its production. Moreover, nutrition research in all its branches had to receive sufficient attention and support as a part of programme of improvement of the health of the nation.

Hitherto, the colonial Government in India had been concerned mainly with the supply of minimum quantity of cereal grains needed to sustain the population at a low level of nutrition. But the War forced the Government to have a new outlook on the problem of food. It became necessary to give due consideration to all the foods which were required to make up a well-balanced and satisfactory diet essential for the maintenance of good health. The Government now became committed to provide a satisfactory diet for the entire population. This was greatly necessitated by the War. Consequent upon the development of new outlook on food the people now began to think in a different way. They were now eager to know what they should eat and why. The Government, therefore, began to pay more and more attention to the science of nutrition. Active steps were taken to stimulate thought and knowledge on the subject of correct diet and to produce and supply individual items of diet which were essential to remedy deficiency. Dr Aykroyd, the eminent nutrition expert, arranged short classes of instruction in nutrition for food officers and social workers in India. The Government was planning to find ways to bring science to help food industries secure a better food for India.[29] It was for the first time that the Government had taken up the problem of feeding, clothing and housing of the Indian population in a decent manner. It was trying to explore resources of production with sympathies which transcended the narrowness of provincial and inter-state boundaries. Indeed, it meant a radical change in the outlook of the Government. The Hot Springs resolutions on food and agriculture were an undertaking by every member of the United Nations to bring nutrition to their people up to standard required by health and to cooperate in bringing about the same standard in every part of the World.[30] This was a solemn undertaking. As a member of the UN, India was also bound to implement it. Hence, it was desirable for the Government to set up organizations to educate the Indian public in nutrition matters and to encourage the adoption of a better standard of diets.[31] As a matter of fact a new India was in the process of making and nothing was to stop it. India needed not only more food but better food. Science was going to play a big role in this noble task. During the War the idea of food requirement had also been revolutionalized. Previously, the people interested in food requirement had studied man as a machine. Appetite had been the natural guide to the amount of food required. So if people had enough food to satisfy hunger, they were regarded as adequately fed. But the experience in the later part of the War had shown that this was no longer true. The caloric intake of food must be carefully studied.[32]

At the end of the War India was in the process of food revolution as a consequence of a revolution in agriculture. The ICAR was playing a key role in revolutionizing agriculture in all aspects since 1942. A Fruit Research Institute was established at Lyallpur to develop fruit product industries all over India. Experiments in hybrid vigour had been conducted on maize, bajra, brinjal, tomato and tobacco. Hybrid crops yielded an extra produce of 50 per cent.[33] Research was also undertaken on the problem of animal nutrition from the breeding point of view. Steps were also taken for dairy development in the country. A wider introduction of fodder crops into Indian agriculture was to effect great improvement in yields and in total output. More food for animals meant more manure and enhanced fertility of soil.[34]

Realizing the need for development of fisheries as a source of essential protective food and its importance in "Grow More Food" Campaign, the Government of India appointed a fisheries development adviser in May 1944 and subsequently a deputy adviser for marine fisheries. To increase production of fish as a short term measure, various schemes were drawn up. Fisheries Training Courses were conducted at Calcutta and Madras to train candidates in all aspects on fishery development.[35]

The demand for fresh vegetables of all kinds increased considerably during the War, particularly in urban centres where there were large concentrations of industrial and defence personnel. Measures were taken to encourage the cultivation of European vegetables of both summer and winter varieties all over the country. Consequently, there had been a considerable extension in the area under vegetables. This presented a problem of procuring vegetable seed of all kinds. War dislocated the supply of seeds of European vegetables from the UK, USA and other foreign countries. Hence, arrangements were made to produce seeds of the European varieties of vegetables from the "mother seed" available in the country. Climatically suitable areas like Kashmir and Baluchistan were selected for the purpose. In 1943–44 nearly 1200 acres were utilized for the purpose which yielded 600,000 lbs of seeds.[36] Dr William Burns had already indicated the possibility of vegetable seed industry in India as a national asset after the War. Consequently, India managed to do without imports of vegetable seeds from abroad. Plans were also made to persuade rural areas to grow and consume more vegetables.

There was a tremendous scope for growing fruits in India. Most of the provinces and states had adopted fruit development schemes during the War to meet food shortage. During the War the Government felt the necessity of establishing a Central Horticultural Institute with substations all over India. Instructions were given to plant fruit trees along roads, public highways and canals. As the War created a great demand for fruits and vegetables the problem of storage and transport had to be tackled. A scheme of research on fruit and vegetable preservation was carried out at Lyallpur in Punjab. The Central Institute of Fruit Technology was established there. Ultimately, the Government had to recognize the importance of processed food in the economy of the country. The achievements made during the War in this respect had to be maintained and improved upon in the interests of preservation of food stuffs, general nutrition and industrialization of the country.[37] Canning of fruits had been started on a large scale in NWF. Province for the army. One up-to-date canning factory with a capacity of 300 tons had also started working in northern India in 1943.[38] The new industry of dehydration had also been greatly developed in India as a result of the War. Vegetable dehydration had travelled all the way from Canada to India. It was now placed in the top rank of processed foods. In time of war, however, they had a definite value as emergency rations and ships' stores.[39] Peaches and other fruits were dehydrated. Jams and marmalade were prepared locally for army canteens and messes. A laboratory was set up to test the samples of processed food and to give proper advice to the industry. The food manufacturing industry had a good prospect in post-War period as the demand for biscuits, butter, condiments, jams, marmalades and a large variety of other foodstuffs was likely to increase. To meet the most serious deficiencies of tropical diets the food yeast manufacturing industry was started in India. It could be added to any liquid food like soup, milk or mixed with flour for bread. It could also be added to the diet of children, aged and those suffering from vitamin B deficiency.[40]

One of army's most important war-time contributions to the preservation of food stuffs had been expansion of cold storage facilities in India since 1943 when there were only small cold storage installations at Calcutta, Bombay and Madras and about 30 smaller units scattered all over India.[41] Of course, even before the War cold storage facilities were available at the port towns, but they were not generally availed of except at Karachi. There were several reasons for this indifference. Firstly, the people had not yet realised the advantages of cold storage and few had seriously thought of utilizing them for storing cheap and perishable commodities such as potatoes. Secondly, the ports were at long distances from the main producing centres. Moreover, the cost of transportation to the cold storages and rents were rather high. The importance of cold storage for potatoes was, however, gradually realized. Hence, cold storages were erected exclusively for potatoes at important producing centres like Meerut, Sialkot, Patna and Jammu. In Sind the main producing area was within a few miles of Karachi and growers had already begun to make use of the facilities of cold storage both for table and seed potatoes. The storage of potatoes on commercial scale was started in Karachi in 1932.[42] But after the War widespread use of cold storage facilities appeared to be the only way of regulating supplies and prices. The Government took steps to encourage construction of cold storage in rural areas to facilitate collection of milk and also in urban areas for the storage of milk to facilitate distribution. Such stores were generally placed in cooperative sector.[43]

Refrigeration was considered to be the best method of preservation of perishable materials like fish, meat, vegetables etc. The Government took interest in popularizing this method of preservation of foodstuffs. As soon as the War ended some sixty new cold storage plants were erected for preservation of seed potatoes and other perishable materials. A number of ice-manufacturing plants were also set up. Cold storage plants varying from 3000 to 30,000 mds in capacity were set up at forty different centres and their total capacity ranged to nearly 1½ million maunds. The UP had the credit of having the largest number of cold storage plants, numbering 40 constructed mainly to store seed potatoes. Some cold storage plants were set up for storing various articles like fruits, vegetables, meat, fish, milk products, eggs etc. A few were specially marked for fish.[44] Refrigeration was a better method of preservation than canning or dehydration for retention of the original quality of foodstuffs. In post-War period its popularity increased considerably with the growth of education in India.

The development of the hydrogenated oil industry got a great spurt during the War. In 1941 there were only two factories of vanaspati industry but by the end of the War the number increased to 23. To overcome the shortage of fat in the general diet the Government thought it advisable to encourage this industry. The food value of vanaspati was hotly disputed at that time. Some asserted that it affected the optic nerve. But Dr W.R. Aykroyd, Director of the Nutritional research had certified that there was nothing objectionable from the nutritional point of view.[45] As soon as the War ended its demand was more than doubled.

Possibilities of a well organised food industry during the War were immense. Good many things were achieved by the application of science and technology. Food had even been produced from wood and fats had been made from coal.[46] To meet the needs of the army processing of food was started in India but it formed an integral part of general production and planning. The main purpose was to give storage life to perishable articles of food. Generally, people were much averse to its use. That restricted its demands. But the Government wanted to put food processing on the industrial map of India. Consequently, as soon as the War ended the Government undertook the planning and development of about 40 food industries. Some of them asked for protection while others were for the time being protected under the Import Control Regulation. Several schemes were undertaken such as the erection of a plant for preparation of soyabean milk, a plant for treatment of grains, improvement in the manufacture of foreign liquor produced in India and the use of seed cakes as human food.[47]

During the War the Central Government was very much conscious of its responsibilities to increase the supply of cattle for agricultural purposes as well as for milk. It created two important sections; namely, Dairy and Livestock under an adviser with necessary staff. The Army in India had already introduced a self-sufficient poultry scheme to organize independent production of eggs for its own requirement. The increased interest in poultry farming during the war was a new phenomenon. The poultry research section of the Institute (IVRI) at Izatnagar was doing its best to enhance this interest by research, teaching and advisory work. The Institute prepared taxoid and serum for tetanus for the military authorities in India.[48] The development of dairy industry was something new to India. The Army took the initiative for its development. The Government established the Imperial Dairy Research Institute at Bangalore to train necessary staff for the industry.

Thus, by the end of the War the colonial Government in India had to change its old outlook regarding its functions in relation to economic life of the people. The people were no longer left alone to solve their own economic problems. In May 1942 during the War the Government of India gave an assurance to the cultivators that if necessary, they would step into the market and purchase foodgrains to prevent a slump in prices. After re-examining the position in 1943 the Government repeated the assurance that should the prices of foodgrains go below a reasonable level, they would be prepared to intervene and buy at fair prices all the foodgrains offered to them in open market. This was really a departure from the earlier policy. The Government was now anxious to secure a reasonable return to the cultivators for their labour.[49] Subsequently, the Government appointed the agricultural price sub-Committee headed by Sir V.T. Krishnamachari on 21 February 1945. The Famine Commission (1944) had indicated that any repetition of the agricultural slump of the thirties would be disastrous to India and might bring progress to a standstill. Hence, it recommended an active price control policy which would ensure to the ryot a fair price for his produce in all circumstances. Taking this into consideration the V.T. Krishnamachari committee recommended that the state must guarantee minimum remunerative prices for selected agricultural commodities and ensure that the benefits reach the small cultivators as well as agricultural labourers. The state should also undertake other measures of agricultural and general economic development accompanied by a complementary policy for maintaining adequate employment, income and purchasing power.[50] The policy of minimum and maximum prices for major foodgrains and commercial crops should be enforced by the state. It also recommended that the Government should appoint an Agricultural Price Board to fix the fair prices of major agricultural products from year to year. It was really a radical departure from the old concept of *laissez faire* in economic matters. Hence, in 1946 a comprehensive document embodying the agriculture and food policy in India was prepared by the Government. It highlighted the objectives to be achieved and the measures to be adopted. It was to promote the welfare of the people and to secure a progressive improvement in their standard of living. This included the responsibility for providing enough for all, in sufficient quantity and of requisite quality. In order to achieve this end high priority was given to increasing the food resources of the country and particularly to reducing dependence on the vagaries of nature. Its aim was not only to remove the threat of famine but also to increase the prosperity of the cultivator, to increase the level of consumption and to create a healthy and vigorous population. The cardinal objectives of the policy were, first, to increase the production of foodgrains and protective food required to meet the basic needs of the population and to reduce dependence on imports; second, to secure for agricultural produce an assured market at a price remunerative to the producer and fair to the consumer; third, to improve the standard of living of the rural population and to solve the problems of rural economy which stood in the way of agricultural improvement; fourth, to stimulate the production of raw materials of industry, both for domestic manufacture and for export; fifth, to promote nutritional research and nutritional education as a prominent part of the public health programme and sixth, to enlarge the market for agricultural produce and augment the national wealth with a view to improving the national diet and to promoting industrial development.[51]

For attaining these objectives, the first essential was the enlargement and intensification of the measures already taken during the War for the purpose of food production. The results of research on improved methods of cultivation were to be made available progressively throughout the country. The production and distribution of improved varieties of seed needed expansion to cope with the demand. Health and increased employment be brought to the villages by such measures as the provision of education in the widest sense of the word, especially for women, eradication of endemic diseases, improvement of village communications, promotion of co-operative marketing and credit and encouragement to village industries. An adequate marketing organization was to be set up to ensure that middlemen's profits should be related to services rendered and the producer was to get a fair share of what the consumer paid. Communications between villages and markets, and methods of preservation of perishable foodstuffs were to be improved. Space for the storage of foodgrains was to be multiplied and improved. Assistance was to be given for the establishment of food processing and preservation of foodstuffs. Moreover, the standard of the quality of foodstuffs was to be improved and enforced. Facilities for obtaining special beneficial foods for mothers and children were to be increased. School feeding and industrial canteens were to be extended. The consolidation of holdings was to be encouraged and the fragmentation of holdings discouraged. Last but not the least important was the consultation with provinces to be undertaken regarding the existing system of land tenures which impeded the full productive use of land and the remedial measures to be taken. Thus, this policy statement on Agriculture and Food in India was a classic document. It embodied all that had happened in agriculture between 1926 and 1946 and also the outline of the course of action to be taken for achieving the objectives in full.

Thus, the planning for development of Indian agriculture during the War opened up a pandora's box of social problems. Dr William Burns gave a stern warning that India's population growth of over 5 million a year was far in excess of possible food production increase.[52] The Royal Commission on agriculture had frankly stated that all the proposed improvements would merely postpone the growing pressure on the soil. Sir Leonard Hill said: "Freedom from want in India and China can be obtained only by education and a wise measure of birth control".[53] Sir Edward Gait too concluded that the growth of population in India was like a glacier. It was irresistible and it would take years or generations before a tendency in that direction could be turned back. It seemed to him that development of irrigation and growth of industry could not possibly enable a decent standard of life to be maintained in the face of the rising pressure of population growth. Edward Thompson too concluded that the population growth if unchecked might reduce India to the status of one vast rural slum. Prof. A.V. Hill estimated in 1944 that the Indian population would increase to 730 million in next thirty years. If all these people were to be fed properly, the country would have to augment its food production three-fold.[54] Dr Henry Fairchild of New York University rightly commented that in ten years India had increased its population by 50 millions – a rise which even the best developed and most resourceful country could not afford without facing extreme disaster whenever an emergency situation such as War arose.[55]

Notes

1. *IASSI Quarterly*, January-June 1942, Vol. 10, pp. 8–9.
2. C.N. Vakil, *Poverty and Planning*, Allied, 1963, p. 14.
3. Ibid., p. 78.
4. ICAR, *Organization and Functions*; Delhi, 1948, p. 6.
5. Ibid., p. 66.
6. *Commerce*, 22 July 1944, p. 114.
7. *Asiatic Review*, Vol. XLII, January 1946, p. 36.
8. Ibid., p. 37.
9. *Indian Farming*, November 1942, p. 559.
10. Ibid., 1 May 1943, p. 259.
11. Ibid., August 1943, pp. 387–88.
12. Ibid., January 1944, p. 5.
13. Ibid., January 1945, p. 40.
14. *Asiatic Review*, April 1944, p. 162.
15. *Indian Farming*, October 1942, p. 559.

16. *Indian Information,* 15 January 1944, pp. 68–69.
17. T.N. Kaul, *Reminiscences*, New Delhi, 1982, p. 116.
18. *Asiatic Review,* October 1944, p. 434.
19. Ibid., July 1944, p. 260.
20. *Indian Farming,* March 1947, p. 140.
21. *Commerce,* 16 February 1946, p. 279.
22. Ibid., 6 July 1946, p. 9.
23. Ibid., 10 November 1946, p. 842.
24. Ibid., 1 July 1944, pp. 2–3.
25. Ibid.
26. Ibid., 15 April 1944, p. 262.
27. *Final Report of Famine Inquiry Commission*, p. 388.
28. Ibid., p. 400.
29. *Indian Information*, 15 December 1945, p. 670.
30. Ibid., 1 August 1943, p. 96.
31. Ibid.
32. Ibid., 1 November 1944, p. 481.
33. Ibid., 1 April 1944, p. 356.
34. *Final Report of Famine Inquiry Commission*, p. 342.
35. *Indian Information,* 15 September 1945, p. 283.
36. Ibid.
37. Ibid., 15 October 1945, p. 410.
38. Ibid., 15 July 1943, p. 43.
39. *Indian Farming,* December 1942, p. 660.
40. *Indian Information*, 15 January 1945, pp. 55–57.
41. Ibid., 15 May 1946, p. 614.
42. Ibid., 1 May 1941, p. 246.
43. Ibid., 1 January 1947, p. 24.
44. Ibid., 15 July 1948, p. 72.
45. *Commerce*, 22 March 1947, p. 629.
46. *Indian Information*, 15 May 1945, p. 629.
47. *Commerce*, 2 November 1946
48. *Indian Information,* 15 June 1941, p. 339.
49. Ibid., 1 June 1943, p. 428.
50. *Commerce*, 23 August 1947, p. 338.
51. *Indian Information,* 15 February 1946, p. 176.
52. *Asiatic Review,* Àpril 1944, p. 262.
53. Ibid., April 1943, p. 148.
54. *Commerce*, 15 July 1944, p. 98.
55. Ibid., 8 Febraury 1944, p. 160.

CHAPTER 4

New Horizon of Science and Technology in India

The Second World War was essentially a war of science and technology. Science played a vital role and ultimately decided the fate of the War. Both sides yoked the best talents of science for final victory. But the role of science in furthering human welfare was more spectacular and successful than its winning the War. British enterprise and American production methods created new world records in the arena of scientific achievements. A number of scientific developments in their destructive avatar appeared on the scene. But the wartime medical developments proved a blessing to humanity in normal time. The human sciences, medicine and surgery witnessed such achievements as never before. The War gave no less impetus to these sciences than to any other. The perfection of blood-transfusion methods and the manufacture of dry plasma on a large scale saved innumerable lives. The discovery of penicillin was a crowning glory of the efforts of the Allied scientists. DDT and gammaxene and other wonders of the War in the field of insecticides have contributed no less than penicillin to the health of mankind. All the world powers spent huge amounts on scientific research. Science became a proper concern of governments all over the world. This was in a sense a scientific age, where there was an ever increasing recognition throughout the world of the importance of science to national development.[1] A number of great nations were spending huge amounts in financing scientific and industrial research and benefiting greatly. Much attention was being paid to industrial processes and also in conducting research in pure science which might ultimately lead to the start of new industries. Supporting science adequately by planning and organization became the national policy all over the world.

At the beginning of the War in 1939 India was very backward in her industries and the government had no positive science policy at all. The needs of British administration and the influence of the Royal Society of London had led to the creation of scientific departments under the Government of India, namely, the Trigonometrical Survey, the Geological Survey, the Department of Meteorology, the Botanical Survey, the Imperial Forest Service and the Indian Medical Services.[2] But as War progressed, the government came to realize that only planned industrial research on many problems of the chemical, metallurgical and engineering industries could harness the country's vast resources for the prosecution of the War. This realization was given effect to by the creation of the Board of Scientific and Industrial Research in 1940 and subsequently by the creation of the Council of Scientific and Industrial Research with a government grant of Rs 5 lakhs a year which was later on raised to Rs 15 lakhs for all research work including war research spread over the whole of India. India's scientific contribution during the War was creditable. The organization of fundamental and applied research in India was put on a realistic basis.

With a meagre grant from the government Indian scientists started to build a new India alive to the demands of the War. Under the CSIR twenty-six research committees covering all the essential branches of science and technology were formed to plan and carry out research helpful to various industries and to the prosecution of the War. Research projects were also financed in Indian universities. Laboratories of CSIR were organized to conduct scientific research. They became a live centre of the research activities of the CSIR. Over two hundred research problems were investigated by the Council in the short period of the War. A number of new industrial processes were discovered to reinforce India's war efforts on the scientific side. The efforts of the CSIR made Indian industrialists aware of the importance of scientific research and thus helped in building of a new India.

The greatest achievement of science during the War worth remembering by posterity was the creation of an entirely new outlook on science by society. The scientist was now definitely acknowledged as a man who sought to organize the relations between nature and his fellow beings. The war-time achievements of men of science and their usefulness in peace increased their importance in society considerably. It was now realized that science must be organized like departments of state and there must be a flow of ideas and products in a continuous manner to keep science a living and useful thing. It was also realized that ordinary citizens and civil servants must be given insight into scientific matters. No planning and development of any government could be undertaken without the fullest consultation and active participation of the scientists. The happy collaboration between pure and applied research was one great achievement which caused far-reaching effects on human progress. In the USSR science was recognized as one of the essential mainstays of culture and was accorded a leading position in the development of technology and national economy.[3] During the War many physicists were learning for the first time that there was as much thrill and satisfaction in applying physical truths as in discovering them.[4] A new India was in the process of making and nothing could stop it. India was in the grip of a struggle between medievalism and modernism due to the all-pervading influence of science. This struggle had entered politics, science, agriculture, industry and even social life. Science was proving a catalyst for social changes in India. Nothing was expected to help more in this modernizing process than the pursuit of scientific and industrial research on a really extensive scale. Application of science to Indian problems was the only remedy. Scientific and industrial research in India was a virgin and fertile field. Hence, India needed science in abundance to solve her problems.

Till the middle of the War India had no definite science policy for industrial and scientific research. It was in August 1943 that she woke up to realize its necessity and asked the Royal Society of London to send a representative to India to advise about scientific matters, particularly in relation to industry and reconstruction and in bringing Indian scientific organizations into closer contact with those elsewhere. The Royal Society sent Prof. A.V. Hill, Secretary of the Society, to India for the purpose.[5] The British scientists had already established close contact and cooperation with scientists of the USA and Dominions for scientific research for successful prosecution of the War. There had been a continuous exchange of ideas between them. On arrival here Professor Hill did a commendable job as scientific adviser to the Government of India and tried his best to bring Indian scientists in contact with work done in other parts of the world. He felt strongly that the great long term problems of India were biological ones related to agriculture, health and population. No doubt industry, transport and the need for raising the standard of life all round had their bearings on these problems too. He believed that the brotherhood of science knew no frontiers or barriers of countries, creeds or races. The pursuit of knowledge, he said, for the welfare of mankind was one of the greatest agents of goodwill between men in every land. Hence, he recommended close scientific and technical liaison between India, Britain, USA and the Dominions. To implement it an Indian scientific office, be suggested, should be set up in London with specialists in agriculture, defence, engineering, industry and medicine. Representative Indian scientists should be attached to the British Commonwealth scientific office in Washington.[6] Young Indian teachers, research workers and members of technical staff must be provided with facilities for advance study abroad, especially in Great Britain. He recommended full-time teachers and research workers in all subjects in medical colleges. To provide first rate medical research centre in India, an all India medical centre should be established in Delhi entirely free of racial, religious, political or provincial bias. It was to have the finest of teachers and research workers and thereby produce a first rate doctors for India. There would be special hospital for the clinical study of malaria. Existing research institutes would be brought into close touch with medical colleges. The necessity of surveying the natural resources of India was strongly felt. Hence, he recommended the setting up of a Research

Board on Surveys and National Resources. He regretted that in a country like India, where breeding of animals and plants was of utmost importance, there was not a single chair in genetics in any of the Indian universities. Moreover, he said emphasis on quality of scientific research which, he laid, could be obtained by selecting and training only the best people, by setting up and maintaining a certain number of institutions of a very high standard.[7] He further indicated the four distinct lines of scientific development for India, namely, education, research, development of experimental trial and production for large-scale application. As a matter of fact these four processes concerned almost every aspect of national development. He also pointed out the importance of social medicine, which was one of the modern developments likely to have a bigger application in India than in European countries. It considered man in relation to his whole social environment instead of curing him when he fell ill. This was one of the many recent trends with which India, through its scientists and medical men, should keep in close touch. The greatest need in India at that time was the training of men. Indian industry and agriculture both required Indians trained in original research and with technical experience. This required technical institutes of a very high order in the country. This was the direct result of the War. Agriculture, being the greatest industry in India, required the resources of engineering and technology in addition to special agricultural research. Proposals for the development of fundamental research in meteorology had already been accepted and it was to be attached to a central organization for scientific research. It was urgently felt that there should be a proper scientific organization of research for the fighting services for all times to come. There should be a scientific adviser to the C-in-C with an organization similar to that of the Advisory Committee for Scientific Research in the Ministry of Supply in the UK. There should be a central organization for scientific research under a Minister without ordinary departmental duties with six boards, for Medical Research, Agricultural Research, Industrial Research, Surveys and Natural Resources, Engineering Research and War Research. Members of the boards would be research scientists and at least an equal number of professionals.[8]

As Professor Hill had great influence in the corridors of power in India, his recommendations were accepted easily. It was nothing short of a magic that some of his progressive schemes had been sanctioned within a few months. As scientific and industrial research activities were scattered over various departments, a mechanism for coordinating them was found in the creation of a scientific consultative committee at a high level. There was a sea-change in the attitude of the bureaucracy in India. Moreover, the War brought into focus the interdependence of industry and agriculture. Any large-scale programme of agricultural development should at the same time envisage a correspondingly large-scale development of those industries intimately connected with agriculture. Of these, power and fuel developments were the most important because it was impossible to introduce new methods of increased agricultural production without power and the facilities for transport if full economic use was to be made of agricultural efforts.[9]

During the War the idea of a great and imaginative plan of national development for India was in the air. If it was to succeed it might need all available resources whether of men or material and in that task science was to play an important part. Many of the great problems in agriculture, food, health, natural resources, power, transport, etc. needed first class scientific and technical knowledge for their solution. Large-scale industry or agriculture without adequate research was like a battleship or cruiser without an escort of destroyer or aircraft – it was pretty likely to get sunk.[10] A scientific outlook was needed in administration. The more a government office was staffed by persons having an appreciation of science and research, the more progressive and adaptable to changing circumstances it was likely to be. To neglect research was to invite calamity. Hence, it was suggested that India should spend at least one per cent of the total value of industrial production on scientific research.[11] Professor Hill also advised that opportunities must always be provided for the pursuit of science as a thing in itself and for its own sake and a scientist must be valued for his capacity for original thinking and discovery, not for the financial or practical value of his results. He also suggested that the whole business of planning should be put under a single national authority with a proper planning staff so that every aspect of national development could be properly looked into. On the whole Professor Hill helped the Government in formulating a science policy for India. Indian scientists were greatly encouraged by his visit. On his suggestion a mission of Indian scientists was sent to UK and some were made Fellows of the Royal Society.

It was strongly felt in the corridors of power that modern scientific knowledge and research together with modern industrial methods must be adopted to bring India at par with the other industrialized countries of the world. Indian industry must also play its part in laying a firm foundation for a stable society by providing the necessities of eduction, health, food and other things needed for a better life. Consequently, a progressive industry in India would need far more science and technology in future as its basis both in respect of tools, machinery and equipment and also in the education and training of those who would direct and operate it. India was capable of producing excellent scientists, technologists, engineers and workmen if given the training, education, experience and opportunity. The talent was there to exploit if only the opportunity and incentives were to be given. Somehow a sense of national purpose was to be created which would give the drive and initiative required.[12]

The War led to a number of salutary changes in India. It caused a large expansion of industry and thereby created a great demand for technicians of all grades. The Labour Department of the Government of India drew up a plan for technical training schemes and opened as many as 300 centres for the purpose. By 1945 as many as 80,000 technicians were trained and most of them were absorbed in the army.[13] Many of the young men who would not otherwise have embarked on a technical career had been recruited under these schemes and the prejudice against industrial employment had been breaking down. The process was likely to be accelerated with the expansion of technical education in the country. During the War the Bevin-boys' scheme was launched to train the Indian artisans in UK in batches of 50. This scheme was complementary to the scheme of the Labour Department of the Central Government. The Bevin-boys' scheme contemplated the more intensive training of artisans who were already skilled and employed. The first batch of Bevin-boys included Hindu, Muslim, Anglo-Indians, Sikh and one or two Parsis. About two-third of them had their previous experience in engineering industries such as railway workshops, in factories, in power houses and elsewhere. A good many of them were of middle class families, a few were sons of landowners and most of them were the sort of men who, a generation ago, would have been more likely to go in commerce or agriculture than in engineering. This indeed was one of the signs that India was changing and naturally they were aware of that change. On return some of them wanted to help India to industrialize. Under the Bevin-boys scheme some 800 technicians were trained in UK. On return many of them were employed on important war jobs and also in supervisory work in civil industries. Some were lucky to have been appointed as commissioned officers in the Corps of Indian Engineers. Others were employed as instructors in technical training centres or held technical posts in the army.[14] They formed a nucleus of genuine trade union leadership in India because they had received a course of lectures on the working of trade unionism in UK.

Before the War technical education was limited to catering to the demands of such sectors as railways, ordnance and a limited number of industries. The number of courses was limited and the subject was yet to become an integrated part of the whole educational system. But the War changed the whole outlook. Importance of technical bias in education was now considered essential. Technical education was now recognized as a branch of education. It now became an integral part of the educational system and not merely a special training for industrial employment. It was War that propelled the unprecedented demand for technical education all over the world. Its scope was widened. In India the technical education committee of the CABE felt strongly that technical education must be a wider and more liberal form of training than it had been in the past. It should include the study of design and distribution as well as the actual processes of manufacture. It must comprehend the scientific principles underlying the processes of manufacture as well as the processes themselves. It must link up the science of production and business organization with the art of design and salesmanship. It must also take cognizance of social science in relation to the effects of industrial development on the life of a previously non-industrial community. Moreover, it must not even neglect the provision of purely cultural and recreational facilities as an antidote against mental and moral stagnation for those workers who are destined to remain the semi-skilled servants of the machine.[15] It must now form a link between education and industry and must at the same time receive a separate consideration as a form of mental training. Moreover, technical education must include commercial education as well as art-in-industry and also agricultural education. This marked a new era in the history of technical education in India. The committee on agricultural education found the existing facilities for agricultural education wholly inadequate to meet the requirements of the country. Hence, it recommended a comprehensive and planned system of agricultural education from school to university stage. It also recommended the establishment of central institutes of advanced research in agriculture. In order to ensure the proper standard of instruction and training the ICAR was advised to set up a council of agricultural education. If agricultural education was to play the proper role in impending development of the country, it must be improved considerably and at once.[16]

To meet the impending requirement of technical personnel in the country a comprehensive system of technical education at all stages was called for. This was to meet the needs of the industry and commerce as well as to provide a suitable form of education for those whose natural abilities could be developed by instruction on particular lines. It was to be an integral part of the general educational system of the country.[17] It was perhaps the first effort to study the subject in such a wide perspective with regard to national interest. Its perception of the subject in the context of socio-cultural obligations really reflected a change in the colonial attitude. The formation of the Association of Principals of Technical Institutions (India) had been welcomed as an important step in the direction of coordinating technical institutions on all India basis. Appointment of a committee on higher technical education under the chairmanship of Shri N.R. Sarkar to advise on the matter was recommended. This committee recommended the setting up of the four Indian Institutes of Technology on the pattern of MIT of USA to meet the impending need of the country for technical personnel. It also recommended the creation of the All India Council for Technical Education which was to become the apex body of technical education in India. Thus, during the War there was a definite shift in the policy of the Government. For the first time it took up the matter with some seriousness in a wider context and initiated a policy with a long-term objective which was to usher in an era of great social changes in India. An earnest effort was made to organize and standardize technical education on all India basis and a beginning was made to promote it as a means of progress in the country. Commerce, agricultural education and art-in-industry became the parts of technical education.

The establishment of Delhi Polytechnic in 1941 was a landmark in the history of technical education in India. Its aim was to become a people's university. John Sargent was the architect of this scheme. The polytechnic idea applied main principles underlying basic education at a higher stage of instruction. It was to help the industrial India of the future. 'Learning by activity' was the basic philosophy of this scheme.[18] Services of Messrs Wood and Abbot were requisitioned from the UK for this purpose. The Delhi Polytechnic did not confine itself only to those subjects which people wished to study for improving their prospects. It was also to offer instructions in subjects like art and music and also to provide opportunities for further education for grown-up people who missed such opportunities in their youth. Thus, in this polytechnic an attempt was made to adapt Indian needs to a new educational principle already tried in Western countries. A centre for training of village craftsmen was also opened by the Delhi Polytechnic. The crafts to be taught included handloom weaving, leather work, oil pressing, soap making, brass work, carving in wood and ivory, gold and silversmithy and pottery.[19] The Delhi Polytechnic was the first of its kind. Similar institutions came up in other parts of the country later on.

The colonial government at last concluded that finance should not be so much of a bottleneck in post-war development as dearth of technical personnel. The government was aware of its responsibility and was willing to meet the situation in a big way. But the success of the technical education of every type depended on three factors, namely, recruitment of proper staff, selection of proper students and planned dovetailing of education into gainful employment.[20] Thus, there was a sea-change in the attitude of the Government. This miracle was brought about by the War.

To meet the growing demands of industries in India the CSIR decided in December 1943 to set up a committee under Sir R.K. Shanmukham Chetty to make a comprehensive survey of the existing facilities for scientific and industrial research in India and to recommend necessary measures for co-ordination, control, direction and development of research by various agencies and also steps necessary for planning of such research in post-War India.[21] The committee strongly recommended that the Government must take initiative to set up a suitable machinery for development of scientific research on sound lines, strengthen the science departments of Universities and existing research institutions. It should forthwith set up a central research organisation to be called the National Research Council representing scientists, universities, industry, labour and administration. It should also organise and maintain national laboratories and establish and maintain specialized research institutes. In order to remove the dearth of technical and research personnel the Government should provide for scholarships available in India and abroad immediately. Scientific teaching and research in Universities should be strengthened. A Board of standards and specifications should be set up to stimulate and encourage research in industry. A research Board was to be set up for administration of the work of the National Research Council. It was to be in charge of all research laboratories and institutions set up by the council. It was to prepare comprehensive plans for research programmes and to encourage the industry to set up research institutes of its own. The council was to be given a bloc grant of Rs 6 crores for five years for research and award of scholarships to train a sufficient number of technical personnel. It was suggested that the National Research Council must also work in close collaboration with the department of industrial planning so that industry and research would stimulate each other. Nine new specialized institutes were to be set up to deal with problems of basic research relating to food technology, metallurgy, fuel research, glass and silicate, oils and paints, buildings and roads, leather and tanning, industrial fermentation and electrochemical.[22] The committee also recommended the establishment of a first class technological institute on the pattern of MIT (USA). It was strongly felt even in the White Hall that India could never be prosperous or strong enough to maintain a free national life until she developed her industrial as well as agricultural resources.[23] Thus, a new path of social change was charted for India during the War.

Lord Wavell took a positive interest in the post-War planning in India and made the Government fully conscious and alive to the problems of industrialization. The dearth of trained technical personnel was the crux of the problem. As soon as the War ended the Government took steps and initiated a scheme to send abroad 500 scholars each year for higher technical training. The recommendations of the N.R. Sarkar committee on higher technical education were accepted immediately. It was really an epoch-making decision. Steps were taken to establish four higher technical institutions on the pattern of MIT (USA) to ensure adequate supply of high grade technical personnel for post-War industrial development. The first two were to be step up in the neighbourhood of Calcutta and Bombay to provide facilities for instruction of about 2000 under-graduates and 1000 post-graduates and research students. They were also to provide facilities for training men for fundamental and industrial research in engineering and technological subjects. The establishment of IIT went a long way towards meeting the dearth of technical personnel in India and ushered in an era of far-reaching social changes. The Delhi polytechnic was upgraded into a first class technological institute. The Indian Institute of Science, Bangalore, was also strengthened to provide facilities for training of power engineers. Steps were also taken to strengthen the three Central Universities of Delhi, Aligarh and Banaras. Provincial schemes regarding higher technical education, training for teachers and educational facilities for ex-servicemen received high priority.[24] The AICTE also decided to make available facilities for higher technical education at 14 technical institutions in India to be financially assisted by the Government. Students from all over the country were to be admitted to these institutions but needs of the backward provinces were to be essentially kept in mind in selecting students for admission. The rush for technical education was unprecedented. The extra facilities thus created were to be available to students from the whole of India. The existing higher technical institutions were strengthened to make them up-to-date in teaching and equipment. All efforts were made to upgrade the technical education to keep it at par with modern requirements. Thus, the Government was ready to face the challenge of the situation and changed its old colonial outlook. The AICTE also evolved a scheme for training of engineers and technocrats in business as well as in industrial administration, which was so essential if they were to take their rightful place in executive positions in the country's industry.[25] Thus, the age of management trained technocrats began.

Six hundred scholarships by Central and Provincial Governments for study abroad in 1946–47 were awarded.[26] A high powered selection board consisting of Sir Maurice Gwyer as chairman and Sir S.S. Bhatnagar and Sir John Sargant as members was created. The Government took special care to get the scholars admitted in different institutions in UK and USA and provided necessary foreign exchange. This prompt action to meet the shortage of technical personnel was highly creditable. It heralded the beginning of a great social change in India. Specialized knowledge and technical skill were to harness the power of science to the material development of the country. The application of technical knowledge to the needs of everyday life was the key to the economic well being, not only of the individual but that of the nation as a whole.

The Government was fully conscious of its responsibility in

the matter. A special sub-committee under Sir S.S. Bhatnagar as chairman was set up in 1947 to recommend certain urgent measures for the immediate improvement and expansion of facilities for scientific and technical training in Indian Universities and in special institutions. These were to be given the highest priority and to be initiated immediately. Recommendations of this committee were embodied in six sections dealing with scientific education, training of personnel for scientific and industrial research, industrial training, technical training for defence, shortage of equipments, housing etc. and steps to expedite government projects.

The committee recommended that the Government should utilize the existing resources to the full, viz. the universities, special institutions and the individual concerns by helping to create in them adequate facilities for higher education, research and practical training. Such help should come in the form of grants for scholarship on a liberal scale, the purchase of equipments, the opening of post-graduate departments in the universities which did not have such facilities at that time and the working of double shifts in places where scientific education was imparted. Besides, the several educational development plans in the offing must be pushed through immediately. Thus, education in science subjects got an unprecendented boost. Science teaching and technical education were co-related and they got a great upward swing. The Government had to plan for at least a four fold increase in the output of all categories of technical personnel to meet the needs of the country. Hence, both short term and long term programmes had to be initiated immediately. The short term programme included a proposal of a co-operative undertaking by the industries concerned and the technological institutions to give intensive training to M.Sc.'s and graduates in technology for a period of 12 months. Moreover, proposals for a three years course in engineering and of a double shift system in engineering colleges were recommended as short term measures. It was a crash programme for producing engineers within the shortest possible time.[27] The committee further urged the Government to begin work on the Eastern and Western IIT immediately. Similarly, it was suggested, the opening of power-engineering department in the Indian Institute of Science, Bangalore, must be expedited and the training of 'C' grade technicians proposed by the Ministry of Labour should be put into operation immediately. It was also recommended to levy a statutory cess (1/16 per cent) on industrial production to supplement the grants from the Government on research. A bloc grant of Rs 6 crore for five years for the establishment of various national laboratories and to provide funds to universities and special institutions was recommended. A system of keeping a register of all employable technical personnel was recommended. The creation of a scientific service equal in status and emoluments with administrative services was recommended.

Ultimately, the Government of India set up with effect from 1 June 1948, a department of scientific research under the Prime Minister. It was to include in its fold the CSIR, the Board of atomic research and such other functions of the Director of CSIR which the Government might decide to transfer to it. It was also to co-ordinate the scientific activities of other ministries. The Department was to be assisted by a co-ordination committee consisting of prominent scientists.[28]

Before the War, geology, mining and metallurgy were treated as Cinderellas among science subjects in universities and high grade technical institutions. Only a handful of students went in for training in these subjects and those who eventually passed out, had to run from pillar to post to secure even the smallest of jobs, carrying not more than bare pittance as remuneration. This was inevitable in a regime of *laissez faire* and almost complete inaction in the field of mineral development. But the War changed the situation. Expansion of industries now demanded large-scale mineral development under centralized control. The mineral policy of the Government had to be changed to suit the needs of the country. A large cadre of mining and metallurgical technicians was needed to speed up industrialization in the country. Two measures were adopted. Firstly, the fullest use of existing supply of manpower was to be made. Secondly, there was to be a rapid increase in the out turn of Indian universities and technical institutions in these subjects to meet the expanding demands.[29]

During the War the need for mineral development was strongly felt and the Government was obliged to take some steps in this direction. The Geological Survey was strengthened and a utilization branch was set up to develop the mineral resources of the country. During the War India was being combed for minerals essential for war purposes. Minerals which had not been worked for over a century were being now examined. Industrialists and scientists now became fully aware of the importance of minerals of various kinds in the development of the country.

Reorganization of the Indian School of Mines, Dhanbad, was undertaken. Its standard was to be raised to that of Royal School of Mines, London. The annual intake of students was to be increased from 24 to 60, consisting of 48 mining and 12 geology students. The three-year certificate course was to be abolished and the four-year course either in mining engineering or geology was to be introduced.[30] Special attention was given to subjects like fuel technology, oil technology, refractory and ceramics, metallurgy and physical prospecting.

During the War the Government took steps to enlarge the geological studies by opening of geological faculties in some of the Indian universities. Schemes of advanced training in geology and mining in some foreign countries were worked out and put into operation. On the advice of Dr A.N. Wadia, a national mineral policy was outlined.[31] The need for accelerated mineral development was recognized in the industrial context of the country. The Government created scholarships for Indian students for overseas studies in Geology and Metallurgy – 22 in Metallugry, 18 in Geology and 3 in Geophysics. It really marked a great change in the outlook of the colonial Government.[32] The American Chemical Society also offered 10 scholarships for chemists and chemical engineers to pursue advanced studies in USA. But the selection of candidates was entrusted to UNESCO.[33]

National Metallurgical Laboratory was established at Jamshedpur. It was the need of the hour. Dr George Sachs of Cleveland, Ohio, USA took charge as its director on 1 April 1948. The NML was to cover all aspects of metallurgical research work on ores, minerals and refractories. Special consideration was given to research work on non-ferrous metals like copper, aluminium, manganese, zinc, titanium and berrylium – which India had in abundance and for the production of which large power resources were also available. Moreover, steps had already been taken to set up the Central Glass and Ceramic Research Institute at Calcutta, the Central Fuel Research Station at Dhanbad, the National Chemical Laboratory at Poona and the National Physical Laboratory at Delhi. These national laboratories of science provided infrastructure and stimulus to Indian scientists who were to play an important role in building up a new India.

As soon as independence came the national Government planned to expand the Geological Survey of India to more than five times its pre-War cadre. The War had changed the whole perspective of mineral policy. As industrialization was coming up in a big way at the end of the War, it was imperative on the part of the Government to be ready for the programme of mineral development and to be equipped with the trained personnel and modern equipment for exploration and utilization of mineral resources. Efforts were being made for increasing the technical manpower in the country relating to mining by reorganizing the Indian School of Mines, Dhanbad, and by aiding the geological and mining faculties of universities and by sending abroad scholars and officials on scholarship and on deputation for higher training in Mining, Geology, Geophysics and allied subjects. The Government attached the greatest importance to the mining and metallurgical development in the country and to removing the shortage of technical manpower of all grades.

To meet the impending need of industrialization the Government of India accepted the following basic principles of mineral policy:

(a) attainment of metal and mineral self-sufficiency as far as possible;
(b) central regulation and control of mineral development;
(c) acquisition by the state of mineral rights from private holders;

(d) regulation of international trade in minerals of key importance;

(e) encouragement of local utilization of the products of Indian mines.

To carry out this policy the Indian Bureau of Mines was being organized.[34]

As soon as the War ended, on the recommendations of CSIR, a committee was constituted under the chairmanship of Dr H.J. Bhabha to explore the possibility of finding out raw materials in India for generating atomic energy and to suggest ways and means of harnessing them and to keep in touch with similar organizations in other countries. The other members of the committee were: Dr S.S. Bhatnagar, Dr K.S. Krishnan, Dr M.N. Saha, Dr A.N. Wadia, Dr Nazir Ahmad and Dr Jivraj Mehta.[35]

A plan with regard to the uranium and thorium deposits discovered then in India was worked out by the Atomic Research Committee and a Uranium Unit under the Geological Survey of India.[36]

Thus, the way was paved for the creation of the Atomic Energy Department in India. A technological revolution was indeed in the offing. Science and technology were becoming the hallmark of progress in India.

Just at the end of the War a five year scheme for development of Anthropological Survey of India was approved. The impending changes in the social and administrative services of India required expert advice for a properly developed Anthropological survey department, if the country was to assimilate about 25 millions of the aboriginal and tribal people in a satisfactory manner in her general system. It was aimed at ensuring the steady growth of competent Anthropological Survey Department to fulfil the need of the country. The tribal problem was really a new challenge for the Indian administration and it needed a new outlook.

The War had to its credit many blessings. One of them was the Operational Research. It was an inter-disciplinary activity that originated solely to meet the practical needs of the Second World War in the UK and USA. It is the scientific study of processes and methods of work in the field, office, or on the bench in order to increase their efficiency. It naturally implies a friendly criticism of existing state of affairs. It was initially designed to apply science to the service of War in an entirely novel way. It was concerned not only with the investigation of technical problems arising in the use of new equipment and devices, but also with the scientific analysis of actual performance of equipment under field conditions and the development of new uses for them. The technique of operational research has vast possibilities during peace time. Within the framework of industrial organization, Operational Research deals with the organization of production system in accordance with quantitative checks on the efficiency of each step. This approach meant to develop a scientific model of system, incorporating measurement of factors such as chance and risk in order to predict and compare the outcome of alternative decisions, strategies and control. The purpose is to help the management to determine its policy and actions scientifically.[37]

The manufacture of internal combustion engines in India both for civil and defence purposes and also for research engaged the attention of the CSIR. It was the pioneer body in ushering in technological revolution in India. It decided to establish a national internal combustion engineering laboratory for type testing of internal combustion engine for land transport, stationary engine for power purposes and small size engines for water transport including diesel-electric generating sets, testing and research on fuels and on metals and alloys. It was decided to send fifteen students abroad for advanced study and training in internal combustion engineering in order to meet the needs of the national laboratories, industries and technological institutions.[38] The CSIR took special interest to speed up the manufacture of internal combustion engines in India as early as possible.

As India had under active consideration a number of extensive hydro-electric and irrigation schemes just on the eve of independence, the demand for electric motor increased considerably. Before the War the electric motor industry was hardly in existence, but in 1948 the industry was firmly established and was in the process of being expanded so as to meet the country's needs. The total annual capacity of the five large producers of electric motor was about 9,21,000 HP which covered 90 per cent of the annual consumption of the types of motor produced in India.[39] Electric motor revolutionized the life of people. Lord Wavell gave full support for development of the country by hydro-electric schemes, irrigation, road-making and other engineering activities connected with agriculture and industries.[40] Hence, emphasis was focused on the importance of the electrical machinery industry to make up the deficiencies in various sectors.[41]

The War focused the attention of the Government of India on the development of electric power in India for the army as well as for civil population. Its potentialities for economic development had been well recognized by all. The total electricity generated in India in 1943 was about 3578 million kw about the same as the weekly production of energy in USA at that time. In the USA about 130 times as much energy was used per head of population as in India, while in UK the figure was about 100 times as much.[42] These comparisons indicated the vast scope and need for the augmentation of electrical power in India.

In 1943 Mr H.M. Mathews, the Electrical Commissioner with the Government of India, convened a conference of leading power engineers in India to consider post-War power development. The conference prepared a schedule of heavy power equipment required by India for electrical development immediately after the War. In addition the conference passed resolutions concerning:

(a) electrical power development in the Provinces and Indian States;
(b) constitution of Central Technical Power Board;
(c) investigations to be carried on in certain prospective power development projects; and
(d) railway electrification, manufacture of synthetic fertilizer and rural electrification.

It was the first occasion on which power development programme of the country was reviewed as a whole.[43]

The Government acted promptly and constituted a Central Technical Power Board on 8 November 1944 with Mr Mathew as chairman and Mr Voordwin as member. Its function was to act as a Central Government Engineering Planning Agency to be available to the Central, provincial and state governments for preparation of multi-purpose hydro-electric and thermal power schemes. It was also to provide economic studies and to recommend the course of action necessary for implementation of the various projects. The Board acted purely as a technical advisory body without any mandatory powers.[44]

Thus, the infrastructure for electrical power development in India had been erected during the War itself. Consequently a social change of much significance was in the offing. The Central Technical Power Board had a triple-action programme: (a) creation of large-scale power stations located in the main industrial areas under the control of public supply undertakings; (b) construction of transmission system with smaller secondary lines attached to it for tapping agricultural and other outlying areas covering the entire region in a power ring; and (c) standardization of frequency within the region to be developed by the power system.

This triple-action programme constituted the foundation of the 'grid system'. The Government of India prepared a scheme for sending ten engineers to receive training abroad on the commercial and administrative side of the electric supply industry. Two more such batches were to be sent for training in the technical aspects. Thus, the Central Government was very much alive to the problems of electric power development and took timely action to implement the programme. Equitable use and distribution of electricity was expected by the adoption of the 'grid system' and the establishment of provincial electricity Board was perhaps a new thing in the history of electricity generation in India:[45]

The 'Grid system' meant, in effect, a regionally coordinated scheme of electrical development which transcended the geographical limits of a municipality, cantonment board or a notified area committee and in order to make it effective it envisaged the erection of large-scale power stations located at suitable places within a particular region and the construction of a main transmission system with smaller secondary lines attached to it for tapping in agricultural and other outlying areas. This necessarily called for the establishment of provincial electricity Boards to perform two-fold functions. Firstly, they were to promote all-round development of electricity within the limits of their jurisdiction and secondly, to effect rationalization in supply of power. The Board was also to establish new generating stations or control existing ones and also to inter-connect the stations by means of main transmission lines. The Board was also to buy electricity in bulk from the owners of controlled stations or sell it to them and to other licensees.

Just on the eve of independence in 1947 the hydel power potential was estimated to be about 30 to 40 million KW. The total installed capacity at that time was below 2 million KW. In the first stage the Government planned to increase the power resources to 3.7 million KW till 1955 – an increase of 170 per cent in the course of next seven years or eight years.[46] At that time the annual per capita consumption of electric power in India was 9.2 KW hours as against 906 in England, 1470 in the USA, 3090 in Norway and 3510 in Sweden. Of even this low output and consumption of electric power nearly 50 per cent was accounted for by the four cities of Bombay, Calcutta, Kanpur and Ahmedabad which together contained less than 1.5 per cent of the country's population.

Out of 412 electricity undertakings in India in 1947, 300 belonged to private companies, 249 of them to British India and 51 to the Indian states. In terms of installed capacity 73.19 per cent of it belonged to privately owned companies and the rest of municipalities and the Government.

The comprehensive powers invested in newly created provincial electricity boards over private undertakings constituted a step towards nationalisation rather than an obstacle to it.[47] There was an urgent need for a national power policy in the changed circumstances. The demand for power was expanding very rapidly in view of the rising pace of industrialization in India. Even during the War the Government had planned to increase the output of electrical energy three times on a really widespread scale and not merely concentrated in urban areas only. There was enough scope for expansion of electricity in

India. Only 7 per cent of the electricity used in India was consumed on domestic premises. Over 42 per cent of electrical energy throughout India was utilized till the end of the War in the cities of Calcutta and Bombay alone.[48] In 1944 a conference of power engineers recommended that in planning for further development of electricity the essential needs of the rural community should be adequately catered for. Cheap power was essential to encourage cottage industries in India.[49] Thus, the huge potential of electrical power in India called for a major expansion of facilities for higher training of power engineers – civil, hydraulic, mechanical and electrical. The electrical commissioner felt the necessity of establishing a new power engineering college in India. Electricity was to bring notable social changes in the life of the people. The slogan of the national government was "every village to have electric light and every home a radio".[50]

A large number of trained power engineers were urgently needed just after independence. Hence, it was decided to start a power engineering department in the Indian Institute of Science, Bangalore which had special advantages for such a course of training because of its post-graduate departments in allied sciences and technology and its proximity to several hydraulic power stations. The proposed department was to be provided with adequate laboratory equipment and also with an installation of heavy power plant on which the students of power engineering were to do the work of operations, maintenance and repairs in order to obtain complete training as power-engineers.[51] Even the Advisory Planning Board set up in 1946 had pointed out that there was a serious lack of electrical engineering personnel, equipment and raw material. There was a grave deficiency of electrical engineers in the experience of designing as distinct from operation and also the lack of irrigation engineers with experience of high dams. The Board recommended the requirement of foreign assistance in the matter and also to make arrangement for training young Indian engineers so that within a reasonable time foreign personnel might be replaced.[52] American experts came to advise the CTPB on generating hydelpower on the dam sites in the Damodar project.[53]

Thirty Indian technicians representing different industries were included in a team of American and British experts who were sent to investigate German industrial and technical processes after her surrender in May 1945.[54] This proved highly advantageous to Indian industries. Thus, by the end of the War there was a complete change in the outlook of the Government towards Indian industries – from apathy to active encouragement. This was a fallout of the War.

Anticipating the needs of the country the Central Government established the Central Water and Power Commission in 1940 and its research station near Pune. Subsequently, the Central Waterways, Irrigation and Navigation Commission was set up in 1946. These institutions proved of much significance in independent India.

To meet the demands of the civil industries after the War the Government prepared a training scheme for artisans leading to national certificate of craftsmanship recognizable all over India. A significant feature of the scheme was emphasis on general education and apprenticeship in the factory under government supervision. A tripartite agreement was to be executed by the apprentice, employer and the government. Regional technical training committees were constituted in the provinces. They were in charge of apprenticeship training within their respective areas.[55] Sir William Stampe, irrigation adviser to the Government of India, outlined a scheme to prepare a ground-water contour map of the whole of alluvial India in cooperation with the Geological Survey of India and the staff of CWINC. He had also conceived a plan to sink 5000 tubewells in northern India.[56] Thus, by 1947 India was well poised for social changes of much significance.

NOTES

1. *Indian Social Reformer*, 3 February 1945, p. 103.
2. Ibid.
3. *Indian Information*, 15 June 1945, p. 827.
4. Ibid.
5. Ibid., 15 December 1943, pp. 342–43.
6. Ibid., 1 March 1945, p. 305.

7. *Commerce,* 15 April 1944, p. 600.
8. *Indian Information,* 1 March 1945, p. 306.
9. *Asiatic Review,* January 1945, p. 15.
10. *Indian Information,* 1 May 1944, p. 476.
11. Ibid., 15 January 1944, pp. 68–69.
12. Ibid., October 1944, p. 354.
13. Ibid., 15 September 1945, p. 253.
14. Ibid.
15. *Report of the Technical Education Committee of CABE,* 1946, p. 4.
16. Ibid., p. 64.
17. Ibid., p. 14.
18. *Indian Information,* 15 April 1943, p. 345.
19. Ibid.
20. *Commerce,* 6 April 1946, p. 595.
21. *Indian Information,* 1 October 1945, p. 366.
22. Ibid., p. 368.
23. *Indian Information,* 15 June 1947, p. 177.
24. *Commerce,* 1 May 1948, pp. 738–39.
25. *Indian Information,* 15 January 1946, p. 102.
26. Ibid., 15 September 1947, p. 181.
27. Ibid., 1 July 1948, p. 47.
28. Ibid., 15 February 1947, p. 152.
29. Ibid., 23 August 1947, p. 330.
30. Ibid., 1 February 1947, p. 86.
31. Ibid., 1 April 1947, p. 322.
32. Ibid.
33. Ibid., 15 August 1948, p. 91.
34. Ibid., 15 February 1946, p. 193.
35. Ibid., 15 March 1947, p. 269.
36. Ibid., 1 March 1944, p. 246.
37. Ibid., 15 September 1947, p. 189.
38. Ibid., 1 July 1948, p. 33.
39. Ibid., 15 December 1944, p. 776.
40. Ibid., 15 May 1947, p. 465.
41. Ibid., 1 March 1945, p. 296.
42. Ibid., 15 February 1945, p. 235.
43. Ibid., 15 November 1946, p. 336.
44. Ibid., 15 January 1948, p. 95.
45. *Commerce,* 10 April 1948, p. 602.
46. *Indian Information,* 15 January 1948, p. 95.
47. Ibid., 15 March 1945, p. 296.
48. Ibid., 1 February 1947, p. 92.
49. Ibid., 15 January 1948, p. 95.

50. Ibid., 15 August 1946, p. 95.
51. Ibid., 15 February 1947, p. 135.
52. Ibid., 1 April 1946, p. 403.
53. Ibid., 15 May 1946, p. 619.
54. Ibid., 15 March 1945, p. 375.
55. *Asiatic Review*, April 1947, p. 99.
56. Ibid.

CHAPTER 5

The Depressed Class Movement Goes Radical

Ever since its inception the Indian National Congress had scrupulously avoided discussion of social problems at its annual sessions. Such problems were discussed in the social conferences held just after the Congress sessions. But in 1917 the situation was different. It was the most crucial year of the First World War. The British were very anxious to secure the support of the Indians at large for the War. Hence, on 20 August 1917 Montagu, the Secretary of State for India, announced the policy of 'gradual realization of responsible government in India as an integral part of the British Empire' as the ultimate goal of the British rule in India. It aroused hopes and aspirations all over India. The War had already stirred the Depressed Classes. In November 1917 they organized two meetings in Bombay and passed two resolutions praying to the British Government to protect their interests by granting them right to elect their own representatives to the proposed councils in proportion to their numbers to ensure their civic and political rights. They also prayed for adoption of a system of compulsory and free education for the 'Untouchables' because social elevation of their community depended upon the universal spread of education among them. They also asked the Congress to pass at its forthcoming session a distinct and independent resolution for removal of all disabilities imposed by religion and social customs on the Depressed Classes as part of the bargain to support the Congress-League scheme of reforms.[1] Thereafter the Congress at its annual session in 1917 passed a resolution for removal of social disabilities of the Untouchables. But this was nothing more than a measure of political expediency and nothing came of it.

In the spring of 1918 the 'Untouchables' decided to assert themselves. They were holding conferences at frequent intervals which were attended by all classes of people. One such conference was held in 1918 at the time of Montagu's visit to India. They once again demanded that in the proposed constitutional reforms they be given separate representation in provincial and imperial legislatures. Moreover, they demanded a Royal Commission to enquire into the grievances of the depressed. A special resolution congratulating Dr B.R. Ambedkar on his return from the USA after completing his education was also passed.[2] Henceforth, he began to take interest in the Depressed Classes movement. It was a significant event in the history of India. The tone and temper of the movement underwent a radical change. B.R. Ambedkar emerged as a passionate fighter for the cause of the 'Untouchables' and he stood for social reforms for them not as an act of philanthropy and charity but as a matter of right. He exhorted them to stand on their own feet. In 1919 in his evidence before the Southborough Committee he pleaded for a separate electorate for the Untouchables.[3] At the Nagpur conference of the Depressed Classes in May 1920 the first organized attempt for uplift of the Untouchables was made. It laid the foundation of Ambedkar's future work as champion of the Untouchables. He took up the work with a missionary zeal and launched a weekly paper *Mook Nayak* to champion the cause of the Untouchables. It articulated the views and aspirations of downtrodden and prayed to the British Government to treat all Indians as equals. Later on, he founded another fortnightly Marathi paper entitled *"Bahiskrit Bharat"* in Bombay. To create socio-political consciousness among the Untouchables he also founded the Bahiskrit Sabha which became their main organ to spread education, to improve economic conditions and represent the grievances of the Untouchables to the proper authorities.

In 1920s the time had changed. Political parties began to include abolition of untouchability in their programme. As soon as M.K. Gandhi came at the helm of affairs in the

Congress he adopted a constructive programme of social-amelioration which included the uplift of the Depressed Classes. To him the removal of untouchability was the most powerful factor in the process and attainment of Swaraj.[4] Similarly, the National Liberal Party of the Central Legislative Assembly in 1922 had declared its objective to promote the well-being of the untouchables as well as protection of the interests of minorities.[5]

The Montagu Report recognized the problem of the untouchables and pledged to make arrangement for their representation in the proposed legislatures. But the South Borough Committee provided them representation in legislatures by nomination in the absence of satisfactory electorate. The Depressed Classes were allotted only seven seats to be filled by nomination out of a total of eight hundred in provincial and central legislatures. The Government considered it quite inadequate and recommended seats for the untouchables to be doubled. Thus, their right to special representation in the legislature under the Act of 1919 had been accepted and adopted in the Constitution. This principle had been extended to District Local Boards, School Boards and Municipalities, too.[6] Under this provision Dr B.R. Ambedkar was nominated as a member of the Bombay Legislative Council in 1927. This provided him with a good forum to voice the grievances of the untouchables. Previously, social workers aiming at the uplift of untouchables were motivated by humanitarian ideals only. They tried to improve the conditions of the untouchables by means of propaganda, opening of schools and hostels for them. But Ambedkar's method was quite different. Undoubtedly, he wanted all that the reformers were doing but he wanted the untouchables to be self-reliant and be prepared to fight for political rights as for their improvement in social, educational and economic fields. He did not like the untouchables to depend on the charity of others. Moreover, Ambedkar advocated open revolt in the form of direct action against Hindu established order. He himself became the symbol of revolt. He was now fully convinced that petitions and protests had failed to move the Hindus. In 1920s the Government had declared all public utilities and public institutions open to all citizens including the untouchables. But owing to the opposition of the caste Hindus the Untouchables were not able to make any use of them. To meet this situation the Untouchables under the leadership of Ambedkar decided to take direct action to get their wrongs redressed. One such direct action was taken in 1927 in case of Chodar tank at Mahad in Colaba district. Ultimately, the Hindus had to yield and the tank was opened to all. Later on, he also initiated the Kalaram temple entry satyagraha at Nasik and the Guruvayur temple entry in Malabar. Such direct actions were the best way of energizing the Untouchables and making them conscious of their rights. This was just a method to awaken them. Ambedkar also organised the burning of the *Manusmriti* to denounce the caste system of Hinduism. But he asked the Depressed Classes to concentrate their energy and resources on education and political rights. He wanted to make them a force in Indian politics. Hence, his whole emphasis was on political awakening and the need for effective organisation. His slogan for his community was "educate, agitate and organise".[7] He was fully convinced that the problem of the Depressed Classes would never be solved unless they got political powers in their own hands.[8]

In 1927 the Simon Commission was appointed to investigate into the working of the Act of 1919 and report upon such changes as might be necessary. As no Indian was included as member of the Commission, the Congress and the liberals decided to boycott it and launched an agitation against it. Ambedkar thought otherwise and decided to cooperate with the Commission. He took it as a great opportunity to represent demands of his community before the British Government. He urged most emphatically that the Depressed Classes should be treated as a distinct community, entirely different from the Hindus and should be classified as a minority like the Muslims and the Sikhs for the purpose of election. He pleaded for sufficient safeguards for his community in the proposed constitution. In a memorial to the Simon Commission the Bahiskrit Hitkarini Sabha pleaded for adequate protection of the civil rights of the Depressed Classes as a minority and proposed that their education should be recognized as the first charge on the revenue of the Bombay Presidency and an equitable proportion of the total grant for education should be earmarked for them. Their right to unrestricted recruitment to the Army, Navy and the Police should be recognized without any limitation as to caste. They also pleaded for the right of the Depressed Classes to priority in the matter of recruitment to all posts in all civil services and also for their effective representation on the local bodies.[9] Dr Ambedkar specially pleaded for greater political protection for them than any other community in British India on account of their being educationally, economically and socially very backward and also because they suffered from certain grave political disabilities from which no other community suffered.[10] Dr Ambedkar was very much critical of the Nehru Report (Motilal) because it made no special provisions for representation of the Depressed Classes in the legislatures although it conceded the right of the Muslims for separate electorate. Hence, he took special care to acquaint the Simon Commission with the grievances of his community.

To consider the recommendations of the Simon Commission regarding the constitutional reforms in India the British Government convened a Round Table Conference of the British political parties, Indian political parties and Indian princes in November 1930. The Depressed Classes were allowed to be represented separately by two delegates, namely, Dr B.R. Ambedkar and Dewan Bahadur R. Srinivasan. This meant the Untouchables were regarded not merely a separate element from the Hindus but also of such importance as to have the right to be consulted in the framing of a constitution for India. It was really a landmark in the history of the Depressed Class movement to be represented at such a conference. Dr B.R. Ambedkar took up this opportunity to submit a scheme of political safeguards for the Depressed Classes in the future constitution of India at the Round Table Conference. In this scheme he particularly emphasized that the Depressed Classes must be given sufficient political power to influence legislative and executive action for securing their welfare. They should be given right to adequate representation in central and provincial legislatures by adult suffrage and separate electorate for the first ten years and thereafter by joint electorate and reserved seats. This joint electorate must not be forced upon them against their will unless such joint electorate was accompanied by adult suffrage.[11] He also demanded adequate representation for them in services and in the cabinet. He emphasized that unless their representatives were included in the cabinet, the work of social uplift and removal of untouchability would not be effectively implemented. He even gave a warning that unless their demands were met in a reasonable manner, the Depressed Classes would not consent to any self-governing constitution for India.[12] The Congress was not represented at the first Round Table Conference due to its launching of the Civil Disobedience movement. But it participated in the second Round Table Conference held in September 1931 with Gandhiji as its leader. He claimed in his own person, to represent the vast mass of Untouchables in India and opposed tooth and nail the demand of Ambedkar for separate electorate for the Untouchables. He clearly stated that he could tolerate the proposal for separate electorate for the Muslims and the Sikhs only as a necessary evil, but it would amount to positive danger for the Untouchables because that would ensure their bondage in perpetuity.[13] The demand made by Ambedkar on behalf of the Untouchables for separate electorate was to him the unkindest cut of all.[14] He even declared in all seriousness that if he was the only person to resist this thing, he would resist with his life.[15] Gandhiji became sentimental and did not look at the problem from the angle of the Untouchables. At the back of his mind he was determined to prevent the disruption of the Hindu society. Moreover, the separate electorate for the Untouchables would have weakened the mainstream of Indian nationalism.

As the majority and minority parties at the second Round Table Conference would not reach a common agreement regarding distribution of seats in proposed legislatures, the matter was entrusted to the British Prime Minister for arbitration. On 17 August 1932 Ramsay Macdonald, the British Prime Minister gave his decision, which was known as the Communal Award. He conceded the demand of the Depressed Classes for special representation in a limited number of seats in which only members of that community would vote for their own representatives along with their right also to vote in the general Hindu constituency. Thus, they were given the right of double vote. This was quite different in conception and effect from the separate electorate granted to the Muslims and the Sikhs. A Muslim could not vote or be a candidate in a general constituency, whereas any electorally qualified member of the Depressed Classes could vote and be a candidate from the general constituency. This was provided solely to keep the Hindu society unimpaired and at the same time to secure at least a minimum number of seats for the Untouchables. But Gandhiji became too sentimental and regarded this limited separate electorate for the Depressed Classes as the injection of poison calculated to destroy Hinduism.[16] He was against their statutory separation even in a limited form. Under the Communal Award the Depressed Classes were to remain part of the Hindu community and were also to vote with the Hindu electorate on an equal footing in the general constituencies but for the first twenty years, they were to get special representation in limited constituencies just in order to safeguard their rights and interests. Gandhi did not look to the logic of the Award and began his 'fast unto death' as a protest against the Award on 20 September 1932 in the Yervada jail. The whole of caste-Hindu India rallied round to save the life of Gandhi. The only way to save his life was to alter the Communal Award. But the British Cabinet was not to withdraw or alter it of its own. They were ready to substitute it for a formula agreed upon by caste-Hindus and the Untouchables. All eyes then turned to Dr B.R. Ambedkar. He found himself in a baffling situation. As he had the privilege of representing the Untouchables at the RTC, it was assumed that the assent of the Untouchables would not be valid unless he was a party to it. His position as the leader of the Untouchables of India had been by then accepted as a fact. He had to make a choice between two different alternatives. There was the duty which he owed as a part of the common humanity to save Gandhi from sure death. There was another alternative for him to save the political rights of the Untouchables which the Award had given them. He responded to the call of the humanity and saved the life of Gandhi by agreeing to alter the Communal Award in a manner satisfactory to Gandhi. He met

Gandhi in Yervada jail and agreed to a formula known as the Poona Act (24 September 1932). Under the Award the Untouchables were given 78 reserved seats out of about 1500 in the provincial legislatures to be elected by separate electorate. But the Poona Pact increased the number of reserved seats for the Untouchables from 78 to 148 to be filled by joint electorate. This took away the right of double vote of the Untouchables. This increase of seats under the Poona Pact was no compensation for the loss of the double vote whose value as political weapon was beyond reckoning. The second vote given to the Untouchables by the Award was a priceless privilege. With this vote they would have been in a position to determine, if not to dictate the issue of the general election. No caste Hindu would have dared to neglect the Untouchables or be hostile to their interests. By the Poona Pact, 18 per cent of seats allotted to the general electorate for British India was to be reserved for the Depressed Classes. The Pact also specified that in every province out of the educational grants, an adequate sum would be earmarked for providing educational facilities to the members of the Depressed Classes.[17]

The Poona Pact evoked mixed reactions. The Hindus in general did not like it but they had not the courage to reject it. There was a common feeling among them that the cost of saving Gandhi's life had been a great one. Disliked by the Hindus and disfavoured by the Untouchables, the Poona Pact was given recognition by both parties and was embodied in the Act of 1935. The difference between the Communal Award and the Poona Pact was in the nature of the electorate. The joint electorate of the Award was intended to enable the Untouchables to take part and influence the election of the caste Hindu candidates while the joint electorate of the Poona Pact was intended to enable the caste-Hindus to take part and influence the election of the untouchable candidates. This was the real difference between the two. The Award was intended to free the Untouchables from the domination of the Hindus. But the Poona Pact was designed to place them under the domination of the Hindus. The Untouchables all over the country felt that the Poona Pact had been a trap and in reality they had been cheated beyond imagination. Ambedkar was greatly disillusioned by the working of the Poona Pact in the subsequent elections and lamented that the Pact gave a death blow to the self-reliant movement of the Untouchables. The Congress sucked the juice of the Poona Pact and threw the rind in the face of the Untouchables.[18] The 'politician in Gandhi became successful and the Mahatma was defeated. So effective and crushing was the victory of Gandhi that he deprived Ambedkar of all his life-saving weapons and made him a powerless man as did Indra in the case of Karna'.[19]

As soon as the Poona Pact was signed, the All India Anti-untouchability League was formed with the blessings of Gandhiji. Later on, it was re-named as the Harijan Sevak Sangh. Gandhi began to call the Untouchables as the Harijans and started a weekly paper – the *"Harijan"*. Hence, this paper became the mouth-piece of his social and political ideas. The objective of the Harijan Sevak Sangh was to reform the Hindu society through persuasion and to improve the lot of the Untouchables through education and welfare activities like sinking wells, opening schools and dispensaries etc., for them. Its programme was mainly motivated by philanthropic ideas. On the other hand Ambedkar had a purely political approach to the problem of untouchability and sought remedies through a purely political mechanism itself. Gandhi and Ambedkar differed on the agency through which the abolition of untouchability should be effected. Gandhi wanted that it should be done by the Hindus within the Hindu society, whereas Ambedkar wanted that it should be done by the Untouchables themselves under constitutional safeguards and outside the Hindu society, if necessary. He concentrated on the elevation of the status of the Untouchables as a matter of right through law and statutes. Gandhian approach was humanitarian and very limited, whereas Ambedkar's approach was radical and emancipative. His approach was not a religio-social but basically a politico-economic one. He was not for social reform approach, all by itself, like temple entry, inter-dining etc. He wanted adequate opportunities for the Untouchables to enable them to have an effective share in the political power of the country. He believed in political and constitutional safeguards to bring them on par with others.

As the elections was to be held in the Provinces in British India under the Act of 1935, Ambedkar organized the Independent Labour Party to safeguard the interests of the Depressed Classes who mostly formed the labour population. His party won 41 seats in the Bombay Presidency and seven seats in C.P. and Berar in the election held in 1937. In the Bombay Presidency Legislature he was the leader of his party and sat in opposition. But he was very much sore about the way the Congress formed ministries in the seven provinces in which proper representation was not given to the Depressed Classes in the cabinets. The Congress was bound by the terms of the Poona Pact to give representation to the Untouchables in the provincial cabinets but it did not implement it faithfully. Ambedkar was so much disgusted with the working of the Congress ministries in various provinces that he too decided to observe the 'day of deliverance' along with the Muslim League on the resignation of the Congress ministries in October 1939.

The outbreak of the Second World War in September 1939 was a great opportunity for Ambedkar to advance the cause of the Depressed Classes in India. Hence, he at once decided to cooperate with the British in the War and to utilize this opportunity to improve the prospect of his community. He offered total support of his community to the British in the War. The Mahars had helped the British in the conquest of western India in the early nineteenth century as sepoys but their recruitment in the British army had been discontinued since 1892 in view of the new recruitment policy which divided the Indian people into martial and non-martial races. Bengalis, Madrasis and non-Punjabis were greatly affected by this policy. The Mahars were very sore about it because their exclusion from military service greatly affected their status in the society in western India. They represented their case to the Secretary of State for India and sought employment in the lowest grades of public service in the rank of police sepoys and of soldiers in the Indian army. They had been employed in the Indian army from the very beginning of the British raj in Western India and had risen to the highest positions by their valour and good conduct. The ban on their recruitment had been most prejudicial to the interests of their people. They offered to serve in any capacity in the military even as menial servants or mule drivers, if they could not be employed again as sepoys.[20] The ban was lifted in case of the Mahars and the Mazhabi Sikhs during the First World War but was re-imposed after the War. In 1927 in a speech at the Koregaon memorial Ambedkar had accused the British of ingratitude towards the Mahars who had earlier helped them in their battles in Western India. This was the theme which he repeated several times during this period.[21] During the Second World War Ambedkar impressed upon the British to recruit the Depressed Classes in the Army. As the British felt the necessity of a huge expansion of the Indian Army, his efforts bore fruit. The Government removed the distinction between martial and non-martial people in the army recruitment and even allowed the Depressed Classes to be recruited. On 1 October 1941 the first battalion of Mahar regiment was raised. Subsequently other regiments of the Depressed Classes were raised. This greatly improved the social and economic condition of the Untouchables during the War. Ambedkar did his best to exhort his people to join the Army in large numbers and thereby to render service to the British Empire at the most critical period of its existence. He even called upon members of his community to suspend their studies and try to get commissions in the Army because this was the prime need of the hour. He even thought it improper to bother the British with any other thing during the War. He did not entertain the idea of taking advantage of the plight of the British either for the benefit of his community or even for the liberation of India. So he wanted to cooperate with the British in the War which was likely to improve the position of his community both economically and politically. He feared that the overnight exit of the British under pressure of the freedom movement might harm the interests of the minorities in India beyond repair. Hence, he wanted that before the transfer of British power in India there should be adequate provisions for constitutional safeguards of the interests of the minorities. Like the Muslims, he too feared Hindu domination in India after the exit of the British.

The year 1942 opened with disasters for the Allied Powers in the Far East. European colonial empires in the area were lost and the Japanese army came at the door steps of India. In Europe too the War was at a critical stage. Hence, the British Government became anxious to resolve the political deadlock in India. In March 1942, they sent Sir Stafford Cripps with some proposals to win over the main political parties in India to the cause of the War. The Cripps proposals envisaged Dominion Status and a Constituent Assembly for India after termination of the War immediately. It even conceded to the Muslims the right to have a separate state after the War. But the proposals did not contain any safeguards for the Untouchables. This came as a great shock to Ambedkar. He took it as a breach of faith and called the Cripps proposals 'a sudden *volte face* on the part of the HMG'. The insistence on prior agreement among various communities was sacrificed in the proposals. He denounced the proposals in most unequivocal terms and nothing but handing over the Untouchables to caste-Hindus, bound hand and foot. To him, the proposed Constituent Assembly was nothing but a betrayal of the Untouchables which would have no voice in it. He was of view that the proposal regarding a treaty for safeguarding the interests of minorities was a mere eyewash. The British would not be here to enforce it. Hence, Ambedkar rejected the Cripps proposals outright and called upon the British to withdraw it. He was totally opposed to the composition of the Constituent Assembly which was not likely to bring into it progressive elements. He feared that the system of proportional representation in the proposed Constituent Assembly was likely to give the right to nominate the representatives of the Untouchables to the caste-Hindus. Hence, he opposed the idea of a Constituent Assembly and supported the adoption of the Government of India Act of 1935 itself with suitable modifications. He pleaded that in India constitutional ideas and forms were ready on hand. Much of the Indian Constitution was written in the Act of 1935 which should be adopted with some modifications only. As a matter of fact he was very much obsessed with the idea of Communal deadlock and in his anxiety to find a solution to it, he was opposing the Constituent Assembly. Here he was quite unjustified.[22] He should have demanded separate representation of Untouchables on it, as he did at the time of the Cabinet Mission.

As soon as the Cripps proposals were rejected by the parties concerned, Ambedkar decided to hold an all India Depressed Classes Conference at Nagpur in July 1942. It was a historic conference of the untouchables. At the conference, Ambedkar denounced the Cripps proposals as a great betrayal for the Depressed Classes because they were denied separate representation in the proposed Constituent Assembly and thus thrown at the mercy of the caste-Hindus.[23] He further affirmed that the Untouchables were a separate and distinct element in the national life of India and they had the same justification as the Muslims to seek special political rights to safeguard their own interests. This was the key to his politics. The Nagpur Conference reiterated that no constitution would be acceptable to the Untouchables unless it was formulated with their consent. They also demanded that in the budget of provincial governments an annual sum should be set apart for promoting primary education among the children of the Scheduled Castes and another sum for promoting higher education among them and such sum should be declared to be the first charge on the revenues of the province. They insisted on representation of the scheduled castes in Central as well as provincial governments in proportion to their number, needs and importance. They also asked for their representation in the public services such as judiciary, police and revenue subject to the minimum qualifications. They demanded their representation in the legislatures and local bodies in proportion to their population through separate electorate. They put forward the demand for their representation in Public service commissions both central and provincial. After long and mature deliberations the Conference concluded that a radical change must be made in the village system then prevalent in India and new villages for scheduled castes should be set up independent of Hindu villages at public cost. A statutory body should be set up to undertake this work and the Central Government should make a minimum grant of Rs 5 crore per annum for this work. All government land cultivable and unoccupied should be handed over to the Commission in trust for making new settlements of the Scheduled Castes.[24] The Conference also passed a resolution for the formation of the All India Scheduled Castes

Federation. Thus, the Nagpur Conference in 1942 marked an important milestone in the long and weary journey of the Untouchables to a better and brighter future. It was the first national political party comprised exclusively of the Untouchables. It provided a new impetus to the awakening among the Untouchables and helped them to pick up confidence for their liberation.

At that very time Ambedkar was appointed as Labour Member in the Viceroy's Executive Council on 20 July 1942 and held this office till March 1946. As Labour Member of the Viceroy's Council he rendered a great service to the cause of labour as well as to his own community. First of all, he impressed upon the Government to recruit members of the Depressed Classes in the army. As the army needed huge expansion, the Government listened to his advice and six scheduled caste regiments were formed. Participation in military affairs is usually related to the intensity of warfare and the consequent rate of social change. The Second World War was a high intensity one and caused social changes unheard of before. It brought 'the pungent sense of reality' among the people. It elevated the position of the Untouchables in the society. Ambedkar was fully aware of the fact that the War was a golden opportunity for the Untouchables to improve their position and status in the society. He submitted a memorandum to the Governor-General on 29 October 1942 outlining the political, educational and other grievances of the Untouchables. He focused on the inadequate representation of his community in the Central executive as well as in public services and in the Federal Service Commission. In the Central Cabinet of 15, there was only one member of the Scheduled Caste while the Muslims had three members. He suggested some remedies: Scheduled Castes must be declared a minority and their proportion in the annual vacancies of central services must be fixed; their age-limit should be raised; Examination fees for them should be reduced and Scheduled Caste officers should be appointed to see whether the provisions had been carried through. Due to his efforts the scheduled castes were granted $8^1/_3$ per cent reservation in Central services in August 1943. Subsequently, it was raised to 12½ per cent in 1946 to bring it in accord with the population ratio. Moreover, by a resolution passed in the Central Legislature the restriction on the Untouchables holding post of officer in the army had also been removed in October 1943.[25] Through the efforts of Ambedkar a scheme for training suitable scheduled caste boys as artisans in the printing industry at the Government presses was introduced for a period of five years and 20 boys were selected every year as apprentice for training in various branches of printing trade.[26] Through his efforts the Central Government also sanctioned a grant of Rs 3 lakh per year for five years for giving scholarships to scheduled caste students pursuing education in scientific and technological subjects both in India and abroad. Such facilities were for those who passed the high school stage. Till 1947 about one thousand scholarships had been granted to scheduled caste students under this scheme. Later on this scheme was extended to the students of the aboriginal and hill tribes also.[27]

Dr B.R. Ambedkar had three main objectives in his life. Firstly, he wanted to spread education among the Untouchables as widely as possible; secondly, he wanted to secure more representation to them in the government services; and thirdly, to improve their condition in the villages. He was fully convinced that as long as the Untouchables would not be ready to leave villages, their condition would not improve. Hence, he advised them to move towards urban areas to make their livelihood. As regards education, there had been a persistent demand from the Untouchables for compulsory and free education since 1918. Similar demand was included in the Poona Pact of 1932 and at the Nagpur conference of the Scheduled Castes in July 1942. Education was the key to progress and power. Hence, they insisted on it. When the Congress ministries were formed in July 1937, they tried to implement the education clause of the Poona Pact half-heartedly. At last the beginning had been made. But Ambedkar was not satisfied with the progress of education among the Untouchables. To speed up education among them he established the People's Education Society in July 1945 and established the Siddhartha College of Art, Science and Commerce in Bombay and also the Milind College of Arts and Sciences at Aurangabad. Later on, a number of educational institutions were established under the auspices of the Society to meet the needs of the Untouchables.

As soon as the War ended in 1945 the possibility of transfer of British power in India loomed large on the political horizon. Elections to central and provincial legislatures were held in early 1946. These elections proved disastrous for the Scheduled Castes Federation. The party was completely routed by the Congress. The caste-Hindus in general did not vote in favour of the Scheduled Castes Federation candidates in joint electorate because they had become very much hostile to Ambedkar due to his activities during the War. This greatly weakened his position at a time when the Cabinet Mission came to negotiate for the transfer of power in India. On behalf of the Scheduled Castes Federation he submitted a memorandum outlining their demands to the Cabinet Mission. Finally, he claimed that the Scheduled Castes Federation should be recognized as the only party representing the interests of the Untouchables. Secondly, the Scheduled Castes should be represented separately and adequately in legislatures, executive and services. Thirdly, all the special facilities meant for Scheduled Castes should be an inseparable part of the Constitution itself. Fourthly, the Scheduled Castes should be represented in the proposed Constituent Assembly through separate electorates. But the Cabinet Mission Plan of 16 May 1946 contained no reference to the demands of the Scheduled Castes. It recognized the Muslims and the Sikhs only as separate elements, but had lumped the Scheduled Castes together with the Hindus. The Cabinet Mission, on its part, justified its action on the basis of the general election of 1946 in which reserved seats for the Scheduled Castes were mostly captured by the Congress. Hence, the Scheduled Castes were not given the right to nominate their representatives in the Interim Government as had been done in the case of the Muslims and Sikhs. They had also not been given the right to separate representation in the proposed Constituent Assembly. Ambedkar was very much shocked at this discrimination and felt that the Mission had done it only to pamper the prejudices of Gandhi, who had all along been opposed to the recognition of the Untouchables as a separate element in the national life of India. The Untouchables were left entirely at the mercy of the caste-Hindus in the proposed Constituent Assembly. Hence, the Untouchables now began to demand the restoration of the separate electorate and the abrogation of the Poona Pact. But it was a cry in the wilderness. The Mission went ahead with its plan and the Untouchables were left high and dry. In October 1946 Ambedkar went to London to plead his case for the Untouchables but he failed in his mission. He lamented: "The British in spite of their promises to us for the last fifty years, in the end, discarded us in not recognizing the scheduled castes as a separate entity".[28] At last Ambedkar realized the political realities of the time and was quick to grasp the new trend and consequently, moved ahead with a spirit of cooperation. He was elected to the Constituent Assembly. He became the Law Minister in the first Cabinet of independent India and was also made the Chairman of the Drafting Committee of the Constitution. Thus, he became the architect of the Constitution of free India. Ultimately, this Constitution decided in favour of joint electorate with reservation of seats for the Scheduled Castes for a period of ten years.

Notes

1. *B.R. Ambedkar's Writings and Speeches*, Vol. 9, pp. 14–18, Government of Maharashtra, 1990.
2. Fisher B. Fred, *India's Silent Revolution*, 1919, Macmillan, New York, p. 110.
3. K.N. Kadam (ed.), *Dr B.R. Ambedkar, The Emancipator of the Oppressed*, Popular Prakashan, Bombay, 1993, p. 148.
4. *B.R. Ambedkar's Writings and Speeches*, op.cit., p. 36.
5. H. Claude Tyne Ven, *India in Turmoil*, Delhi, 1985, p. 53.
6. *B.R. Ambedkar's Writings and Speeches*, Vol. 5, p. 312.
7. M.S. Gore, *Ambedkar's Social and Political Thoughts*, New Delhi, 1993, p. 85.
8. *B.R. Ambedkar's Writings and Speeches*, Vol. 2, p. 506.
9. Ibid., p. 442.
10. Ibid., p. 465.
11. *B.R. Ambedkar's Writings and Speeches*, op.cit., Vol. 9, p. 51.
12. W.N. Kuber, *Ambedkar, A Critical Study*, People's Publishing House, New Delhi, 1991, p. 104.
13. *B.R. Ambedkar's Writings and Speeches*, Vol. 9, p. 71.

14. Ibid., Vol. 5, p. 315.
15. Ibid., p. 316.
16. Ibid., Vol. 9, p. 87.
17. Ibid., p. 89.
18. Ibid., p. 102.
19. M.S. Gore, op.cit., p. 138.
20. P. Stephen Cohen, *The Indian Army*, Oxford, Delhi, 1990, pp. 60–61.
21. M.S. Gore, op.cit., p. 85.
22. A.M. Rajsekhariah, *B.R. Ambedkar, The Quest for Social Justice*, New Delhi, 1989, p. 134.
23. W.N. Kuber (ed.), op.cit., p. 114.
24. *B.R. Ambedkar's Writings and Speeches*, Vol. 9, pp. 403–6.
25. K.N. Kuber (ed.), *Dr B.R. Ambedkar, The Emancipator of the Oppressed*, Popular Prakashan, Bombay, p. 162.
26. *Indian Information*, 1 March 1944, p. 452.
27. *Indian Information*, 15 August 1948, p. 120.
28. M.S. Gore, op.cit., p. 181.

CHAPTER 6

Indian Women's March to Progress

In the early 1920s Indian intelligentsia began to feel that something had to be done to improve the social and educational status of women in India. Gandhiji gave his first long and well thought out speech on women in 1918. He appealed to the social workers to work for social reform, female education and new laws to give women their natural rights. At that time 85 per cent of Indian women lived in poverty and ignorance. Gandhiji felt that they should be awakened to their essential equality with men, their rights to freedom and liberty and to a supreme place in their own sphere of activity. In 1919 he asked women to join the satyagraha movement so that men could be fully involved.[1] He urged women to take swadeshi vow, the promise to give up foreign goods and to spend a certain time of each day spinning thread. He also asked women to know the causes of India's poverty and to fight for its removal on equal terms with men. He proposed that rich and upper class women should take a vow to spin and act as a model for the mass of women in the country. He urged women to do whatever they could even from the home. He made women believe that they counted. Gandhiji wanted women from the higher classes to take the *swadeshi* vow because they could be emulated by other women. It was in the Civil Disobedience movement of 1930–32 that the women participated actively in large numbers and earned a place for themselves in history. But the ground had in fact been prepared between 1925 and 1930. It was during this period that women's organizations and their networks were founded, enabling them to respond to Gandhi's call.[2] A valuable stimulus was coming from women themselves. They had already founded the All India Women's Conference in 1926 and every year since then they had been emphasizing the need for the education of women.[3] Gandhiji indeed was a great emancipator of women in India. During the Salt Satyagraha many women of all ages came out to join the movement. Majority of them were not westernized or even educated Gandhi's appeal was a phenomenal success. Women were made to feel equal of men. That feeling dominated both educated and uneducated women.[4] Thus, the women's movement in India entered a new era in 1930–32. Gandhiji asked them to undertake picketing on shops dealing in foreign cloth and liquor. It was a clear and specific programme of action and women responded promptly. Large numbers of women in Bombay and Calcutta came forward to participate in the programme of Civil Disobedience movement. Many foreign cloth merchants were faced with the reality of women picketeers and had to sign a pledge not to sell foreign cloth until an amicable settlement had been made for the country. Women processions were organized peacefully. That was really a stirring time for the country. And it amazed eveyone.

After the establishment of the All India Women's Conference in 1926, the agitation for improvement of status of women in India took an upward swing and became well organized. Enlightened Hindu opinion ever since 1919 had begun to feel that Hindu laws regarding women's right to property and laws and customs concerning marriage needed immediate reform. In 1919 V.J. Patel introduced the Hindu Marriage Validity Bill in the Imperial Legislative Council.[5] Education, travel, contact in cities with people of other castes and various other factors widened the outlook of the younger generations, when ideas of marriage, home and life were generally broadened. They generally resented the antiquated Hindu laws concerning marriage and succession. Hindu laws were not moving with the times. Even inter-caste marriage among the Hindus was not permissible. Education and communication are the most potent factors of modernization in the society. Many Hindu intellectuals strongly felt that the time had come to bring about radical changes in Hindu laws to suit the needs of the society.

Dr R.P. Paranjape felt that there should be compulsory registration of all marriages. He also felt that polygamy should be penalized by laws and a second marriage should almost automatically give the first wife the right to divorce her husband.[6] Various women's organizations were also demanding reforms in Hindu marriage laws. The Bombay Women's Council passed a resolution recommending registration of marriages.[7] As a matter of fact the All India Women's Conference and associations attached to it had been doing immense service to Indian womanhood. From 1937 onwards a number of private Bills or resolutions were brought up in the Central Legislature for improvement of the status of women in society. Dr G.V. Deshmukh, a great champion of women's rights had tabled a number of resolutions in Central Legislative Assembly for upliftment of women. Hindu public opinion was moving rapidly in the direction of monogamous marriage. Dr Deshmukh tabled the Hindu Women's Divorce Bill in the Central Legislative Assembly in November 1940. His intention was to make a second marriage by a husband as one of the grounds of divorce for a woman. He also brought another Bill giving women the right to separate residence and maintenance in case of a second marriage by a husband. Some measures had already been passed due to his efforts in respect of women's right to property, particularly of widows in Hindus society. Till then they were at the mercy of the other members of the household even for a morsel of food. But their position improved when the widow got a right in her husband's property. As a matter of fact social and legal status of Hindu women had been restricted on account of archaic rules or conventions being practised for centuries. They were inelastic and had no relation to the existing environment of society. There were two forces which militated against the progress of Indian womanhood. The first was the pursuit of out of date customs and the tendency to maintain inherited traditions and the second was the preservation of archaic Hindu laws by judicial decisions. The remedy against the first was education of public opinion by means of the press, the public platform and social meetings. The laws of inheritance and marriage in Hindu society had become fixed and rigid as a result of judicial rulings and these rulings were in force throughout the country. The only remedy against the mischief caused by archaic laws preserved by judicial decisions was through legislation. The stage was now set for the Government to come forward to undertake a legislation for improvement of Hindu women's social and legal status. The Government appointed the Hindu Women's Rights Committee consisting of Sir B.N. Rau, D.N. Mitter and Principal J.R. Gharpure of Poona Law College to examine the whole matter and to make recommendations which would help the legislature to pass an act which would cover the whole of India. Accordingly, the Hindu Law Bill on marriage and interstate succession was introduced in the Central Legislative Assembly on 23 March 1943. Mrs Renuka Ray was nominated as member of the Central Legislative Assembly as representative of the AIWC for participation on discussion regarding Hindu Code Bill. Mrs Renuka Ray rightly observed: "Women did not succeed in changing social laws before but they had won a psychological victory, an important section of public opinion was convinced that change was essential. Gandhiji had pointed out the necessity for changing social attitude. His encouragement of women's emancipation and women's own participation in the national movement brought this about".[8]

The campaign for a uniform civil code for all women was first of all undertaken by the All India Women's Conference and other leading organizations in the thirties. It was a twofold programme: public opinion had to be convinced to pass the relevant legislation. To achieve this a vigorous campaign was started by AIWC. To mould public opinion in its favour, meetings were organized and processions were taken out throughout the country with Calcutta and Bombay as the major centres of the campaign. They were in many ways in the forefront of women's emancipation. An insistent demand for changes in the Hindu law in support of women's rights was voiced in the Central Legislative Assembly which ultimately sought to remedy the disabilities from which women suffered. There was a spate of private Bills on the anvil of the Central Legislative Assembly. Consequently, the Government had to appoint the Hindu Law Committee under the chairmanship of Sir B.N. Rau. Sir Sultan Ahmad, the then Law Member, took interest in the matter. Their labours resulted in the introduction of Bills on Hindu marriage and Hindu intestate succession in the Central Legislature in March 1943. Mrs Renuka Ray, as representative of the AIWC in the Central Legislative Assembly acknowledged on behalf of Hindu women the debt of gratitude which they owed to Sir Sultan Ahmad, the Law Member, who had taken not only so much interest but had also nominated one of their representatives to voice their opinion in the legislature. He had actually brought in a new policy and a new outlook on the part of the Government. It was the beginning of a new era of social reform for India.[9] Six associations of women wanted these Bills to be passed as they were all in agreement so far as the broad principles were concerned. All branches of organizations of women had accepted the Bills *in toto*.[10] The National Planning Committee had also agreed with the main principles of the Bills. Both the Bengal and Bihar Governments were of the opinion that the Bills might be postponed till after the War because the time was not opportune for such radical legislation. Renuka Ray countered it by saying that the Bills would not come as a surprise to anyone. The vast majority of opinion on the Bills was in their favour. She maintained that it was not necessary to wait for the new election to discover how far the country was in favour of the Bills. The Hindus were not only willing to support the Bills but they would also go much further.[11] A four-day conference was organized by National Council of Women to discuss the legal status of women. Mrs Sarojini Naidu in a message urged that the conference should demand for a complete and radical revision of the Hindu law which was "outworn, unwieldy, too intricate and too rigid a system that acts frequently as a boulder of obstruction in the stream of modern progress".[12] M.R. Jayakar was looking forward to the day when there would be one legislation for all women of India because religion had little to do with property rights. Divorced from religion a civil Bill of property rights covering all communities would be an ideal one. He hoped that in the not too distant future India would have a simplified law governing marriage and inheritance. He urged the National Council of Women to wait for some time more when the legislature would be completely representative of the community. He feared that the Bill then in the legislature would emerge in the most defective form.[13] As a matter of fact the Rau committee had done a great service to Indian womanhood by providing rules of inheritance and marriage which were in consonance with justice and equity. It also provided that monogamy should be the rule and legalized the intercaste marriage.[14] Jawaharlal Nehru too thought that a uniform civil code for the whole of India was essential. But this could not be imposed on unwilling people. The urgent need was the extension of the civil marriage Act to cover marriages between any two persons, to whatever religion they might belong without any renunciation of religion, as at present. No change could be imposed from the top. It was the duty of the Government of the time to try to educate public opinion so as to make it accept the changes proposed.[15]

As a matter of fact the Hindu Law Committee wanted codification of the Hindu Law by stages, beginning with the law of succession and the law of marriage. The Government accepted this view. The Bill was circulated for eliciting public opinion. Some of the opinions were critical and even hostile. On the whole the opinions were in favour of the principles of the Bill. The controversy mainly centred round the question of introducing monogamy and the application of *sagotra* marriage. The Government did not contemplate any precipitate action on so important a matter touching the Hindu community. The recognition of intercaste marriage in Hindu society was welcomed. In reality the Hindu Law Committee had evolved order out of chaos and in doing so always kept steadfastly in view the basic principles of Hindu Law. It did not propose any drastic changes as might be wholly or vitally antagonistic to the essential concept of Hindu inheritance. The general opinion even among women appeared that daughter's share should be half of a son. The chief virtue of the Bill was that it was merely a pointer in the proper direction and nothing more. It touched only a small proportion of Hindu property. It did not touch the ancestral property of a Hindu governed by Mitakshara law. The Bill was not revolutionary in character. It was not going to disturb the fundamentals of Hindu society or materially change its structure.[16] There was only one reform of any significance and that was the abolition of polygamy and insistence on monogamy. Sir Sultan Ahmad considered it a privilege that he brought forward a legislation (Hindu Code) which was found to improve the status of the country both internally and internationally.[17] Mrs Renuka Ray while supporting the Bill observed: "Hindu Law, if it is to be preserved, must get rid of the deadly influence of outworn customs which like dead wood are choking up the very life springs of Hindu society. Those who today want to bind and better the Hindu Law will one day be responsible for its complete disintegration.[18] Women in general desired that polygamy should be prohibited not only because it was wrong and caused much suffering but also because it was highly detrimental to the peace and happiness of family life. Dr G.V. Deshmukh gave full credit to the Government of India for creating public opinion with regard to the proposed change in Hindu Law.[19] The Indian press as a whole had given full support to the Bill. But most of the judges found that this new code would undermine Hindu Law and create a sort of revolution in the Hindu society, which it had not experienced for the last thousand years.[20] They took it as a kind of revolution in the change of the fundamental principles of Hindu society. One of the judges went so far as to say that the object of the Bill was to satisfy those persons who were fond of slogans such as 'complete independence for women and sex-equality between men and women'.[21] Despite such orthodox opinions, there was a strong feeling growing in the country at that time that marriage laws should be simplified and be less expensive. The Congress election manifesto of 1937 stood for removal of all sex disabilities whether legal or social in any sphere of public activity. Under the Act of 1935 women got special representation in Provincial Legislatures and some of them became ministers too. They stood for reforms in Hindu society. The result of the election in the provinces proved that the country supported the policy in an overwhelming manner. Even in remote villages the urgency and importance of the legislation for social reform was recognized.[22] Some members of the House wanted to make the Bill more comprehensive by providing for dissolution of marriage on certain definite grounds and for the residence and maintenance of the divorced partner and for the custody of children. It was erroneous to think that such legislation would lead to disintegration of the family. As a matter of fact Hindu public opinion was moving rapidly in the direction of monogamous marriage.

As the war neared its end, political matters engrossed the attention of the Government and the people. Moreover, the Government feared that the axis powers might use this to influence the minds of the Hindus against the British. The Bill was allowed to lapse and could not be enacted in law. Later on, when India became independent the same was taken up by Dr B.R. Ambedkar with some modifications. Hence, the credit now goes to him for getting the Hindu Code Bill enacted in law. The background had been prepared by the colonial Government. During the whole of 1940s women's organisations in India were very active in the agitation for removal of disabilities of women. Indeed, India was passing through a period of social transition.

The Second World War was really global in character. It was a highly intensified war and a large number of people, both civil and military were involved in it. Women too had to come forward to participate in the war effort in different capacities. In Great Britain women made up about half their labour force by the end of the war. There were about 5,00,000 British women in armed forces, another 2,00,000 in the women's land army and well over 3,00,000 in the civil services.[23] Almost similar was the case with Russian women. Almost all able bodied males in Russia were drafted for military services and the civil services were mostly handled by women. In America, more than two million women had volunteered for Red Cross work during the war.[24] Women had to take to trousers for war work. Consequently, women's purchases of trousers in the USA jumped five times since the beginning of the war. Large shops were opening departments for trousers for women. This indicated the extent to which women were going into war work. Women working in war plants needed to make this sensible change of clothing.[25] Mrs Roosevelt congratulated women of the USA for the way in which they had come forward and taken their place in industry, often undertaking jobs which seemed beyond their strength or known skills to perform.[26] In India the situation was different because there was no dearth of male-power in the country. Still some educated women came forward to participate in war efforts. Previously women doctors were not admitted into the Army medical service. After a considerable hesitation the Government agreed to admit women doctors to the Army medical service on the same terms as men. British as well as Indian women doctors were declared to be eligible for selection but they were liable to serve both in and outside India.[27] By March 1943, 35 lady doctors had been appointed to the women's branch of the Army medical service. During the war there was a demand for trained nurses in the Armed forces. A number of nurses had volunteered for military service in India and overseas. Among the tribals of North-east India the Khasi girls were the first to volunteer for nursing service abroad and joined the Auxiliary nursing service. Many tribal women joined the women's voluntary service also.[28] The Indian Military Nursing Service was constituted and by March 1943, 288 girls had joined it. The Auxiliary Nursing Service was also constituted to provide a reserve of nurses sufficiently trained to be immediately useful in case of emergency in military or civil hospitals. At that time there were about 5,000 fully trained nurses in India. This number was quite inadequate for a country like India. The War provided a good opening for Indian girls to join the nursing service but only the tribal and Christian girls came forward to avail of this opportunity. The women's voluntary service was also organised in India. They rendered useful service in organising canteens which served refreshments to troops. They also served army families, looked after soldiers in hospitals and helped with other odd jobs. When the Auxiliary nursing service was started in 1941, over 15,000 applications were received for admission to the course. One-third of these were from Madras, 1450 from Bengal and 1300 from Bombay. Madras Presidency had contributed nearly one-third of total number of nurses and Bombay nearly one-fifth. 603 were Europeans, 543 Indian Christians, 143 domiciled Europeans, 123 Hindus, 24 Parsis, 5 Sikhs and 11 Muslims.[29] At that time there were fewer nurses in the whole of India than there were in London. For the whole of India, there was one nurse to 65,000 of the population and in UP there was only one trained nurse to every 2.5 lakh people.[30]

Many women of good social status in the Punjab came forward to volunteer for the post of Fauji Sevadarni – women military welfare worker. Their work was voluntary and unpaid. They maintained contact with families of soldiers in the villages under their charge. They were to keep up the spirit of soldiers' families and persuade them to write encouraging letters frequently to their relatives overseas. They also helped in despatch of parcels to serving soldiers. They were also to offer sympathy and help and to secure redress of any grievances and to disseminate accurate information and to contradict false rumours. About 500 Sevadarnis were appointed in an area which covered the districts of Jullunder, Ferozepore, Ambala, Ludhiana and Hosiarpur. It came to about one Sevadarni to every 20 villages. They were chiefly ladies whose husbands or other relatives were in the army and who could command respect and confidence of village women. This experiment was bound to be instructive and was bound to open a new field through which Indian women of position could render useful national service.[31]

During the war women joined colours also. Women Auxiliary Corps was organised in USA and Great Britain. In March 1942, the Women Auxiliary Corps was started in India too. It was recruited on voluntary basis. They were paid but their service was for the duration of the War only and limited to the confines of India. They were whole time workers. All women between the age of 18 and 50 who were British subjects or subjects of Indian states, were eligible for enlistment. Among the duties they might undertake were those of switchboard operators, telephone orderlies, wireless operators, clerks, drivers of staff cars, dieticians etc. These covered 45 distinctive types of occupation. Eighteen hostels had been set apart for them. Their number grew up rapidly because there was a rising demand for WAC (I) in all three services – Army, Navy and Air Force. Not a single new post was created to accommodate them. They merely replaced men who were released for service abroad. By September 1942, the strength of the WAC (I) was 90 officers and 200 auxiliaries.[32] This scheme gave women of all races and creeds in India an opportunity for national service. Even the Nepali girls joined the corps and proved to be a valuable addition to it.[33] Some of them worked in signal units. There was a great demand for signal girls in communication branch of the Army. The WAC(I) was unique in having women from nearly every part of the world united together in common cause. Women of 27 different nationalities were represented there. Not only were all castes and creeds of India represented and of neighbouring countries, like Burma, Malaya, Ceylon, Java, and China, but also serving by the side of their Asiatic sisters were women from UK, Russia, Canada, Australia and several European countries. Despite their differences of culture and outlook these women formed a union of loyalty and service to a common cause. They played their part as individuals in a great team.[34] The strength of WAC(I) reached a peak of 11,000 consisting of all ranks.[35] Women of all castes and creeds found it possible to work together in this corps. It was not a small achievement. Serving in naval wing of WAC(I) were women from Madras, Bengal, Rajputana, the Punjab, Bombay and other provinces and states as well. There were Hindus, Muslims, Parsis and Christians working together. Several persons levelled charges against the corps but General Auchinluck countered them forcefully. He found the criticism ill-informed, false and malicious. He appreciated the value of the services done by the WAC(I).[36]

With the War nearing its end in 1945, the problem of disbandment of WAC(I) loomed large. The programme for their rehabilitation was being drawn up. At this very time the *Blitz* demanded an independent official enquiry into the charges of racism and all-round neglect and scandals of the corps. One hundred women of the corps signed an open letter to conduct an open enquiry into the working of the corps. They described the entire organisation as a rotting mass of racism, incompetence, shameless immorality and waste without parallel. They also alleged intolerable discrimination between English and Indian girls in promotion, salaries, amenities such as hospital treatment, of cases of venereal disease and unwanted maternity. The fear of demobilization hung like the Damocles' sword. They feared that 50 per cent of the Indian girls would have to walk straight from the disbanded corps into brothels, being uneducated, unprepared, unequipped for any decent means of livelihood. During the War they had become used to a higher standard of life. As a consequence of demobilization, they were likely to be thrown on streets. They appealed to the Government to undertake the responsibility of peace time reconversion of the corps. Their principal charge, however, concerned the absolute irreparable mess this war time organisation had made of the lives of young Indian girls.[37]

The Government took steps to train them in various professions likely to absorb them in the mainstream of society. But in general the Indian society looked with suspicion on the girls who had served in the WAC(I). More than one thousand Anglo-Indian girls had joined the corps. Mrs Hansa Mehta in her Presidential speech at the AIWC in 1945 expressed her deep anxiety and concern for these girls who were likely to be thrown out of employment after demobilization. She appealed to the AIWC to appoint a special committee to investigate into their problems and to find out ways and means to help these women. She advised that services of these women should be utilized for education and social work in rural areas.[38]

War had a liberating influence on women all over the world. The AIWC and other women associations continued to play their part in general awakening of women in India. Educated women, instead of being tied to their homes began to take active interest in social and political work in a way that was really astonishing. They had become alive to their social problems and wanted to work for their solution. All this produced a wider field for their talents, broke the relative segregation of women as a sex, relaxed the restrictions that otherwise narrowed their functions. Mrs Kamaladevi Chattopadhyay wanted the focus on women to shift from sex to social genre. She had never been in tune with feminism as advocated in the West where men and women had lined up in confrontation, as though they were irreconcilable elements. In India women's problems had been treated as social part of a malaise in the body of society. Men and women had been struggling to rectify this for half a century or more as a joint battle to better the whole society. She struck a new note by affirming human value of a housewife in economic and social terms. Women's contribution as a basic cohesive element in the family and therefore in society and the nation needed recognition; whether she held a job and contributed monetarily or not she was entitled to an equal status with her husband.[39] Thus a new light was thrown on the problem of women in India. The women's movement in India was essentially a social movement and part of the process of enabling a constituent part of society to adjust itself to the constantly changing social and economic conditions. Thus, it operated as an integral part of the progressive social movement in the broadest sense.

The War afforded opportunities for educated middle class girls in India for jobs in the various offices of the war department as well as in commercial firms in big cities. Middle class girls in India till World War II seldom went to work even in Bombay. The pioneers were the Anglo-Indian and Christian girls, who first took to nursing as a profession; then in Bombay came the Parsi girls, more Westernized than the average. These girls turned to secretariat work in European commercial offices, while the first profession the Hindu girls entered was teaching. With the spread of education among girls demand rose for women teachers and there was no objection to teaching as it did not involve working alongside men. There were no shop girls in those days and there are very few even today. The factories hardly employed any women. Textile mills took some but only the uneducated illiterate kind at less than twenty rupees per month. But the war had opened up some opportunities for educated girls. They were encouraged to take up jobs and had to move from villages to cities for the purpose of employment. This created a problem of their accommodation in cities. After the war hostels for working women had to be set up in big cities. Thus, the War opened a new chapter in women's liberation movement in India.

Notes

1. D.A. Low (ed.), *The Indian National Congress: Centenary Hindsinghts*, Oxford, Delhi, 1988, p. 65.
2. Ibid., p. 71.
3. *Report of the Royal Commission on Indian Agriculture* (Abridged), p. 522.

4. Zareer Masani, *Indian Tales of the Raj*, Bombay, 1987, p. 109.
5. *Indian Year Book,* 1919, p. 618.
6. ISR, 20 April 1940, pp. 408–9
7. ISC, 17 February 1940, p. 293.
8. Renuka Ray, *My Reminiscenses*, Allied Publishers, New Delhi, 1982, p. 63.
9. *Proceedings Central Legislative Assembly*, 24 March 1943, p. 141B.
10. Ibid., p. 1556.
11. *Bombay Chronicle Weekly*, 25 March 1943.
12. Ibid.
13. Ibid.
14. *Indian Annual Register*, 1944, pp. 276–84.
15. S. Gopal (ed.), *Nehru an Anthology,* Oxford, 1980, p. 54.
16. *Proceedings of Council of State,* 1 April 1943, p. 510.
17. BCW, 2 April 1943.
18. *Proceedings Central Legislative Assembly*, 3 March 1944, p. 829.
19. Ibid., 10 November 1944, p. 591.
20. Ibid., 3 April 1944, p. 1896.
21. Ibid.
22. Ibid., p. 1895.
23. Asha Briggs, *Social History of England*, London, 1983, p. 269.
24. BCW, 31 May 1942, p. 23.
25. Ibid., 17 May 1942, p. 19.
26. *Proceedings Central Legislative Assembly*, 17 November 1944, p. 960.
27. ISR, 17 January 1942, p. 20.
28. *Asiatic Review*, January 1944, p. 9.
29. *Indian Information,* 15 April 1943, p. 353.
30. Ibid.
31. Ibid., p. 243.
32. Ibid.
33. *Indian Information,* 15 June 1944, p. 612.
34. *Indian Information,* 15 September 1945, p. 290.
35. *Indian Information,* 15 April 1947, pp. 398–99.
36. *Indian Information,* 1 May 1946, p. 582.
37. ISR, 2 March 1946, pp. 211–12.
38. Ibid., 5 January 1946.
39. Kamala Devi Chattopadhyay, *Inner Recesses, Outer Spaces,* Memoirs, Delhi, 1987, p. 293.

CHAPTER 7

Development of Transport and Communications

Roads and road transport in India are as old as her civilization. But prior to the nineteenth century there was probably little or no artificial surfacing outside towns and very little bridge building. Large-scale road building began in British India in 1830 when the Grand Trunk Road and other large works were undertaken and the Public Works Department was created. Road-building, however, had but a short start in time in comparison to railways. The first railway from Bombay to Thane was opened on 1 April 1853 and others quickly followed. Railways had three effects on roads. Firstly, they duplicated many of the better roads, because usually they followed the most active traffic roads along which roads had often first been made. Secondly, the importance of roads fell in the general estimation and thirdly, the railways created immense new road traffic. As a result, by 1920, when the rural motor transport began there were about 50,000 miles of metalled roads against nearly 30,000 miles of railways; many of the metalled roads and railways served the same routes. There was a network of about 1,30,000 miles of earth-roads maintained by public authority, but generally in a very bad state.[1] Many of the roads and even some railway lines were constructed mainly with the purpose of bringing raw materials like cotton, linseed etc. to the ports for export to Great Britain.

Before railways came up traffic on local roads was light and seasonal. Farming was for subsistence and the village a self-contained unit. As emphasized by the Royal Commission on agriculture in India, it was the railways that revolutionized agriculture by making possible the growing of money crops which swelled the volume of exportable staple. Railways again led to heavy industries and large urban population to be fed and later to mutual stimulation of industry and agriculture. Railways and public health measures together greatly reduced the ravages of famine and disease in the country. Moreover, railways opened new prospects of travel, of migration of labour to industrial towns, of pilgrimages etc. All this greatly increased the movement of men and material on local roads. There were nearly six and a half million bullock carts in British India in the 1940s and there were probably 1,30,000 motor vehicles of all sorts.[2]

Under the Government of India Act of 1919 the popularly elected district boards were put in charge of roads, education and public health. They had meagre resources to meet these responsibilities. It was not possible for them to maintain roads in proper order at a time when motor traffic together with carts caused greater wear and tear to roads. By 1926–27, 80 per cent of all roads and 57 per cent of metalled roads were under the charge of district boards. With the exception of Madras the condition of district board roads was notoriously bad. Motor traffic on road was increasing. At first it operated on short stretches very often on earth roads between towns and outlying places off the railways. Later on new buses began plying on main roads profitably. That attracted competition. The Government in 1927 set up a committee of Indian Legislature presided over by Mr M.R. Jayakar to advise on road development. The Royal Commission on Indian Agriculture had already pointed out that there was urgent need of good communication together with efficient marketing arrangement for improvement of agriculture. Efficient communication by cutting down the time taken to transport a commodity had an important role to play in its price determination. Good communication would bring new crops within the range of profitable cultivation. It also concluded that bad communication imposed a constraint on the health and stamina of the draught animals and seriously reduced their efficiency for all important work of cultivation. The income of the cultivator largely depended on the efficiency of communication. Besides, the social and political effect of good communication especially on the rural population was no less important. The Road Development Committee concluded that the development of road system in India was desirable because it would go a long way towards improving the economic, social and political advancement of the rural population on which the future of the nation so much depended.[3] Eventually in 1930 on the recommendation of the Committee the Central Road Fund was created by an addition of two and a half annas to the taxes of Customs and Excise per gallon on petrol. 15 per cent of this fund was to be reserved by the Central Government for discretionary grant, research and intelligence, the balance to be allocated to provinces and states on the basis of their petrol consumption to be used on schemes of development. The Central Road Fund had in 1945 been in existence for fifteen years and was used for construction and improvement of internal roads necessary to the prosecution of the War, for which, of course, other large sums were also provided. A great deal of construction and improvement of bridges, particularly in Madras and Central Provinces and considerable construction and improvement of surfaced roads was financed from the fund. From 1930 to 1945 the mileage of surfaced roads increased from 57,000, mostly ordinary macadam to 70,000, including 12,000 miles of modern surfaces, an increase of 23 per cent in fifteen years. In 1945 there was approximately 1,45,000 miles of earth roads in the charge of different public authorities but still in very poor state making up 2,15,000 miles of roads of all sorts.[4]

Long years of neglect, to which India's road communications had been subjected, had inevitably resulted in a glaring disparity between India and economically advanced countries of the world during the War. In the USA, 75 per cent of all traffic was carried on roads and the position was not different in other progressive countries. But in India roads did not carry even 10 per cent of the total traffic in 1948. In this process of continued neglect, agrarian development of the country had been throttled which in turn had slowed down the growth of traffic. Development of roads in India now began to be felt as essential for economic, social and cultural development of the rural areas. Even during the War the Government took some positive steps to meet the situation.

As a follow-up of the recommendations of the M.R. Jayakar Committee the Indian Road Congress was created in December 1934. It was designed to promote interchange of ideas and experience, promote standardization and advise on research. It is a private association of engineers employed on road work under the central and provincial governments, states and local bodies. Road research got a new orientation through its efforts. The central road research station under CSIR is directly concerned with the improvement of India's road transport. It was mainly due to its efforts and initiative that the Nagpur plan was drawn up which provided the blue print for all the development projects concerning road transport in India.

In the eighth session of the Indian Road Congress at Gwalior on 4 October 1943, the idea of planning post-War road development was mooted. The War brought into special prominence the necessity of an integrated road system in India. The IRC Council in October 1943 passed a resolution which paved the way for the conference of chief engineers of provinces and states to be held at Nagpur in December 1943 to prepare a road development plan for the whole of India. The conference produced the "Nagpur Report" which marked the real beginning of road planning and development on all India basis.[5] Sir Kenneth Mitchell, Controller of Road Transport, at the Gwalior session of the IRC gave a detailed survey of what he hoped would be the basis of a balanced scheme of road development in the future – a scheme so designed that whether it be a great national highway or a humble village road, each would be well adapted to its purpose and traffic and equally well-maintained. The War had forced the Government to think of road development in India on scientific lines. He emphasized the need of a national highway system and frankly admitted that India could not do without it. He particularly pointed out that the village roads and district roads had not only not progressed but had deteriorated with the increasing traffic of more cash crops, more people and more travel arising from security needs and general awakening.[6] He pointed out the general neglect of the link between the village and public road and stressed the need for strengthening it. The people in villages were the primary producers of crops and revenue. Every maund of exportable foodstuffs, cotton etc. originated in the village and started the journey to markets along the village or unmetalled district roads and the service which the people got from these roads was quite inadequate. Village roads were generally incharge of Union boards and they were not properly provided for. In this competitive world every means of communication to markets was as essential to the primary producer in the village as to the great manufacturer in the town. Hence, the need for improving the village and district roads. Sir Kenneth Mitchell was strongly of the view that no village with a population of 1000 and over should be more than half a mile from a public road. But the district boards in charge of them had neither the money nor the taxing capacity to discharge properly all the expanding functions that had devolved upon them, in education, public health as well as roads. It was realised during the War that the financing of post-War development and the overtaking of years of neglect would be quite beyond the existing and potential resources of local bodies. Sir Kenneth Mitchell suggested that if the business was financially beyond them, they should be relieved of it. The large sums for post-War development were to come from sources other than local rates and if maintenance was later neglected, those large sums or a good portion of them, had better not have been spent at all. It would be most unwise for provincial governments to spend large sum on development and leave maintenance of this asset to others. The status and service conditions of district board engineers were not such as to make for efficiency. Hence, it was suggested that the first step towards the improvement of district roads was to transfer them to expert provincial highway department which would absorb the efficient district board engineers and make for efficiency all around. The War had revealed many weaknesses or missing links, particularly in the all India highway system. In order to rectify them it was thought essential to plan for a national highway system and this matter was referred to a special meeting of chief engineers of provinces and states held in Nagpur in December 1943.[7]

The Nagpur plan envisaged linking up of the remotest parts

of India with a well-planned road system. A system of national highway was projected. Two American road experts (General Fleming and Mr Thomas H. Macdonald) toured the whole country from Khyber to Madras and from Bombay to Calcutta and made valuable suggestions. They were impressed with the fact that Indian road problems were very similar to American problems in 1916 when they were coming out of the "horse and buggy age" and when they first created their department of public roads and rural engineering, afterwards called the public road construction. Motor traffic in India had increased considerably between 1920 and 1940. Compared to this the increase in surfaced roads had been very far from satisfactory. The progress in simple type road surfacing in the pre-War period was not in any way commensurate with the growth of commercial motor traffic. During this period the metalled roads increased in mileage from 58641 (1928) to 60496 (1938) or by a meagre 3.7 per cent only. On the other hand there had been an increase of 98 per cent in commercial vehicles or a total increase of 43 per cent in all types of motor traffic in a space of ten years.[8] The situation called for urgent attention from the Government. Hence, it was decided at Nagpur to pay more attention to low type surface. The road user wanted first as large a mileage as possible for all weather roads and thereafter only roads of higher surface types. The Nagpur plan envisaged that India would need 4,00,000 miles of road, half of it all weather surfaced road in order to bring all villages reasonably close to a planned road system. The estimated cost to execute such a plan would be Rs 450 crores. The system of national highway would serve as a framework within which to fit a network of provincial, district and village roads. In the national highways were included certain trails to open communication through large under developed tracts which were not the particular concern of any province or state. To coordinate and direct and to execute the plan for building a national system, nearly five times the existing 80,000 miles of metalled roads in India in 1943, the conference recommended setting up of a road board.

The bold and imaginative road development plan envisaged two great new roads and improved highways radiating from Bombay. One big highway was to run from Bombay to

Khyber pass via Ahmedabad, Karachi and Peshawar and the second from Bombay to Cape Camorin hugging western coast. Moreover, there was to be one highway from Bombay to Madras and Vizagapatnam. In addition there were plans for three new highways from Calcutta. A road into Assam to link up the military road built in China and the Lushai hills and ultimately with the Burma road to China. Another road was to connect Calcutta with Chittagong and join up with the new military road to the Arakan and ultimately to Akyab. Delhi, being the capital of India, was one of the most important focal points with five national highways radiating from it.[9] Thus, India was to have a mammoth network of highways stretching from north to south and east to west connecting India between Persia in the west and China in the east. This bold plan of national highways really marked the beginning of social change of deep significance for the country.

Lord Wavell emphasized that the first step in all schemes for the social progress of India was the improvement in means of communication not only in respect of the main roads but the minor district and village roads. After the War it was expected that motor vehicles would play a far greater part in transportation. There were likely to be many vehicles and many drivers available almost at once from the military organization after the end of the War. Even during the War a start had been made in developing motor transport. The Central Government distributed new motor vehicles imported under lease-land system for civilian use. The development of motor transport in rural areas was likely to be of great advantage and benefit to the rural population as well as the trade, industry and general prosperity of the country as a whole. The picture of the future rural India was one in which motor transport was to penetrate to the remotest villages connecting them with the main transport system and was to play a gradually increasing part in marketing between village and market town and in distribution between town and village. Thus, the villager in post-War was likely to have at his disposal modern means of transport, readier communication with the outside world, medical attention and other social services to no less a proportionate degree than the town dwellers. To achieve this social change, active development of roads and constructive development of road transport were necessary.[10] Circumstances were favourable for introducing and establishing motor transport where it was needed. It was a golden opportunity for Indian agriculture and business to make a greater use of mechanical transport to improve their prospects. Hence, it was essential even during the War to plan for a system of national highways to serve as a framework within which will fit in a network of provincial, district and rural roads. This was expected to bring a great social change in the country. In the scheme of post-War planning Lord Wavell gave precedence to communication. Lord Wavell said: "Transportation is civilization. War is transportation. In peace . . . the improvement of communication has always led the way into social progress. After the War it must be expected that motor vehicle will play a far larger part.[11] In the wake of roads would follow the development of health services, the extension of educational facilities, the opening of schools, better exchange of information through improved postal system and extension of travelling cinema. Accordingly, the improvement of communication fell within the sphere of both economic development and social progress. He put the social services in the following order: communications, health and education.[12] He did not see how it was possible to effect any improvement in health or education in the villages unless they could be reached surely and quickly at all times. The National highways plan had given adequate attention to this aspect and provided for building and improving provincial, district and rural roads. The objective of the plan was that no village should be in future more than five miles from an all weather road and more than 100 miles from a national highway.[13] As a matter of fact Lord Wavell thought that the first step in all the schemes for the social progress of India must be the improvement of the means of communication.

Before the War there were 5000 Army vehicles but the number swelled to 50,000 in 1942. The number was increasing in view of the establishment of SEAC command in India. In 1943 thousands of special chassis (in parts) were obtained from Canada and USA under Lease-lend system. These were assembled by Indian workmen. By January 1945, there were a quarter of a million military vehicles then in use in India.[13] The call for mechanization and yet more mechanization and the immense need of mobility such as gave the Allies triumph in African campaign, had brought forth an urgent demand for motor vehicles of all kinds and trained personnel to drive and maintain them. Practically every cantonment in India had a training centre for motor drivers so that each of them should be able to maintain his vehicle. In every province there was at least one centre to train driver mechanics who could repair serious damages to motor vehicles. So there were about 2.5 lakh motor driver-cum-mechanics in the army in 1945 and a good number of them were to be demobilized at the end of the War. Thus the army had a good reservoir of transport drivers, mechanics and other semi-skilled technicians. On demobilization they were expected to give a spurt to the transport industry. After the War motor transport was likely to play a larger part in the life of the civilian population. Many army vehicles were to be released for disposal and many drivers and mechanics too would be available almost at once at the end of the War. Thus, in post-War period India was to experience a big social change resulting from the unprecedented expansion of road transport. After the First World War a few motor vehicles released for disposal from the army had helped in starting motor transport service in moffusil areas in a small way. But after a quarter of a century the situation in India had completely changed. The population had increased considerably and people were becoming travel-minded. The urban population too had increased. There was a demand for city-bus service in big cities and that was proving virtually a gold mine for transport operators. The demand for bus-services in moffusil areas too was increasing. Motor-transport was to become an important sector of the national economy. In each province a whole time transport commissioner was appointed to deal with the problem. All this had tremendous effect on social life of the people.

The National Highway scheme was put into operation on 1 April 1947 with the Government of India undertaking full responsibility for its construction and maintenance. The Nagpur plan envisaged the development of about 3,11,000 miles of roads in divided India including Indian states and was estimated to cost Rs 375 crores. In covered national highways, provincial highways, major and minor district roads and village roads. The National Highways aggregated about 11200 miles in the provinces and 2650 miles in the states. About 500 important bridges, 22 of 3000 ft. in length, were to be built under the scheme. The Indian Road Congress sponsored annual deputations to the USA of serving road engineers to study the latest methods of road and road bridge construction. Forty-two officers had benefited under this scheme in 1946 and 1947.[15]

The War witnessed unprecedented expansion of another means of communication, viz. the radio. Both sides used it as a means of propaganda as well as for educating the people. In India radio broadcasting began on 5 May 1932 and the government decided to place it on a permanent footing in 1935. Mr Lionel Fielder from BBC was appointed as the first Controller of Broadcasting. In 1936 it was named as AIR (All India Radio). Broadcasting made rapid progress in India and the number of licences rose from 10872 in 1933 to 92782 in 1939 and 6,67,130 in 1952 and subsequently rose to 20,64,097 in 1961.[16] In 1945 there were about 2.5 lakh listening sets in a population of 400 million. It was quite inadequate. Over 40,000 radio sets were imported from the USA under Lend and Lease. The department of information and broadcasting was created in 1941. The War had given enormous impetus to the development of internal services as well as external services covering the whole of Asia and beyond in 24 languages. The government took steps for manufacture of cheap radio sets in India. A ban on import of complete radio sets was imposed. The CSIR had financed several schemes of research for the purpose and a good measure of success had been achieved. The government was very much keen to achieve mass production of cheap radio sets in India and consequently, encouraged indigenous manufacture of radio components.[17]

The War also proved a boon to the newspaper industry in India. People in general became news-hungry and eagerly awaited arrival of newspapers both in urban and rural areas during the War period. Circulation of both English and vernacular papers increased considerably and their income from advertisement soared high to make most of them self-sufficient. In 1937 there were 32 dailies and 22 weeklies in English but in 1947 their number increased to 51 dailies and 258 weeklies in English.[18] The number of vernacular newspapers also increased considerably and some of them covered the rural areas also. The influence of press in moulding public opinion increased considerably throughout India.

The War brought about a tremendous increase in telegraphic and telephone traffic which had to be met by an expansion of telecommunication facilities. In 1942–43 the Government decided to increase these facilities and sanctioned one crore rupees for it. But it was found quite inadequate. Hence, a new Rs 8 crore plan was formulated. It was meant for the development of telecommunication for the defence services during War-time and also a doubling of existing civilian circuits. A telecommunication development board was set up with the Director-General himself as chairman. But the Rs 8 crore plan was found inadequate to cope with the phenomenal rise in traffic. Hence, a new Rs 16 crore scheme was sanctioned and undertaken. This involved the construction of a number of principal routes linking up major cities in India with interconnections radiating between larger and smaller centres. Previously, telegraph lines had been laid mostly along the Railways, because India had very few good trunk roads and reliable mechanical transport was not available. But during the War, conditions changed. A radical departure was made when telecommunication scheme was planned along roads. Alternative route was built to prevent complete isolation of any centre. Thus, trans-continental routes were built linking up major cities in India. The line from Bombay to Delhi was erected along the Bombay-Delhi trunk road which not only provided three alternative routes but also doubled the number of telegraph and trunk circuits existing before the War. The route from Calcutta to Delhi was constructed during the War along the Grand Trunk Road. It provided three alternatives between these two cities and increased the number of circuits considerably. The other four main lines were constructed between Bombay and Karachi, Bombay and Calcutta, Bombay and Madras and Madras and Calcutta. All these lines were constructed along roads except for part of Bombay and Karachi route where no road existed. The needs of northern and southern India had not been forgotten. Main telecommunication lines were constructed between Delhi and Lahore, Lahore and Karachi and Lahore and Peshawar increasing the pre-War facilities manifold. In Madras area, the lines constructed not only provided alternative routes but also linked the city of Madras with places like Bangalore, Coimbatore, Trichinopoly and stretched southward to Ceylon and in most cases doubled the existing facilities.

The requirements of big business in Bombay also found a place in the scheme. With the completion of these lines Bombay had outlets – both trunk and telegraph – double the existing telecommunication facilities before the War to Surat, Ahmedabad, Akola, Nagpur, Poona and other places. The increase in the number of telecommunication channels had been made possible, not only by the construction of new lines but also by the extensive application of that modern wonder of telecommunication engineering "carrier working" – the principle of radio-broadcasting applied to telephone trunk circuits. Automatic telephone facilities were also made available in big cities like Delhi, Lahore, etc.[19] Nearly 20,000 miles of new telephone and telegraph lines had been added to the railway network and radio communication between headquarters and division had been introduced.[20] The expansion of telecommunication had its impact on social, economic and political life of the country.

Notes

1. *Asiatic Review*, April 1947, p. 148.
2. Ibid.
3. *Report of the Indian Road Development Committee 1927–28*, p. 18.
4. *Asiatic Review*, April 1947, p. 152.
5. *Indian Information*, 1 January 1944, p. 38.
6. Ibid., 1 November 1943, p. 248.
7. Ibid.
8. Ibid., 1 March 1947, p. 202.
9. Ibid., 15 October 1945, p. 418.

10. Ibid., 1 May 1944, p. 468.
11. *Bombay Chronicle Weekly,* 11 January 1945.
12. *Indian Information,* 1 February 1945, p. 83.
13. *Commerce,* 15 January 1944.
14. *Indian Information,* 15 January 1945, p. 70.
15. *Indian Information,* 15 August 1948, Independence number, p. 42.
16. E. Roland Wolseley, *Journalism in Modern India,* Asia Publishing, Bombay, p. 163.
17. *Commerce,* 6 December 1947, p. 1028.
18. Kuppuswamy, *Communication and Social Development in India,* Sterling, Delhi, 1976, p. 141.
19. *Indian Information,* 15 September 1945, p. 251.
20. Ibid., 15 January 1945, p. 9.

CHAPTER 8

Impact of the War on Public Health Services in India

Among the social services Lord Wavell placed communications, public health and education in order of priority. Consequently, the Government of India appointed the Health Survey and Development Committee with Sir Joseph Bhore as its Chairman in October 1943. Firstly, it was to make a broad survey of the then position of health conditions and health organization in British India and secondly, to make recommendations of future developments of health services in India. The immediate necessity for initiating such a survey had arisen from the fact that the time had come to make plans for post-War development in the health field. Moreover, such plans had to be based on a comprehensive review of the health services and their problems. Even during the War much progress had been registered in public health in the western countries. But India was lagging behind in public health services abysmally. During the five pre-War years 1934–39 the condition of public health in India was highly shameful. Death-rate for general population in 1941 was 21.8 per thousand. Child mortality was 138 for 1000 births. An average of two million women died annually from causes associated with pregnancy and child bearing. 100 million people suffered from malaria, of which 20 lakh died every year. In terms of money the economic loss amounted to Rs 147 to 187 crore a year. Moreover, five lakh people died of tuberculosis, while 2.5 million suffered from this disease annually.[1] In 1944 in North Bihar alone two lakh people died of cholera and malaria.[2]

Malaria, cholera and tuberculosis were the three most dreadful diseases causing havoc among the rural population of India and the Government had not taken adequate steps to eradicate them completely. It was during the War that special attention was given to control malaria.

Of 47,400 doctors available in India in 1944 only 13,000 were reported to be on the staff of medical institutions maintained by Government and other agencies.[3] The remaining were in private practice concentrated mostly in urban areas. Hence, the rural population were the worst sufferers. The diet of the Indian population as a whole was very poor both in quantity and quality. About 80 to 90 per cent of the food consumed by the people consisted of cereals. The average annual production of cereals in the country in 1939–43 fell short of the necessary requirements of the population by about 22 per cent. In regard to other articles of diet such as vegetables, fruits, milk, meat, fish and eggs the quantities then produced were quite inadequate.[4] People viewed with apathy the sickness and mortality which existed in their midst with apathy and their outlook had no doubt been largely due to the continuance of the existing state of affairs through many generations, to which the inadequacy of the available health services had been an important contributory factor. This outlook had to change if a definite improvement in the public health was to be achieved. The insanitary conditions associated with rural and urban life could be mitigated if the individual felt a sense of responsibility towards his neighbours. The development of civic consciousness was essential if an improvement in environmental hygiene was to be effected. The importance of general education and health education for creating civic consciousness could not be overemphasized. Incidentally, the percentage of literacy in British India in 1941 was only 12.5.

To sum up, the factors responsible for the low level of public health in India in 1943 included among others, the prevalence of malnutrition, and under-nutrition among appreciable sections of the people, the serious inadequacy of existing provisions for affording health protection to the community and a group of social causes consisting of poverty and unemployment, illiteracy and ignorance of the value of hygienic mode in life and certain customs such as the *purda* and early marriage.[5]

According to the Bhore Committee, expenditure of money and effort on improving the nation's health was a gilt-edged investment which would yield not deferred dividends to be collected years later but immediate and steady returns in substantially increased productive capacity. They asserted that a nation's wealth, prosperity and advancement, whether in the economic or the intellectual sphere, were conditioned by the state of its people's health. They further regarded national health as the foundation on which any plan of reconstruction must be based if it was to yield optimum results. The State must ensure the conditions essential for healthful living in town and countryside, viz. suitable housing, sanitary surroundings and a safe drinking water supply. Elimination of unemployment, provisions of a living wage, improvement in agricultural and industrial production, development of village roads and rural communications, as distinct from the great national highways were so many facets of a single problem calling urgently for attention. A vigorous and healthy community life in its manifold aspects, must be suitably catered for. Recreation, mental and physical, played a large part in building up the conditions favourable to sound individual and community health and must get serious consideration. The child's proper nutrition, its health care and health education, its physical development were matters of concern to the state, which must see that where parental efforts were inadequate, the child must not suffer. No individual should fail to secure adequate medical care because of his inability to pay for it.

The attitude of the Soviet Government towards the health of the people epitomized the new trend:

> "Health is one of the goods of life to which man had a right; wherever this concept prevails, the logical consequence is to take all measures for the protection and restoration of health accessible to all, free of charge, medicine like education is then no longer a trade, it becomes a public function of the State."[6]

The ferment of ideas arising out of the World War had resulted in an increasing awareness on the part of the governments and peoples of the need for measures which would ensure social security; health protection was recognized as an essential part of social security. The idea that the State should assume full responsibility for all measures, curative and preventive which were necessary for safeguarding the health of the nation, was developing as a logical consequence.[7]

The Bhore Committee had been greatly influenced by the ferment of ideas arising out of the War. It rightly observed: "We shall be building on unstable foundation, if we hope to secure any rapid or lasting improvement in health conditions without arousing the living interests and enlisting the practical cooperation of the people themselves".[8] The modern trend was towards the provision by the State of as complete a health service as possible and inclusion within its scope of the largest possible section of the community by ensuring the distribution of medical benefits to all irrespective of their ability to pay.

The Committee had taken the countryside as the focal point of their recommendations, because it was the tiller of the soil on whom the economic structure of the country eventually rested. It was from his meagre earnings that the large provinces drew nearly one-third of their total revenues before the War. It was on the produce of his husbandry that the country's balance of foreign trade depended. Yet public services and amenities only occasionally came within the orbit of his daily life.[9] The essential aim of their recommendations was to ensure the health of the masses through the effective working of the centres to be established for rural areas.

The study of disease as a community problem demanded that the approach be on a wider basis so as to include social and economic factors such as housing, nutrition, poverty and ignorance of the hygienic mode of life. A recognition of these facts had led to the emergence of 'social medicine', which had widened the conception of disease by the inclusion of social, economic and environmental factors which played an equally important part in the production of sickness. Consequently, social medicine was beginning to develop its own methods of study of community health problem. This wider outlook brought into the sphere of social medicine many workers besides the doctor. They included the public health nurse, the hospital social worker, the nutritionist, the public health engineers and the statistician.

The modern public health movement has the broader aim of creating an environment in which each individual can develop his potential fully and completely. That was particularly true as regards nutrition. Malnutrition produces ill-health and lowers physical efficiency and is perhaps more serious, being more widespread than the disease itself. To meet the situation agricultural and economic policies must be so formulated as to improve the general diet of the people. A food policy based on nutrition science was essential. The UN Conference on Food and Agriculture (May 1943) endorsed the principle that governments are responsible for introducing general and specific measures for improving the diet of the people. The Conference broadly outlined the method of approach to food policies designed to improve nutritional standards.[10] It suggested that the state of nutrition of the population should be investigated by medical and public health worker. Nutritional advice should be requisitioned in connection with crop planning, production of new varieties of seed and numerous other matters. Emphasis on nutrition became the hallmark of new health policy. In the re-orientation of medical studies, greater emphasis was laid on nutrition. Professorship in nutrition in medical colleges was recommended. That would promote research on prevention and treatment of nutritional disease and broaden medical education in the desired direction.

The Committee specially recommended that the doctor of future should be "social physician protecting the people and guiding them to a healthier and happier life". He should place prevention of disease in the forefront of his programme and should so combine remedial and preventive measures as to confer the maximum benefit on the community. It also recommended that the training of the medical graduate of the future should be so designed as to equip him for all such studies. Moreover, it also recommended that the medical social worker should be recruited in the field of medical service. He should be called upon to use professional skill and knowledge in order to effect desirable changes in the relationship of the patient and his physical and human environment. He should be called upon to help in analysing the social and emotional aspects of the patient. The duties of a hospital social worker may be broadly divided into constructive and semi-negative. He may supplement medical history of the patient with his social history including any defect of heredity, personality, manners of life, home environment, character of employment, etc. He may educate the patient in regard to his physical condition in order that he may cooperate in the programme of treatment laid down by the physician – not only for the cure of illness but promotion of health for preventing disease.

It was further recommended that all large hospitals should employ a trained dietician with high qualifications. Special courses on dietics may be arranged for selected nursing sisters. Graduates of domestic science courses who have taken a course in nutrition may be employed as dieticians after receiving a training in nutrition. In the training of nurses in general, more attention should be given to nutrition. This would help to improve the nutrition treatment of patients in small hospitals which could not employ a full time dietician. All children should be taught simple facts about food and diet as part of health education. The importance of education of the people in general was greatly emphasized.

The Bhore Committee had drawn up a comprehensive health plan in order to provide a reasonably complete health service for the country. The plan falls in two parts, one, a ten year-short term plan to meet the immediate health needs of the country, the other a long-term plan covering a period of 40 years designed to provide for the people a well-deserved service based on new conception of a modern health practice. It also recommended a programme of housing, improved water supply and better sanitation, measures to improve nutritional standards, elimination of unemployment and a living wage for all workers. To make the scheme of national health service effective a comprehensive plan must be formulated to raise the general living standards of the people. It recommended that for each district with a population of 3 million there should be 150 primary units for the purpose of providing both curative and preventive medical attention within their respective areas. Each primary unit normally would serve a population of 10,000 to 20,000. To every group of 30 primary units there was to be attached a secondary unit providing institutional facilities of a high order. Finally, the secondary units (3 to 5) would form the district Health Unit, where ultimately a hospital would be developed, making available medical aid of the highest standard in every department of medical science.

It was estimated that such a plan would cost a non-recurring expenditure of Rs 362 crores. It recommended that municipalities should contribute 30 per cent of their total revenue and rural administration 12 + 2 per cent towards the cost of a health centre. The rest of the finance should be provided by the Central Government. The statutory obligation on Governments in general should be to spend a minimum of 15 per cent of their revenues on health activities. This figure compared favourably with about 8.4 per cent of the revenues then being spent on medicine and health in India. Thus, the recommendations of the Bhore Committee marked an important landmark in the social history of India and ultimately envisaged far-reaching changes in the country.

The Bhore Committee recommended ministry of health at the centre as well as in the provinces and health administration in local areas. Administrative district was to be taken as the area of development of health scheme. Social medicine like suitable housing, sanitary surroundings, safe drinking water, improvement of nutritional standards and health consciousness was to be undertaken. One hospital bed for every 1000 population at the end of the ten years was the target. Malaria Institute of India was to be expanded. Each province was required to have Malaria Organization and Malaria Control Units.

It was also recommended that there should be in each province a Ministry of Housing and Town and Rural Planning to deal with the housing of the industrial population and with the zoning and location of industries. New industries should be dispersed in rural areas so that local inhabitants might derive the fullest benefit from industries being brought nearer to them. The present system of establishing factories in or near big towns was harmful to town-dwellers and workers. Establishment of improvement trusts in all larger cities of the country to deal with slum clearance and re-housing problem was recommended. Every improvement trust was required to employ a town planner on its staff. At the Centre there should be an expert in town planning who, for the purpose of administration may be attached to the DGHS under the Ministry of Health. It was further recommended that an India-wide housing programme should be undertaken giving priority to needs of the lower income groups of population. A water supply programme aimed at providing safe drinking water to the entire population within a period of 35 years was recommended. A programme for the provision of sewerage in all towns with a population of 50,000 and over in 10 years was recommended.[11] It was proposed that the country should aim at producing 4000 to 4500 doctors a year in the first ten years or roughly the double of the output at that time. There should be one standard of medical training of the medical graduates and the training of licentiates should be discontinued within ten years. The medical curriculum should be reorganized in every medical college, there should be a department of Preventive and Social Medicine.[12] It was estimated that for ultimate requirement in India the number of doctors had to be increased five times, of nurses a hundred times, of mid-wives 20 times, and of dentists about 90 times.[13]

The Bhore Committee rightly pointed out that a nation's health was perhaps the most potent single factor in determining the character and extent of its development and progress. It emphasized the need for an improvement in environmental hygiene and preventive measures generally. It also recommended programme for the improvement of living conditions, i.e. of housing and planning of towns in India. The establishment of industrial canteens supplying good food at low cost was also recommended. The extension of industrial canteens was extremely desirable in view of the food and rationing policy of the Government. It helped greatly in satisfying the special food requirements of manual labourers.

The Bhore Committee recommended the establishment of All India Medical Institute at a central place to bring together in one place all educational facilities of the very highest order for training of important types of health personnel and to promote research of the highest order in all the branches of medical science and also to inspire all persons undergoing training with the highest ideals of the profession. The Central Government should be responsible for its establishment and maintenance. The Institute should aim at providing medical training in all its branches and also the training of nurses. It should have as an integral part of it, a medical college with its teaching hospitals and laboratories as well as a college to provide the highest type of nursing education.[14]

The Bhore Committee rightly pointed out that no programme of social reconstruction could afford to ignore the implications of the population problem. In order to reduce the rate of growth of population it recommended (a) raising the age of marriage for girls; (b) improvement in the standard of life; and (c) intentional limitation of growth. It recommended the use of contraception for birth control and also pointed out that it should be the responsibility of the governments to provide instructions regarding contraception in maternity and child care centres, dispensaries and hospitals and any other public institution administering medical aid to women. The supply of contraceptives should be free of cost and the state should have control over manufacture and sale of contraceptives as in the case of food and drugs. It also emphasized that the population problem should be the subject of continuous study.[15]

The recommendations of the Bhore Committee implied social changes of great significance for the country. It gave a new direction to the public health measures and town planning in the country. It focused attention on the inadequacy of medical services in the country and called for opening of a large number of medical colleges to meet the need of the country. Its recommendations became the sheet-anchor of the future health programme of India. For the first time it fixed the responsibility of the State for maintenance of national health.

During the Second World War medical science made rapid headway. Previously blood-transfusion service hardly existed in India. Generally, the medical profession in India was not "blood transfusion minded" and the necessity for such a service as a part of peace-time hospital organization was barely recognized. A new blood bank was established at Lahore in

October 1940. In January 1942 the Government of India led the way by establishing a unit for the manufacture of blood serum at the All India Institute of Hygiene and Public Health, Calcutta. The unit was placed at the disposal of the Director of the Institute. The provinces and states soon followed suit and worked out a scheme to start blood banks.[16]

Blood transfusion may well be regarded as one of the most noteworthy medical advances in the treatment of wounded soldiers that this War had produced. To bring this life saving treatment to all wounded soldiers of the army in India an Army Blood Transfusion Service (India) had been created. Blood depots at Dehradun and Poona had been equipped with modern apparatus for the preparation of blood products and for the assembly and sterilization of the specialized apparatus required for taking blood and giving transfusion.

Modern medicine has become so complex that specialization has become essential. This had been fully recognized in the army medical services in India. The total number of specialists ran into four figures and embraced physicians, surgeons, anaesthetics, radiologists, pathologists, hygienists, psychiatrists, neurologists, oncologists and ophthalmologists etc. The organization of specialists became so complete that serious patients in all regions were assured of expert attention.[17]

Considerable progress had been made during the War in the institution of facilities for physiotherapy and rehabilitation. The importance of these branches of medicine in hastening the recovery of men suffering from wounds and injuries involving bones and joints could not be overestimated. In addition, most general hospitals had to be equipped with facilities for occupational therapy which proved of real value to patients.

Laboratory investigation and diagnosis of disease had long been recognized by the medical services in India as one of the most important branches of medicine. To cater to this need there grew up an up-to-date clinical pathology service staffed by specialists and skilled technicians. The creation of the Central Military Pathological Laboratory was an important step in this direction. During the War some of the finest hospitals were then to be found among the military hospital in India.[18] They set a standard of excellence to be emulated by others.

During the First World War psychiatry was recognized as a branch of medical science. But in the Second World War the number of specialists in psychiatry had been substantially increased and the number of medical officers employed in this branch became ten times greater than that before the War. In the Second World War the psychiatrist was in uniform from the outset, a routine figure and a key specialist in the crucial field of morale. By the time the War was over psychiatry had finally lost its alien overtone. It was not only intellectually but also popularly accepted. The foundation of an up-to-date psychiatric service was laid in the War. In due course the psychiatric specialists, trained in military hospitals with their colleagues in civil practice found ample scope for their professional skill after the War. Army specialists approached the problem of mentally defective children and adults in the civilian population with a background of experience and knowledge.[19] As a matter of fact the military medical services had undergone a radical re-organization and development dictated by the intensive application of modern science to military medical problems which had greatly increased the professional and technical value of the personnel concerned. During the War the utter inadequacy of the medical cover for the expanding Indian army was strongly felt. Hence, steps were taken on an emergency basis to train medical personnel suitable for needs of the army. Seven medical schools were expanded and raised to the standard of colleges and two new ones were started to produce medical graduates. Licentiates of the IMD were put through special intensive courses which brought them up to standard in six months. Women with a reasonable knowledge of English were given three months' basic training in nursing at specially selected hospitals and were then posted to other hospitals for full duty under the supervision of qualified nurses. Similar steps were taken to produce radiographers, laboratory assistants, dispensers, male nursing orderlies and others. By the end of the War India had a good nucleus of specialists, who had been trained by well-known physicians and surgeons from the UK and had also medical technicians of every category. Many of them when discharged from military service were employed as teachers and gave good account of themselves. In the Indian military medical services between 1940 and 1945, the personnel of different categories increased from 9270 to 169325. To treat about 5 million sick and wounded the hospital beds were increased from 11,100 to 1,97,530.[20] The Bhore Committee emphasized the supreme importance of this to the health services of the country. They considered it essential that services of all such personnel should be utilized as far as possible.[21]

During the War milk supply in urban areas posed a great problem. Agricultural marketing adviser to the Government of India strongly felt that the distribution of milk in a city or town should be entrusted to a properly constituted milk marketing organization and special legislation should be enacted for this work. An experimental scheme was to be tried in metropolitan cities like Calcutta, Bombay, Madras, Delhi, Karachi, Kanpur and Nagpur. Mr R.A. Pepperall, Chief Executive Officer of British Milk Marketing Board was appointed as Milk Marketing Adviser to the Government of India. He was to make a rapid survey of the problems involved in the supply of milk to Indian cities, particularly procurement, transport, processing, quality and price control. The problem was one of unparalleled dimension and involved more than 22 million individual producers all over the country. India was the country where the standard of integrity was very low and dairy industry afforded a lot of opportunities for fraud.

The Pepperall report described the prevailing efficiency of the dairy industry throughout India as "probably the lowest in the whole world".[22] The report attributed this to the almost total apathy of the general public in a matter which affected their health and incidentally their pocket. The practice of adding water or other substances to milk was so common as to cause little comment. Consequently, the report suggested that there should be a fixed price for the producer but affordable for the consumer.

The report further suggested that in every province a milk commission should be set up with a paid director and an advisory Board nominated by the Government and at the Centre a coordinated milk policy as part of an all India food policy should be adopted and implemented through a central milk director to be recruited from abroad and given the salary of not less than Rs 3000 per annum as it was really very hard for Indians to take unpopular decisions.

Other recommendations of the Report were: (i) the cow should be developed both for dual purpose of milk and draught; (ii) cattle from city stables should be dislodged and colonized in more natural environment; (iii) *Berseem* should be grown more extensively than at present in irrigated areas; (iv) village areas should be utilized for cultivating and feeding green fodder in preference to grazing; (v) a total ban should be imposed on the export of oilseeds and cakes from India; (vi) dairy utensils and appliances of uniform standards should be manufactured in India; (vii) the existing legal standards for pure milk should be re-examined; (viii) the activities of the military dairy farms should be restricted with regard to manufacture of milk products and their export; (ix) manufacture of milk products should be confined to remote rural areas; (x) export of cattle from Punjab to Bombay and Calcutta for milk production should be replaced by the evaporated milk manufactured there; (xi) manufacture of butter in India should be discouraged and instead it should be imported from New Zealand and the other Dominions; (xii) cheap milk should be provided for priority consumers; (xiii) producers should be organized into cooperative societies; (xiv) manufacture of dairy products should be licensed; (xv) modern dairies should be established in cities and dairy farms should be established.

The Government of India invited the attention of provincial governments to these recommendations. Schemes had already been drawn up in some provinces for setting up milk control boards and appointing dairy development officers.

The ICAR and IVRI at the centre and the various provincial governments had already taken measures to tackle the problem of milk supply and further action was being taken to achieve desired results. Some provinces had started separate departments for dairy development. The technique of artificial insemination under Indian conditions was being perfected at IVRI and work on full scale had been started at a few centres both in farms and in city cattle stables.

The dislodging of cattle from city stables and colonizing them in more natural environments was the accepted policy of the Government and specific steps were being taken by some of the large cities like Bombay, Madras and Calcutta to give effect to it. Berseem was being grown wherever irrigation facilities together with soil and climatic conditions permitted. But most of the areas kept for growing were unfit for fodder cultivation.

Manufacture of simple types of utensils like dairy pails, milk cans, strainers etc., at comparatively low prices had been well established during the War and encouragement was provided for manufacture of high grade dairy equipment. The existing legal standard for pure milk was being re-examined by the ICAR. The manufacture of milk products in rural areas became the accepted policy of the Government.

Schemes for the supply of cheap milk to priority consumers had been in operation in several large cities under the guidance of the Food Department since the outbreak of the War. Concrete schemes for organizing producers into cooperative societies were being taken up by the provinces. The establishment of modern dairies in cities formed part of the provincial schemes. Subsequently, a 21 point programme for increasing the overall supply of milk to the country was adopted. It dealt with problem of procurement, processing, transport and sale of milk.[23] Thus, India was undergoing a process of immense social change on the eve of independence.

Notes

1. *Commerce*, 9 March 1946, p. 409.
2. *Indian Social Reformer*, 16 September 1944, p. 12.
3. *Health Survey and Development Committee Report*, Vol. I, p. 13.
4. Ibid., p. 12.
5. Ibid., p. 19.
6. *Health Survey, Recommendations*, Vol. III, p. 10.
7. Ibid., p. 7.
8. Ibid., p. 4.
9. Ibid.
10. Ibid., pp. 70–71.
11. *Indian Information*, 1 April 1946, p. 353.
12. Ibid.
13. Ibid., p. 369.

14. *Health Survey: Recommendations*, Vol. IV, p. 70.
15. Ibid., p. 82.
16. *Indian Information*, 15 March 1943, p. 250.
17. Ibid., 1 August 1944, p. 93.
18. Ibid.
19. Ibid., 15 January 1944, p. 92.
20. *Seminar*, September 1994, p. 30.
21. *Indian Information*, 1 April 1946, p. 353.
22. Ibid., 15 March 1946, p. 324.
23. Ibid., 1 January 1947, p. 24.

CHAPTER 9

Education – A Potent Factor of Social Change

Under the Government of India Act of 1919 education became a provincial subject in charge of popularly elected ministers. Primary and middle education was entrusted to the care of the local bodies. John Sargent regretted that the decision to hand over education to local bodies was one of the most serious administrative errors ever made in the country.[1] Education being largely a provincial subject there was a permanent need for a national body which could evolve a national plan and establish national standards. To meet this need the Central Advisory Board of Education was created in 1920 to guide and coordinate educational policy in the country as a whole. It became the victim of the economic crunch in 1923 but was revived in 1935. From then on it played an active part in formulating educational policy in India. Apathy and inertia had reigned for long in the domain of education and poverty had been the accepted excuse for leaving undone what ought to have been done. R.A. Butler frankly admitted that the state of education in India was the most serious blot upon the British administration. The percentage of illiteracy in India was 85 per cent after the British rule of 150 years.[2] Sir John Anderson commented that he did not know that the Government of India had an education policy.[3]

The inauguration of provincial autonomy on 1 April 1937 marked a real change in the educational field. The inertia was broken. Provincial ministers undertook the expansion of education with great enthusiasm. There was a common complaint that the Indian educational system was too academic in content. To rectify this a committee on vocational education headed by Abbot and Wood was appointed in 1936. This committee concluded that vocational education was not on a lower plane than literary education since the full purpose of education was to develop the whole powers of the mind, body and spirit so that they might be devoted to the welfare of the society. It also pointed out that general and vocational education were not essentially different branches but the earlier and later phases of a continuous process. The condition of India demanded that business should have its fair share of the best brains available in the country. It also spotlighted the fact that the schools in India devoted insufficient attention to the teaching of Art and there was a serious risk of the artistic traditions of India being weakened. The spheres of the influence of the existing schools of arts and crafts should be enlarged considerably.[4]

In the history of British India the year 1937 is a turning point of the deepest significance. The Government of India Act of 1935 conceding provincial autonomy was put through. It aroused high hopes and aspirations among the Indian people. Even Gandhiji thought that the new constitution despite all its deficiencies could further the programme of village uplift, reduce the burden on peasantry, promote village industries, encourage the use of homespun cloth, extend education, combat untouchability and introduce prohibition. There were at least two items in the legislative programme of the Congress ministries in seven provinces which owed their inspiration almost wholly to Gandhiji – prohibition and education. An education conference representing Congress ministries in provinces met on 22 October 1937 with Gandhiji in chair.[5] He pleaded for craft-centred education with a view to developing personality through productive work. In March 1938, the Congress approved the basic education scheme and the Hindustani Talimi Sangh was founded at Sevagram.[6] Thus, there was a stirring in the educational field with the installation of the Congress ministries in provinces.

Even in East Bengal the inauguration of provincial autonomy started a process of social change of deep significance. For generations the Hindu middle class had kept its finger in every social, cultural and political pie of the area. They had monopolized the services and professions and had a firm grip on municipal administrations, district boards and colleges in urban areas. Being backward in education the Muslims, although in majority, had to stand at the end of a long queue. But with the inauguration of the provincial autonomy the emerging Muslim middle class began to arrive on the political scene with vengeance. The process of unscrewing of the Hindu hold on public life by the Muslim middle class had started. The stronghold of the Hindu middle class fell one after another to the Muslim middle class.[7] To remove the educational backwardness of the Muslims the Fazlul-Huq ministry did some valuable work and accelerated the rise of Muslim middle class in Bengal. Education, reduction of rural indebtedness and land reforms were the three main planks of social reconstruction under the provincial autonomy almost all over British India. Some of the provincial ministers were bold enough to introduce mother-tongue as medium of instruction in schools and colleges. Sir Ashutosh Mukherjee had already shown the way in introducing mother-tongue as the medium of instruction at the secondary stage. This greatly speeded up the expansion of education.

In November 1938 Sir John Sargent was appointed Educational Adviser to the Government of India. India would always remember him for the part played by him in formulating the first integrated and comprehensive plan of national education.[8] Even in the midst of petrified official environment he had succeeded in keeping alive the freshness of a democratic and liberal outlook. He believed that the educational system in India required overhauling from top to bottom. India needed a soundly conceived system of popular education which ought to satisfy both cultural and economic needs of the community whose interest it intended to promote.[9] John Sargent wanted to employ education as an instrument of social change. The education caravan moved on very slowly in India. He undertook to mechanize it and to direct it from a central dynamo. After Lord Curzon no one was as serious about the educational policy as John Sargent. He activized the Central Advisory Board of

Education and made it a tool for implementing his educational ideas in India. During 1937–47 eleven meetings of CABE were held in various important centres in India and except one all were held under his guidance. He was perhaps the first British educationist to conceive of a national system of education for India.

The CABE prepared a scheme of national education for India under John Sargent's guidance and submitted it to the Central Government in January 1944. It is popularly known as the 'Sargent Plan'. It was the first of the Central Government's post-War development schemes to be made public and it set a standard in planning. It can claim to be the first serious attempt to envisage comprehensively India's educational needs from nursery to the university and beyond. The Board's intention was 'to indicate in broad outline the minimum educational requirements of this country and to show how long it would take to satisfy them and roughly what it would cost'. At that stage it was beyond their power to perceive the precise lines which future development should follow, though the endeavour had been made to lay down principles for general guidance. Its object was to lay down certain general principles which could be regarded as valid so far as the establishment of an efficient system of public instruction in any democratic state was concerned.[10]

Its main features were: (i) to provide universal compulsory and free education for all boys and girls between the age of 6 and 14 in order to ensure literacy and the minimum preparation for citizenship. It was estimated that for basic primary and middle schools alone 18,00,000 teachers would be needed. A reasonable provision of education before the age of 6 in the form of nursery schools and classes had to be provided. At least one million sites for nursery schools and classes would be needed. Partly owing to expense and partly owing to the dearth of trained women teachers, who alone could be in charge of children at this tender age, facilities of that kind were practically non-existing in India at that time; (ii) secondary and high school education for those who would show the capacity for benefiting by it. Provisions were to be made in the high schools of various types of not less than 20 per cent of boys and girls in each age group. On this basis a six-year course provision was to be made in high schools for just over seven million boys and girls. At least 3,60,000 teachers would be required for this group of students. This was to be the minimum provision. No boys and girls may be debarred by poverty from further education. Liberal financial assistance in the form of freeships, scholarships and stipends must be provided. There should be variety both in types of schools and in the curricula of individual schools to suit varying tastes and aptitudes of the individual pupils on the one hand and requirements of their future occupations on the other; (iii) providing university education including post-graduate and research for selected students. When the new high school system would be established, about 1 pupil in 15 would be found fit to proceed to a university, apart from those who would opt for technical institutions, training schools and other places for further education. This meant doubling the number of students in universities at the moment, although Indian universities did not make any serious attempt to relate their output to the needs of the community and their examination system did not encourage original thinking and real scholarship; (iv) the higher stages of technical education must be organised and administered on an all India basis and with this end in view advocated the establishment of an all India council for technical education because a considerable development in technical education would be called for in the post-War period. Commerce, agriculture and art in industry were included in technical education and these were to be given proper encouragement; (v) adult education, both vocational and non-vocational of all kinds and standards to meet the needs of those who were denied adequate opportunities in their earlier years or recognize importance of supplementing what they had received. It was proposed to have a plan for making literate all persons below the age of 40 in a period of 25 years. The concept of adult-education had undergone a sea change. Literacy was not the end of it but only the beginning leading to further education.

The plan involved a massive programme of training of school teachers. Over two million additional teachers were required for a national system of education. It was considered desirable that every teacher ought to be trained and adequate arrangement in training and for keeping the teachers up-to-date refresher course was to be arranged regularly. To keep the school children healthy an efficient medical service was to be arranged. Special schools for children suffering from mental or physical disability were to be set up. In a universal system of education their claims could hardly be ignored. The need for a youth movement on all India basis was recognized. Employment bureau to guide school and college graduates into profitable employment and to adjust the output of the schools and colleges to the capacity of the labour market was also suggested. An efficient educational administrative system was to be developed to implement the plan successfully. Provincial governments were to resume all educational powers from local bodies because their inefficiency in the matter had been proved beyond doubt. No western ideas or methods had been adopted in the plan without making sure that they were best suited to India. At all stages of education the training of intellect and training of character had been emphasized. The moral or spiritual side of education had not been ignored. The plan assumed that Indian parents, like other parents, would wish their children to grow up physically fit, mentally alert and morally sound.[11]

The scheme was to cost, about Rs 313 crores per annum. When the estimated income from fees, endowments and other sources would be taken in account, Rs 277 crores gross per annum would remain to be funded from public funds. These figures were based on pre-war standard. In 1940–41 the total expenditure on education was Rs 30 crores, of which Rs 17½ crores came from public funds. The plan was to be completed in a period of 40 years. Moreover, if India wanted to have a proper system of education, she must be ready to follow the practice of other countries and must pay for it. The development of India's economic resources and the expansion of her social services were inseparably connected and must proceed side by side. Even the Bombay plan covered, among other things, the provision of compulsory primary and middle education for all, as well as the liquidation of adult illiteracy. This was the need of the hour. John Sargent was of the view that it was in the world's interests as much as India's that this should be done and done quickly. He even suggested that the government of India should take an immediate loan of such a size as would enable a quick start to be made at once. He further commented that if money in any quantity could be raised in war time, the same should be done in peace time for a nobler purpose. He thought that the government would find it difficult to ignore the very large volume of public opinion both inside and outside India, which was apparently convinced that such action of a comprehensive scale for national education in India could not be deferred any longer. The plan had wide favourable reactions all over India. All castes and communities and all shades of public opinion were ready to co-operate in any constructive effort to deal with one of India's most urgent problems. India could not afford to wait indefinitely for its solution. There could be no half way house between what was and what ought to be done. John Sargent thought that anything less than all meant that India accepted a position of permanent inferiority in the society of civilized nations. India could not expect to compete on level terms with other nations if she was to remain content to go on drawing her leaders and experts from not more than 10 per cent of her potential brain power resources. British practical interests and credit before history demanded that they should do all in their power to help India to fall in by their side. The prophetic words of Disraeli – "Upon the education of the people of this country the fate of this country depends", was very much applicable to India.[12]

The Sargent plan stirred the minds of intellectuals as well as administrators in India and set them thinking. Dr M.R. Jayakar thought that the scheme held out an early prospect of realizing the ideals which Indian nationalists had dreamt of. It marked the right direction in which progress had to be made. The plan was very modest as compared with the British scheme for post-war Great Britain. India had to try and find out the requisite sum for implementing the scheme. He advised the Indian Universities to take active interest in the scheme and not allow it to have the fate of similar ones in the archives of a somnolent secretariat.[13] He was firmly of the view that ill-advised economy in education was particularly undesirable in India, where educational grants had always formed a drop in the ocean. He further thought that the War was the best time for pushing forward educational schemes so that as soon as the War was over, they might be implemented.[14] Similarly, John Sargent also thought that the period of War was just the time when such measures ought to receive the most serious consideration and the necessary planning ought to be put in hand. In UK the Education Acts of 1902, 1917 and 1944 were passed when the country was in the midst of War. There was even stirring of spirit in the imperial secretariat in New Delhi. Mr G.L. Mehta rightly pointed out that the essentials of a sound national economic policy must envisage a greater expenditure by state on nation-building activities. Education and public health ultimately were remunerative and tended to act beneficially on the economic stamina and productivity of the country.[15] Even Sir A. Dalal who looked well ahead of his times, used to remark frequently on the neglect of important studies like those of Dr Burns on agriculture and Sir John Sargent on education.[16] As a matter of fact the Sargent Plan had a surprisingly good response in India, even from those organs of press which had always been critical of the government. Some even described it as a 'gesture of British goodwill'. It was likely to give the provincial governments a greater lever in their demands upon the central government for money.

It was recognized as early as 1935 that a radical reconstruction of school education was essential. The scheme formulated by CABE at its inaugural meeting, righly emphasized the intimate relationship between secondary and technical education. A stage appeared to have been reached when it was equally essential to carry the policy to the logical conclusion by a radical reconstruction of technical education. The experience of the War had already led to a number of salutary changes. It had caused a large expansion of industry and created a greatly increased demand for technicians of all grades. The army too needed a large number of technicians. To meet the needs of technicians the Labour Department organised the technical training schemes in almost every technical institution in the country. Many young men who would not otherwise have embarked on a technical career had been recruited under these schemes and the prejudice against industrial employment had been steadily breaking down. Technical education attracted the attention of young men because it offered opportunities of employment in the impending industrialisation of the country. Technical education acquired respectability during the War. Its scope was widened to include the study of design and distribution as well as the actual processes of manufacture. Technical instruction became a wider and more liberal form of training than it had been in the past. It was now considered an integrated part of the general educational system and not merely a special training for industrial employment. It was now to form a link between education and industry.[17] Technical high school was to become an established part of a selective High School system under the Sargent Plan.

Before the war the agricultural education was neglected. It had not caught the attention of the intelligentsia of the country. War focused attention on the absolute necessity of a strong national agriculture as a basis for every other action. A well considered policy in reference to food production was, therefore, considered an integral part of War efforts. The first Conference on agricultural education in India was held in May 1942. It resolved that the Universities should recognize the science of agriculture as an optional subject for a degree course.[18] The existing facilities for agricultural education were quite inadequate to meet the requirements of the country. Hence, a comprehensive and planned system of agricultural education was called for.[19] Agricultural education including education in animal husbandry and dairying must logically be a branch of technical education.

The reorganization of the Delhi University during the War was an important event in the history of education in India. Sir Maurice Gwyer, the Vice-Chancellor of Delhi University, undertook the task of reorganizing it with a view to transforming it into a first rate university. Till then it had no standing in the academic life of the country. The main inspiration came from John Sargent, the Educational Adviser to the Government of India, who was full of ideas and wanted to improve academic life as far as possible. Under his stewardship an amendment to the Delhi University Act was passed in 1943 and the three-year degree course was launched which later became the general pattern for the whole of India. Higher Secondary education was also reorganized. The reorganization of Delhi University acquired an all India significance. It was an educational experiment of great value. The scheme aimed at creating an all India institution of first rate importance outshining all the provincial universities. Sir Maurice Gwyer contemplated that the Delhi University should be an all India centre of culture and learning and that it should form the main link between India and the outside world.[20] He rightly observed: "We do not seek to rival or compete with other and more ancient universities, but rather to develop an atmosphere, a habit of mind, a tradition . . . of our own. We would like to aim at quality rather than quantity . . . we are willing to learn and we hope that as we have neither provincial or communal affiliation, we may be able to serve India as a whole".[21] To implement this ideal he began building up first rate post-graduate departments in arts and sciences in Delhi University. Chairs in Economics, Physics and Law were created.[22] On the initiative of Sir Maurice Gwyer, Dr V.K.R.V. Rao and Dr D.S. Kothari were appointed professors and heads of Economics and Physics Departments respectively and they made their mark in the academic life of the country. Good students from all over India began to be attracted to Delhi for study and research. It really marked the beginning of a great social change in India. In course of time the Delhi University turned out to be the first rate centre of learning in India. The credit goes to John Sargent and Sir Maurice Gwyer.

During the Second World War Sir Maharaj Singh found unbounded enthusiasm for English education among boys.[23] The rush for government service was even more pronounced than before and the university graduates and even matriculates had very little difficulty in finding suitable jobs. The educated unemployed had almost vanished on account of opportunities for employment in the War. The army needed a large number of skilled and unskilled workers. There was a great demand for technicians of all grades in the army. The inertia in education had already been broken with the introduction of the provincial autonomy in 1937. War gave impetus to the establishment of new colleges and schools all over the country. Inflation resulting from the War was a factor in accelerating the pace of education. The number of degree colleges was still small while the universities throughout India did not exceed a dozen. The demand for new degree colleges and new universities was voiced. In 1913 the Government of India had decided that every important province in the country should have a university of its own. The case of the Bombay Presidency was a peculiar one. Its jurisdiction extended from Dharwar in the south to the border of Sind in the north and it had only one university. Hence, there was a demand for a regional university in Bombay Presidency. In 1937 Dr G.S. Mahajani moved a resolution in the Bombay Legislative Council recommending that the Government should take steps to establish additional universities in the province to meet the increased demand for higher education and facilities for research. In principle the Government had no objection to the creation of such institution provided the necessary safeguards and conditions were present. During the War the Bombay Government belatedly realized that no useful purpose could be served by shirking the issue of regional universities indefinitely. Hence, a committee was appointed under the chairmanship of Mr M.R. Jayakar to study the problem.[24] The Committee recommended that the proposed university should be called the University of Poona and should keep in view the special needs, interests and traditions of Maharashtra and its people. As soon as the War ended, a number of universities were established in India such as the Utkal University, the University of Saugar, the University of Poona and others.

Some beneficial measures were adopted by the Coalition Government of Fazlul Huq in Bengal particularly in the field of education. He was very much conscious of the backwardness of Muslims in education in Bengal. Hence, he was determined to redress the balance. He established the Sakhawat Memorial Girls High School and the Lady Brabourne College in Calcutta for Muslim girls and the Islamia College for Muslim boys. Moreover, he established a large number of schools and colleges in rural areas which greatly benefited the Muslisms.[25] Even some ICS officers like T.N. Kaul and B. Shiva Raman helped in establishing colleges at Unnao[26] and Purnea[27] respectively during the War period.

The demand for science teaching and technical education picked up considerably during the War. Before the War there were in Bengal no fewer than 1700 high schools but there was not a single high school where science teaching was provided with practical work for the students. There were about 3,90,000 students in high schools but the number attending science classes was under 500.[28] During the War the craze for science teaching and technical education picked up considerably. Scientific education was no longer regarded as necessarily non-cultural in India. In 1944 there was frantic rush for science courses of study in Bombay. As the demand for scientific and technical education was likely to increase in the post-War period the problem needed greater attention and planning by the University and Government authorities than it had so far received. The Bombay Government was alive to the situation and arrangements had already been made for admission of 30 students above the usual number to the bachelor of science courses in the Royal Institute of Science that year.[29] This was not only confined to Bombay. The demand for science education became an all India phenomenon and the authorities concerned had to make necessary arrangement for the same. The place of statistics as a potent tool not only of planning but of many kinds of scientific activity had been well-established during the War. As soon as War ended University Grants Commission was constituted under the chairmanship of Sir Mirza Ismail to monitor the grants and academic standards of higher education in India. Lord Irwin rightly observed in 1944: "India comes of age: India became adult for two reasons. Firstly, in a material way she had made enormous progress in industry and in technical knowledge during the War. Secondly, she had become adult in the realm of education."[30]

The early 1940s witnessed a phenomenal rise in the number of colleges and students all over the country. There was a tremendous upward swing in education. The number of colleges rose from 425 in 1940–41 to 593 in 1945–46. By 1949–50 this number had risen to 976 in the post-partition India. The number of men and women graduate students of all faculties in 1949–50 rose to 1,81,134 of whom 77,890 or nearly 42 per cent, belonged to professional colleges and the remainder to colleges of arts and science. The number of undergraduate scholars totalled 1,99,703. Together they formed a total of 3,80,837 in 1949–50. Thus, there was one college student to every 1000 of the population, which was 360 million in 1951. The proportionate increase in the number of graduate students was much greater than before.[31] In the faculty of medicine in 1939–40 there were 12 colleges and 5640 students. In 1949–50 this number rose to 45 colleges and 14097 medical students. In the faculty of engineering in 1939–40, there were 7 colleges and 2509 students. In 1949–50 this number rose to 29 colleges and 12331 engineering students.[32] Thus, during the decade 1940–50 there was a tremendous upward swing in education which resulted in bringing about a social change of deep significance in the country.

In 1921 the total number of literates in British India was less than 15 million. But in 1941 the number of literates had increased to 37 million. The proportion of literates to the total population thus increased from 6 per cent to 13 per cent in twenty years. The annual expenditure on recognized educational institutions was less than Rs 16 crores in 1920–21; in 1940–41 this figure had increased to Rs 30 crores and about half of this expenditure had throughout been met from Government funds. Thus, from 1937 onwards attention was focused on removal of illiteracy in India. The provincial governments were very much alive to the problem of adult education and various programmes were put into operation, although the result was far from satisfactory.

Notes

1. *Report on Post-war Educational Development,* January 1944, p. 19.
2. *Asiatic Review,* July 1944, p. 247.
3. Ibid., p. 244.
4. *Report on Vocational Education in India by Abbot & Wood,* 1937, p. 110.
5. *Progress of India: Decennial Review,* Vol. I, p. 1.
6. B.R. Nanda, *In Gandhi's Footsteps,* Oxford, 1990, p. 248.

7. D.P. Das, *The Untouchable Story*, Allied Publishers, New Delhi, 1985, p. 98.
8. Humayun Kabir, *Progress of Education in India 1947–52*, p. 1.
9. *Indian Annual Register*, July-December 1941, p. 309.
10. *Report on Post-War Educational Development*, January 1944, p. 10.
11. *Asiatic Review*, July 1944, p. 238.
12. Ibid., p. 240.
13. Ibid., p. 241.
14. *Indian Annual Register*, Vol. II, p. 368.
15. Ibid., p. 368.
16. *Commerce*, 13 May 1944, p. 740.
17. Sir A. Dalal, *A Memoir*, Bombay, 1980, p. 81.
18. *Report of the Technical Education Committee*, 1946, pp. 3–4.
19. *Indian Farming*, November 1942, p. 559.
20. *Report on Agricultural Education*, 1944, p. 69.
21. *Council of State Proceedings*, 27 August 1943, p. 270.
22. *Indian Annual Register*, 1943, p. 412.
23. *Bombay Chronicle Weekly*, 1 March 1942, p. 1.
24. V.B. Kulkarni, *M.R. Jayakar*, Publication Division, 1976, p. 309.
25. Tamizuddin Khan, *The Test of Time: My Life and Days*, Dacca, 1989, p. 143.
26. T.N. Kaul, *Remembrances*, New Delhi, 1982, p. 97.
27. B. Shiva Raman, *Bitter Sweet: Government of India in Transition*, New Delhi, 1991, p. 26.
28. *Asiatic Review*, January 1945, p. 6.
29. *Times of India*, 22 June 1944.
30. *Asiatic Review*, April 1946, p. 153.
31. B.B. Misra, *Middle Class*, Oxford, 1961, p. 304.
32. Ibid.

CHAPTER 10

Rural Reconstruction on Anvil

During the second half of the British rule in India (1858–1947) problems of rural life attracted the notice of the academics and administrators. William Hunter's *Annals of Rural Bengal (1860)* and Lal Bihari Day's *Bengal's Peasant Life (1874)* were pioneers in portraying economic and social life in Bengal. Later on, Faridun-ul Mulk's *An Early Analysis of Economic Life of the Peasants of Aurangabad District (1891)*, J.C. Jack's *Economic Life of A Bengal District (1916)*, Harold Mann's *Land and Labour in A Deccan Village (1917)*, Gilbert Slater's *Some South Indian Villages (1918)* and Keating's *Rural Economy of Bombay Deccan (1921)* constituted the next stage in analysis of regional economic life in India.[1] Many studies of a similar kind made in different parts of India came up later.

Even after more than one hundred fifty years of British rule in India the vast majority of the rural masses were in a condition of abject poverty. A low standard of living, an inadequate and non-nutritious diet, meagre and rough clothings, insanitary living conditions, prevalence of diseases, dirt and squalor and above all ignorance and illiteracy were the characteristic features of life in rural India till the end of the First World War.[2] The position had been made much worse by loss of village industries, rural indebtedness, village factions, litigations and drunkenness. The disruption of the village community had led to isolation of the individual farmer and artisan and left them without any defensive organization. Commercialization of agriculture had not brought much profit to the farmer. It only filled the pockets of moneylenders, the lawyers, the traders and other urban classes. Consequently, there had been a considerable increase in rural indebtedness and land had passed on a large scale from the hands of the peasants to moneylenders. The village people had to depend solely on land and followed the traditional method of agriculture. They had hardly any subsidiary industries and were unable to withstand the first shock of a serious famine. The fragmentation of landholdings and unproductive expenditure on social functions made them incur debts. They were denied modern amenities of life such as education, sanitation, communications. Such facilities were available in urban areas. This induced exodus of the best intelligence and enterprise of the village to towns. Educated people of the towns and the landlords residing there did not care much to study rural problems. Thus, the village presented a gloomy and depressing picture of people torn by factions and petty jealousies. Extension of irrigation facilities in some parts of the country improved the lot of the peasant marginally. The cooperative movement had just touched the fringe of rural problems. After the First World War the Government was becoming increasingly alive to its responsibility for welfare of the rural masses and was trying to tackle the problem of rural stagnation, although its efforts were often haphazard, inadequate and uncoordinated. Under the reforms of 1919, education was made a provincial subject and showed signs of reaching the villages. A general mass awakening was coming up due to the forces liberated by the Great War. The peasant came into the forefront all over the world. He was now coming into his own and was not going to be ignored in the political, social and economic aspects of national life. This had its effects on India as a whole.

Rural reconstruction has become the foremost national problem in India in the present century. Some attempts were made by some non-official agencies to tackle this problem. One such attempt was made by Sir David Hamilton in 1903 when he organized the Gosaba Cooperative Reclamation Society in the Sunderbans. 22,000 acres of jungle infested by tigers and crocodiles was reclaimed and made fit for human habitation. As a rule, moneylenders were the constant scourge of village. But they were not allowed to enter the Gosaba. Every village in

Gosaba had a bank and a school. The village cooperative societies numbering 24 were organized with a working capital of £ 3000 and reserve funds amounting to £ 2000. Gradually cooperatives moved beyond banking into a united endeavour to meet the needs of the villagers, producers and consumers alike. Simultaneously, a Central Cooperative Store was also organized. To crown it all came the cooperative rice mill having 600 shareholders. The Rural Reconstruction Institute was also established to educate young men for rural life and service.[3] As a matter of fact Gosaba was rural reconstruction in action. It started almost on a clean slate. But the problem of rural reconstruction in other parts of India was a complex one.

Recommendations of the Royal Commission on Agriculture touched the heart of the problem and led the nationalists, academics and administrators in search of a well-thought national programme of rural reconstruction. But it was a formidable task. The Commission rightly pointed out that it was upon the homes and fields of cultivators that the strength of the country and foundation of its prosperity must ultimately rest. They appealed to the members of Indian Universities to apply themselves to the social and economic problems of the countryside and to prepare themselves to take lead in the movement for the uplift of the rural classes.[4] They were convinced that mere material improvement alone would not bring lasting benefit to the peasant population.[5] Nor would the welfare and prosperity of the rural population come by technical advances alone. Better living could be secured only by a combination of better farming and better business. But it was equally true that the will to live better must furnish the driving power that was required. At the heart of the problem was the development of the desire for a higher standard of living. At that time the will to live better was not a dominant feature of rural India. Indian peasantry was very conservative. For him the life on land was a means of living and not a business. What had been done by his forefathers was the most natural thing for him to do. It was almost a sin to change the method of doing anything. Moreover, the idea of making profit expressed in terms of money out of their activities was an anathema to them. Extreme apathy was found everywhere in the countryside. This outlook of rural India had to be changed for success of any rural reconstruction programme.

Consequent upon recommendations of the Royal Commission on Agriculture several provinces began to take interest in improving the lot of rural masses in one way or another. Even some non-official agencies showed interest in the matter. Rabindranath Tagore wanted to bring back life in its completeness into the Indian village. With this end in view he established the Institute of Rural Reconstruction at Sriniketan and tried to revive old village crafts and industries. He wanted to acquaint villagers with cultural traditions of their own country and to make them competent in the use of modern resources for improvement of their physical, intellectual and economic conditions.[6] Gandhiji fully agreed with his view. Tagore's programme of rural reconstruction was followed later on by other leaders and social workers in the country. The rural development of Punjab began with its Board of economic enquiry, cooperative societies for consolidation of holdings, arbitration and compulsory education. Punjab was the first province to undertake consolidation of holdings through co-operative societies. Sir M.L. Darling did some valuable work in the field of cooperation in that province. His classic book entitled *The Punjab Peasant in Prosperity and Debt* gave a critical analysis of the cause, incidence and extent of debt in that province. He was convinced that no progress was possible in the case of cultivators unless the power of moneylenders was broken in the rural areas. The supreme need of the time was to free the masses from the disabilities of poverty and ignorance and to infuse the people with ideals of progressive life. It was essential to awaken in them a desire for this.[7]

Several provinces evinced interest in undertaking rural improvement programme in the 1930s. The Madras Presidency proposed to establish a special rural development fund for supply of principal wants of rural areas. The Bombay Presidency Government proposed to revive spare time occupations for agriculturists. The Bombay Central Cooperative Institute proposed to take up rural reconstruction work in some villages. Enlightened Indian states like Baroda and Mysore were giving a trial to several rural schemes and contemplated their extension. Even the Government of India made provision in its budget for village improvement work. In 1935–36 it sanctioned a grant of one crore rupees for village improvement to the Bombay Presidency.[8] Now the time was approaching for undertaking rural reconstruction work on a national scale.

Mr F.L. Brayne, an ICS of Punjab cadre, was one of the pioneers in movement for rural uplift and left an indelible mark on the history of pre-independence India. He had not been content merely to state principles or call attention to the importance of the subject but had realized that the uplift of the peasant could be brought about only by his own efforts both individually and in cooperation with others. He exercised all his influence, power and resources of a District Officer in inducing villagers to effect improvement in their surroundings. Whatever the practical result of his work might have been, he had certainly brought home to them one lesson: that the peasant who formed the backbone of India, had a way of living, a way of life and needs and requirements of his own, very different from those of urban people and that he ought to be made a subject of special study.[9] A number of publications, large and small, were issued by him on village uplift in dialogue form. They embody his ideas on rural reconstruction. He was very active in propagating his ideas between 1920 and 1950.

Some most interesting rural reconstruction work had been done on the old Skinner estate within fifty miles of Delhi. Mrs Ingram, Skinner's great grand-daughter had inherited the Gurgaon portion of the estate consisting of 18,000 acres of land spread over 30 villages, having a population of 16,000. Under the inspiration of Mr F.L. Brayne some 600 holdings varying from 5 to 50 acres were created and given over to the peasants for cultivation.[10] For some twenty years this estate had been farmed in the most modern way possible. The system of collection and disposal of manure was probably a model to the whole world. Subsequently, the estate was sold to the peasants on pre-War price. Brayne thought that to secure continuity two things were essential. Firstly, there should be a network of cooperative societies for all needs and purposes, adequately staffed and supervised. The other was to bring women in this business. He believed that unless women came in on this programme, men would be helpless. This required a change of outlook in the society. Involvement of women in rural reconstruction was essential. But Brayne found it very difficult to persuade the officials in India to believe that women's cooperation was essential for all progress in India. The Army in India was more progressive than civil authority in this respect. Every married line in India had a welfare centre for women. Men had their institutions and arrangements for learning farming and management of animals, but women had no place where they could learn, how to run a home and bring up children. According to Brayne the success of all post-War planning depended on their being able to do their share of the work of raising standard of living. He was convinced that so long as programmes of development continued to be for men only, they would fail. Unless the programmes were built round the home and the women, the standard of living would never be raised or the peasant be persuaded to forsake his old ways.[11]

Even during the Second World War the Indian village was still in the middle ages. It had none of the amenities of modern life. Worst of all, women, upon whom depended the standard of living, had been subjected to none of the modernizing influences which had so changed the soldier. The soldier returning after the War was likely to have a different outlook at home. Mr Brayne wanted to use the demobilized soldier as a spearhead of a great movement to raise the standard of living in the whole of India. He suggested that post-War development policy should be built round the land and the people who lived on it. Cottage and rural industries should be expanded and organized because the Indian village was still full of craftsmanship. A savings system both for soldiers and villagers should be organized and safeguarded from attachment in any law court. The cooperative system should be extended as far as possible in rural areas.[12] Brayne also proposed to hold the ex-soldiers together through cooperative and better living schemes. Women, he suggested, should be made to benefit from these activities as well as the modern outlook of their husbands. To raise standards of living a full campaign of publicity should be undertaken. Education should be made compulsory for all.

Girls' education should be brought at par with the boys' and the whole machinery of Government must be harnessed for the welfare of the common people. Farming, industry, health and women's welfare figured prominently in his programme of village uplift. The main objective of all programmes of development was to be to assure the soldiers and villagers of better homes, better living and better livelihood. Utilizing millions of ex-soldiers for rural reconstruction work should be welcomed in the interest of all, as nothing would be more wasteful or extravagant than to allow their knowledge and disciplined energy to be wasted or directed towards wrong ends.

Mr F.L. Brayne made a strong plea for a new order in the countryside in any national programme for rural reconstruction because prosperous agriculture would provide the foundation of a far larger market for industrial outputs. Moreover, he felt that land should be considered as a trust liable to be bought on neglect at a far price by the state, reconditioned and leased to good and active farmers.[13] Hence the Government must look upon the improvement of countryside as being the first priority in the post-War planning. Brayne's idea of village guide was a useful one provided such a person could be obtained and properly used. Mr M.L. Darling also concluded that after education the village needed a strong leader to keep the village together and to save it from disintegration with which it was being threatened by modern forces.[14] To hold his own in the modern world the peasant needed something more than education. In the past the village community had been his bulwark but this had now disintegrated. Some other institution was needed to take its place. This could be done by the Panchayat and the cooperative movement. But the crux of the rural problem was to find out the right type of leaders because *without them* little could be done, and *with them* everything was possible.[15] Moreover, Mr Brayne was convinced that mere increase of wealth would not make people good, clean, happy or peaceful. Man must have ideals and spiritual inspiration. According to him, fair conditions were essential for rural reconstruction – village organization, education, leadership and a spirit of service.[16] Women must also be enlisted in the campaign for better food and better living. As the strongest instinct of women is the well-being of the family, this must be developed and exploited. Being the prime mover in raising the standard of living, she should have far more knowledge and training than she had then. Not only must she have a suitable education but should also have proper training for domestic duties. She should be given training for running a house and keeping it clean, cooking a balanced diet and keeping family in good health.[17] Further Mr Brayne felt that development policy must be built round the land and the people who lived on it. Cottage and rural industries must be expanded and organized.

With the beginning of provincial autonomy in India on 1 April 1937 there began a new chapter in the history of rural reconstruction in the country. Provinces had now become more or less independent units in some matters and could afford to have some chance to work out their own economic salvation. This was really a distinct advance in the political life of the country. Several provinces constituted Rural Development Board as a popular measure but nothing substantial could be achieved due to the outbreak of the Second World War soon thereafter. During the War the post-War reconstruction planning was undertaken by the Central as well as provincial governments that included rural reconstruction schemes too. In 1945 the Central Land Utilization Board was set up with Sir N. Gopalaswami Ayyangar as chairman to plan and coordinate schemes in respect of soil erosion, forestry, land reclamation, irrigation works and other forms of land improvement.[18] These were to envisage a change in rural society. Rural Development Board in some provinces had already been reconstituted as a part of the post-War development planning. The Bombay Presidency Rural Development Board was reconstituted in 1945 with Sir Henry Knight as chairman and Dr D.R. Gadgil as a member. It prepared a comprehensive scheme divided into three five-year periods touching rural life at every facet. The first phase of the plan was to cost Rs 50 crores in five years. All-round development of selected areas was undertaken. Nine districts of the Bombay Presidency liable to famine and drought were selected for all-round development. These areas roughly corresponded with the best recruiting areas for the army. The Governor had given assurance during the War the such areas would be given priority in development.[19] This was likely to facilitate the re-settlement of soldiers and their rapid and orderly absorption into civil life. Rural development centre was established in each district. It was to provide demonstration in improved method of cultivation of crops and training in cottage industries. Demobilized soldiers were to be trained at the centre of development not only to take care of their own lands but as agents of reconstruction in villages. The scheme included instruction of soldiers' wives and families in sanitation, domestic economy and nutrition. Emphasis was on development and improvement of agricultural, forest and waste lands in areas liable to famine and scarcity. Dry farming research centres were established at Sholapur and Bijapur. At Bijapur a centre had already been set up to train 200 students annually in land development, construction of contour bunds and trenches. At Sholapur a scientific dry farming centre was set up to train 100 students each year. Moreover, a comprehensive scheme of building and improving roads based on 'Nagpur Plan' was undertaken. When completed in fifteen years the scheme was to provide 2700 miles of national highways, 5600 miles of provincial highways, 6000 miles of major district roads, 10,000 miles of minor district roads and 14,400 miles of village roads.[20] The contour-bunding experiments in the Bombay Presidency had resulted in an increased yield of crops by 20 to 30 per cent. There was an increase in fodder crop also.

The first notable attempt at rural uplift was made by Sir Fredrick Sykes, the Governor of the Bombay Presidency in 1933 when he inaugurated the village improvement scheme. In 1935–36 the Central Government made a grant of one crore rupees for village uplift to the Bombay Presidency.[21] It marked a significant change in the attitude of the Central Government towards the problem of rural India. At that time the idea of social service in villages was gaining ground among the intellectuals. The Karnatak Sahitya Parishad of Bangalore drew up a scheme for training graduates for social service in villages. They were to visit villages to instruct the people in sanitation, personal and domestic hygiene, civil responsibility, elements of science and economics, social problems, etc. At this very time in 1935 Sir Dorabji Tata School of Social Work was started in Bombay with a two year course for graduates.[22] Gandhiji too was contemplating in terms of devoted village workers as catalytic agents for creative rural change. He believed that revolutionary changes could be brought about in rural areas, if one such devoted worker could be available for each village in India.[23] Thus, the rural development needed the services of selfless workers to guide the destiny of rural population.

During the War the ICAR launched a scheme of village reconstruction in Baroda state where a number of villages had passed into the hands of moneylenders. The Baroda Government was to buy out the five villages from moneylenders who had displaced the ryots from their land. Each of the five villages was to be farmed out in a different system of land tenure. Each was to consist of 1000 acres of land. In the first village each cultivator was to be given a consolidated holding which could not be subdivided subsequently. He was to farm the land according to the programme outlined by the central authority. He was to pay land revenue at four or five times the normal rate, the excess being credited towards the ultimate purchase of his holding after seven or eight years. In the second village similar consolidated holding was to be given to a cultivator but he was to remain a tenant of the state with security of tenure but double the ordinary revenue for cost of improvement. In the third category there were no consolidated holdings. The fourth category was to be for collective farming and the fifth for state farming. The ICAR proposed to examine the results of various systems and to carry out experiments in collective farming, cooperative farming, state farming or by the capitalist enterprise in different places and to see which of them resulted in increased production. That, ultimately, was to be the test of any system.[24]

During the War the urgency of land reforms was strongly felt by academics, administrators and politicians all alike for speeding up food production in the country. Gandhiji declared that the land belonged to those who worked on it and to no one else.[25] The Bengal famine clinched the issue. Ultimately in 1945 the Congress accepted the policy of abolition of all intermediaries between the peasant and the state. What was needed was nothing short of an agrarian revolution if Indian agriculture was to become a sound and profitable industry. The Congress ministries in Bombay Presidency and Bihar were the first to undertake legislation for abolition of landlordism in 1946. This was really a period of social ferment in India.

Even during the War rural reconstruction occupied a prominent place in the thinking of academics, administrators and social reformers in India. All were interested in improving the condition of rural population. Lord Linlithgow thought that technical training and knowledge of ex-soldiers ought to be harnessed for rural reconstruction because majority of them would return to their land in villages after the War. This would provide a good opportunity to push forward agricultural improvement and rural welfare schemes in the country. Of all the factors making for prosperous agriculture, by far the most important was the outlook of the peasant himself. A kind of total war had to be waged against ignorance and apathy of Indian peasant. The War had already focused attention on the absolute necessity for a strong national agriculture as a basis for every other action.[26] The ICAR had already proved itself an effective instrument for promoting scientific knowledge regarding agriculture. It showed how science could be introduced into peasant agriculture. Scientific knowledge regarding agriculture gathered in academic journals since 1929 needed its application into the field. There was a dire necessity of extension services in rural India. Mr N.M. Khan had started new schemes for agricultural development in Bengal. Mr H.S.M. Ishaque too tried to re-train the disbanded jute regulation staff into agricultural extension workers. Lord Wavell too felt the necessity of extension workers for rural population and called upon young men of agricultural background to volunteer for the service.[27] The ICAR had much expanded a great deal particularly in the area of genetic improvement, hybridization and multiplication on farmers' field. The agricultural scientists tried various breeds of rust resistant wheat, hybrid maize and Tanjore rice in research stations and demonstration farms which proved successful during the War. This was the real beginning of the Green Revolution.[28] As a matter of fact Indian scientists had to telescope two centuries of agricultural research into two decades. A process of change and development that had gone on at least from the time of partition in Punjab had its roots much further back in time. The so-called 'Green Revolution' did not come about all of a sudden. It was the culmination of efforts of scientists and administrators for over four decades. 'The Borlaug seeds fell on fertile ground in Punjab and achieved the greatest success. It was due to the building up of an infrastructure which prepared the way for their coming.'[29] Sir M.L. Darling felt that science was now ready to put all the means for improving condition in rural India. He thought that the needs of India were so enormous that they could not afford to wait for political settlement.[30] Pt Nehru laid emphasis on irrigation, agricultural extension and research and land reforms as essential requirements for rural regeneration. He differed from the more orthodox school of thought in his emphasis on science as the catalyst to increase agricultural output and to improve rural life.[31]

Albert Meyer, an American architect and planner proved an imaginative pioneer and a man of new and exciting experiments. He organized the Naini Agricultural Research and Extension Institute near Allahabad. The Etawah Pilot Project was launched by him in September 1948. This was a model rural reconstruction project to be imitated by others. This gave a new thrust to the rural reconstruction programme in India. Principal Sam Higgonbottom and his associates of the Naini Agricultural Institute pioneered research in farm implements, a degree course in agricultural engineering, an early scheme of extension research and an extension project. Under the auspices of the Institute, textbooks on dairying, agriculture and extension were published.[32] The Institute had trained a group of young Indians who eventually provided leadership in agriculture. Wherever they went, they tried to turn wasteland into good yielding land so that there might be enough food. Principal Sam Higgonbottom asked his students to learn all they could about the village, the social structure, the method of agriculture, the size of holdings and attitude of villages towards changes. He was the greatest exponent of scientific agriculture and its study in colleges and universities for improving conditions of farmers and thereby bring about agricultural development in the country.[33]

Gandhiji came on the scene of rural reconstruction in India in the thirties of the present century. He looked upon the rehabilitation of villages as perhaps the greatest of his ambitions. Through the columns of *Young India* he initiated a discussion on causes and remedies of poverty in India. He was fully convinced that poverty of India would never be removed so long as foreign exploitation continued unabated. Even the spinning wheel would bring only partial relief if the terrible drain of India's wealth was not stopped. He thought that spinning wheel and the use of *khaddar* were perhaps the only important remedies available for removal of poverty in India. But keeping in view the great forces of international trade and modern method of manufacture the efficacy of spinning wheel as remedy for removal of general poverty was considered doubtful by economists. In the complex problems affecting Indian agriculture, industry and trade, the spinning wheel had only a secondary place, although Gandhiji claimed for it 'not a point in circumstance but the centre from which could radiate innumerable other things'.[34] As such, Gandhiji's programme of rural reconstruction involved revival of handicrafts, panchayats and removal of untouchability. He wanted panchayats to arrive at decisions on the basis of consensus because ordinary democratic process results in suppression of minority views and interests.[35] Under the guidance of J.C. Kumarappa Gandhiji got All India Spinners' Association and All India Village Industries Association founded at Wardha. It was one of the many steps taken for rural reconstruction in India. But the problem was a formidable one.

The introduction of Provincial Autonomy in India in 1937 was a turning point of the deepest significance in India. It accelerated the pace of social change in British India. It aroused aspirations of Indians to a great height. They looked forward to the programme of national reconstruction with great optimism. In October 1938 Shri Subhas Chandra Bose, the Congress President appointed the National Planning Committee under the Chairmanship of Pt Jawaharlal Nehru. He believed that the pace of development in India had to be forced much like that of USSR and for this planning had to be accepted as an instrument of social change. Pt Nehru too shared this view fully. He particularly emphasized the development of scientific outlook in the country and wanted to build India on a scientific foundation.[36] But the work of the National Planning Committee was interrupted during the War. But its notable contribution was that it conceptualized the whole idea of planning and threw up certain hints which brought into reality the ideals of social and economic justice.[37] The NPC evinced keen interest in science education and research. Pt Nehru particularly emphasized the importance of science as the catalyst to increase agricultural output and to improve rural life. He asked the scientists to find solutions to the main problems of Indian villages and country's poverty.

The *Science and Culture* group headed by M.N. Saha was a great champion of science and technical education during that period. During the War the Government of India adopted planning as an instrument for post-War reconstruction and a high-powered committee of the Viceroy's Council had been constituted to deal with the problems. The Bengal Famine of 1943 forced the Government to have a new outlook on problems of administration in India. Besides, the maintenance of law and order, the duties of modern Government now included within their compass social and economic development in all its aspects. Nation-building activities of the Government now received greater attention than in the past. The whole outlook of the Government underwent a radical change. A Department of Planning and Development was constituted at the Centre and development officers were appointed in the provinces. Thus, a process of social change through planning was initiated. In January 1944 a group of capitalists published the Bombay Plan for the development of the country. It made the entire nation planning-conscious. Even Sir Jeremy Raisman, Finance Member, in his budget speech for 1945–46 observed: "A scheme of national development of the kind contemplated by a number of public leaders and writers, and by the Government, has to be planned for, worked for and paid for".[38] Thus, planning as an instrument of social change was finally accepted in India during the War.

NOTES

1. Hashin Ameer Ali, *The Environs of Tagore*, Indian Statistical Institute, Calcutta, 1960.
2. *Indian Economic Journal*, 1927–28, pp. 412–13.
3. *Asiatic Review*, January 1945, p. 39.
4. *Abridged Report of the Royal Commission on Agriculture*, p. 544.
5. Ibid., p. 499.
6. *Asiatic Review*, January 1945, p. 37.
7. *Indian Farming*, February 1950, p. 88.
8. *Indian Social Reformer*, 9 May 1936.
9. *Asiatic Review*, April 1945, p. 119.
10. *Indian Farming*, January 1943, p. 7.
11. *Asiatic Review*, April 1948, p. 164.
12. Ibid., April 1945, p. 116.
13. *Indian Farming*, April 1945, p. 193.
14. *Asiatic Review*, April 1948, p. 157.
15. Ibid., Vol. 38, 1942, p. 50.
16. *Commerce*, 20 October 1945, p. 328.
17. *Indian Farming*, June 1949, p. 252.
18. *Indian Information*, 15 March 1945, p. 379.
19. *Indian Social Reformer*, 23 September 1944.
20. *Planning for the Future of Bombay's Countryside*, 1945.
21. *Indian Social Reformer*, May 1936.
22. Ibid., 14 December 1935.
23. *IASSI Quarterly*, Vol. 10, July-September 1991, p. 215.
24. *Indian Information*, 1 February 1945, p. 114.
25. Bipan Chandra, *The Epic Struggle*, Orient Longman, 1992, p. 36.
26. *Indian Farming*, October 1942, p. 559.
27. *Commerce*, 1 July 1944, pp. 2–3.
28. T.N. Kaul, *Remembrances*, New Delhi, 1982, p. 116.
29. J.G. Hawkes (ed.), *Conservation and Agriculture*, 1978, p. 195.
30. *Asiatic Review*, January 1945, p. 41.
31. Najma Heptuallah, *India's Progress in Science and Technology*, Oxford, New Delhi, 1986, p. 28.
32. R. Hess Gary, *Sam Higgonbottom of Allahabad*, Virginia, 1987, p. 134.
33. B.M. Pugh, *The Story of A Tribal*, Orient Longman, 1976.
34. C.N. Vakil, *Poverty and Planning*, Allied, 1963, p. 41.
35. M.N. Srinivas, *The Dominant Caste and Other Essays*, Oxford, 1987, p. 21.
36. Najma Heptullah, op.cit., p. 20.
37. Ibid.
38. *Proceedings CLA Debate*, 28 March 1945, p. 874.

CHAPTER 11

Conclusion

The Second World War was an epoch-making event. It brought about scientific and technological revolutions hitherto unheard of. The horizon of science had been widened, and thereby vast possibilities for service to humanity had been opened. The War pushed up the process of industrialization all over the world. It may be said to have caused the second industrial and scientific revolution in the world. Science was accorded a leading position in the development of technology and national economy. As India was the base for supply of men and materials for the eastern theatre of the War and also the base of operation against Japan, it was exposed to social and economic changes of far-reaching importance.

Before 1939 India was industrially very backward in comparison with the countries of the West. Although the Colonial Government had realized even during the First World War that India had potentialities for industrial development and that a stronger industrial India might prove to be a great military asset to the empire, it had not done anything substantial in this area. Before 1921 it was wholly guided by the nineteenth century idea of preserving law and order, leaving the people alone to shape their economic destinies. The talk of industrial development at that time was ridiculed or treated with utmost apathy. India was considered essentially an agricultural country, although even agriculture was not well attended to. However during 1921–37 the old bureaucratic outlook was slowly changing. *Laissez faire* was already dead in England and state intervention in economic matters had come to stay. It was no longer possible for the British authorities to deny the extension of state intervention in the economic life of India. Ultimately, the Colonial Government decided to take positive steps for prosperity of the people in addition to maintenance of security. First, it adopted the policy of discriminating protection in 1924 in favour of those Indian industries which needed it. This afforded some relief to some Indian industries but was not enough to stimulate them. Enlightened Indian public opinion continued to discuss the Indian economic situation critically. In 1928 Gandhiji discussed the problem of poverty in India in his paper *Young India*. This drew the attention of the academics as well as the bureaucracy. But the old bureaucratic outlook was so rigid that it took a process of long education to change it. The great economic depression of 1929–32 stirred the mind of the bureaucracy too. In April 1934 measures for improvement of economic condition of the rural population were considered at a conference of officials and ministers of Central and Provincial Governments, and an intensive programme for developing marketing facilities for agricultural products was formulated.[1] To improve the position of farmers legislative measures were also undertaken by some Provincial Governments. The crop planning conference suggested ways and means for coordination of agricultural production for the country as a whole. Suggestions were made to Provincial Governments for keeping up cultivation of different crops at a remunerative level.[2] Even the Central Government took measures for the economic survey of the country. The Government was moving haltingly, and it was not in a mood to do more than the bare minimum compelled by necessity or circumstances.

A real breakthrough in the political and economic area came with the introduction of provincial autonomy in 1937. The provinces were now supposed to be independent units in charge of certain defined functions. However, the resources left at their disposal were too meagre for any bold scheme of reforms. It was not possible for them to satisfy the growing demand in the country for economic improvements. By 1930s the idea of planning as a tool for economic development was catching the imagination of the academics as well as administrators. Sir M.V. Visvesaraya was the first man to focus attention on planning as an instrument of social change. His slogan was "industrialize or perish". To him, science was a rising force and it was creating a new world. To ignore it was to court disaster. Subhas Chandra Bose and Jawaharlal Nehru both believed that India must use science and technology for national reconstruction and must march determinedly towards industrialization. Two centuries of scientific development in the West must be squeezed into two decades in India. Gandhiji was sceptical about the industrialisation of the country. But Nehru and Bose wanted to build India on a scientific foundation and wanted to quicken the pace of industrialisation in the country. The National Planning Committee under Nehru's chairmanship started its work very seriously in 1939 but its work was interrupted during the War. Nevertheless its greatest contribution was that it conceptualized the whole idea of planning and charted roughly the future course of development of the country.[3] Nehru realized that during the last 150 years the greatest revolutionary force in society had been science which had changed political, social and economic organizations. The people should be made to understand it and must adapt themselves to it.

The War led to some changes in the bureaucratic government at the centre in both composition and outlook. Under instructions from the Whitehall Lord Linlithgow constituted the Reconstruction Committee of his Council which was entrusted with the task of planning for post-War reconstruction in India. At first its functioning was very sluggish but Lord Wavell speeded up the work. Meanwhile, the Bengal famine opened the eyes of the administrators. They were made to realize that besides maintenance of law and order, the duties of modern Government encompassed the function of social and economic development in all its aspects. The nation-building activities of the state had to receive greater attention than in the past. The whole outlook of the Government had undergone radical change during the War. The War was really a great eye-opener. It had a tremendous democratizing effect all over the world. Planning for national reconstruction was recognized in India too as an instrument of social change. In 1944 India had become very much plan-conscious. A number of plans were floated. After independence the Nehru Government too accepted the policy of planning as an instrument of social change and on 28 February 1950 the Planning Commission was formally constituted in India.

War brought mobility in all aspects of national life in India. It really put the country firmly on road to industrialization. During the War India was the most important supply base of men and materials for the Allies east of the Suez and also a fighting base against Japan. The strength of the Indian army increased tenfold. They had to be fed, clothed, trained and sent to the fronts. This necessitated huge supplies of consumer goods for the Indian army. It was a golden opportunity for industrialists and businessmen of India. Many light industries grew up overnight. Many traders became industrialists. They supplied goods to the supply department on contract. Such demands on Indian industry were to the tune of something like Rs 20 crore per month.[4] The expenditure on defence and supply amounted to Rs 1.5 crore per day.[5] There was an unprecedented expansion of engineering industries. India was manufacturing nearly 400 new articles, while the range and output of her existing industries had considerably expanded. Every effort was being made to replace imports wherever possible by indigenous production in order to achieve the highest measure of self-sufficiency in the matter of defence and civilian requirements. During the War India was manufacturing a very large proportion of her defence requirements ranging from ships to shirts, from buttons to bridges, from goggles to guns not only for her itself but for all the other countries of the Eastern group. Over 200 new items of engineering stores were being manufactured ranging from small tools and machine parts to sea-going vessels, heavy calibre guns etc.[6]

Exigencies of the war helped the growth of entrepreneurship in India. "Improvisation provided adventures" in the field of industry as lively as in any storybook. In every factory the scrap-room had become as important as the stockpile and salvage experts used ingenuity and skill to reclaim from the apparent waste the means of further production.[7] During the War import of plant machinery was not possible. Hence the progress of factory industry was held up and other types of manufactures developed. These often involved small commodity producers. Consequently, all the new industries depended in one way or another on the higher factory form of production. They either obtained half-finished products from factories for their own form of production or made parts for big plant equipment and repaired factory made articles. During the War the number of joint stock companies registered in India increased from 11,114 in 1939 to 17,343 in 1946.[8] The number of such companies doubled by the end of 1947 and their paid-up capital increased by 70 per cent.[9]

The War proved a veritable gold mine for the textile industry. The mill-owners of Bombay alone made Rs 920 million in profits on an initial capital of Rs 135 million. The average annual profits were 11 times the pre-War figure.[10] A number of small and middle sized capitalist establishments with powerlooms grew up to meet the demands of the War. By 1949 there were 1830 such establishments. Out of this 1325 were located in Bombay and 332 in Surat. It was a new stage in the development of capitalist enterprise in this small-scale industry. This greatly affected the small handloom weavers scattered among villages. Some had to be closed down because they were not sure of steady supply of yarn from textile mills.

This War led to emergence of Indian capitalism as a powerful influence in the country's affairs. By 1943 Indian capital controlled two-thirds of all the big factories in India. At least 75 per cent of the stock in the British controlled jute industry was concentrated in hands of the Indian shareholders. During the War British companies started dismantling their outfits in India. It was a golden opportunity for Indian capitalists to fill the vacuum. They had already entrenched their position in the Indian capital market by war profits, speculation in shares and other commercial activities. The newly rich millionaires adopted the system of managing agencies and continued to speculate in shares, precious metals, cotton and foodgrains. They built up their strength not only by increasing production in one enterprise or by enlarging factories or purchasing or building new ones but by projecting their operations in other spheres of economy. New capital issues were licensed. This restricted the formation of new companies. There was even a virtual ban on expansion of the existing ones. House-building and import of precious metals practically had come to a standstill. The way was thus opened for canalization of all savings into bank deposits or public loans. Black markets had already created a new rival to bank deposits and public loans. Hence it was in banking that Indian capitalistic development during the War was particularly fast. From 1939 to 1943 Indian joint stock banks' capital doubled, while the deposits rose 3.5 times. In 1943 the six Indian banks owned 1/3 of all paid up capital of joint stock banks. Indian bankers made huge profits. The growth of the major joint stock banks reflected the gains made by the upper crest of India's propertied classes during the War. It was a reflection of the hiked prices, profiteering, the moneylender's profit and landlord's accumulated wealth. The leading Indian joint stock banks swept ahead of all the other enterprises, their assets growing most rapidly. Insurance business too attracted the Indian capitalists. Their capital increased from Rs 206.8 million in 1941 to Rs 717.6 million in 1945.[11]

During the War Indian capital made a great headway. The foreign capital controlled about 28 per cent of Indian domestic market leaving the rest for indigenous enterprises. The Indian capital acquired a dominant place both in industry and in banking by the end of the War. It increased its hold on Indian economy through three processes: firstly, by entering new areas and accounting for new investments in sugar, cement, paper and heavy chemicals; secondly, by edging out Europeans' influence and dominance in banking, life insurance, jute textile, coal, tea and foreign trade; thirdly, through a faster growth in terms of investment and output where Indian capital dominated.[12] Between 1939 and 1942, 38 new banking companies were registered. Most of them began business with inadequate capital and adopted some highly undesirable methods. As there was a glut in the money market seeking avenues for profitable employment, there was a large increase in the deposits with the banks. This resulted in a growing temptation to float new banking companies as one of the solutions to the problem of investing surplus funds profitably. But the Indian capitalist class had thrown caution to the winds and followed a 'get rich quick' policy. Their greediness crossed normal limits. They had no national outlook. Their only interest was profits by any means. Even Gandhiji criticized the Indian capitalist class for speaking and writing against the Government on the one hand and collaborating with them and even profiteering through them on the other. He felt that the urban middle class had let the country down during the War.[13] D.D. Kosambi even pointed out that during the War the really amazing increase was not in production but in profits, particularly speculative gains through profiteering in food, share market operations and the black market in general. The Indian bourgeoisie was a special kind, characterized by 'ravenous greed' and a mania for speculation rather than initiative or efficiency in developing productions.[14]

There was a virtual metamorphosis of the business communities in India during the War and thereafter. Traders became entrepreneurs and industrialists became monopolists. Industrial wealth was being concentrated in the hands of a few. Capitalist production, big banking and trade produced monopolists. The trend for them was to invest more and more in industry, banks, trade, insurance, etc. The Bombay Chamber of Commerce had changed from a gentlemen's club of distinguished and able merchants to a modern professional organization as much concerned with industry as trade. Another significant change was that they were no longer the owners of capital but were usually professional managers with all the difference of outlook. By the end of the War the Birlas gained control over a hundred joint stock companies besides having twenty-two big factories with an investment of Rs 20 crores.[15] Modern form of capitalist enterprise in the field of credit, trade, etc. gained momentum with the big bourgeiosie making money faster than other classes. Their ranks were growing and more and more Indian monopolists were being created.

Gone were the days of non-professional managers of industries. New technology required new type of men to manage industrial units. Labour relations had become very complicated and needed careful handling. Industry and business in India had passed lately into the hands of the people many of whom had neither the background of pioneering industrialists of old nor that of stalwart businessmen of the last few generations. In the changing situation of the post-War it was doubtful whether those veterans would have found it easy to handle the industry. Technique and means of production had been fast changing and the handling of labour problem was becoming more and more exacting. Consequently, those who were to be in charge of management of industrial units now required altogether different equipment. A need was now felt for proper training of personnel management as well as for business research to improve the efficiency of business executives. It was necessary to have proper coordination between technology and administration and also between production and research. In the US and UK institutes had already been created for business administration. In India too the Government recognized the necessity of such institutes and financed the establishment of such institutes at Ahmedabad, Calcutta, Bangalore and Lucknow. Thus, the age of professional managers dawned in India. Industrialists now began to understand the importance of scientific as well as industrial research as distinct from business research. Industry and business both now needed trained personnel to handle the work efficiently. There was a sea change in the attitude of the Central Government towards the growth of industry in India. A new industrial policy was adopted in April 1945. A plan for rapid industrialization with state assistance and under state control was prepared. Central control of twenty key industries was generally accepted by the provinces. The Government also approved the policy that as far as possible financial and administrative control over basic industries should be in Indian hands.

War opened up great opportunities for industrial development and for progress in all directions. It proved the greatest catalyst for all round progress in the country. Before the War the colonial Government had no science policy worth the name for development of the country. But as the War progressed it was realized that the conduct of War required planned industrial research on many problems of the chemical, metallurgical and engineering industries so as to harness India's vast resources for the purpose. This realization was given effect to by creation of the Board of Scientific and Industrial Research and also the Council of Scientific and Industrial Research which put the fundamental and applied scientific research on a realistic basis and thus helped in building of New India. With the arrival of Prof. A.V. Hill as scientific adviser to the Government of India in 1943 the whole outlook towards science changed overnight. He recommended the setting up of Research Board on Surveys and National Resources and also the setting up and maintaining of a certain number of scientific institutions of a very high standard. He indicated four distinct lines of scientific development for India, namely, education, research, development of experimental trial and production for large-scale application. These four processes concerned almost every aspect of national development. At that time the greatest need of India was the training of men both for industry and agriculture. This required technical institutes of a very high order. This was the direct result of the War. Agriculture required the resources of engineering and technology in addition to special agriculture research. Similarly, the scientific as well as industrial research needed proper attention of the Government. Both Great Britain and USA were miles ahead of India in this respect. A.V. Hill impressed upon the Government that modern scientific knowledge and research with modern industrial methods must be adopted to bring India at part with the other industrialized countries of the world. Hence a progressive industry in India needed far more science and technology as its basis both in respect of tools, machinery and equipment and also in the education and training of those who would direct and operate it. Prof. Hill was optimistic that India could produce excellent scientists, technologists, engineers and workmen if given education, training, experience and opportunity. He helped the Government in formulating a positive science policy in India. In accordance with his recommendations a close scientific and technical liaison between India, Britain, USA and the Dominions was established. He brought Indian scientists into contact with the work done in other parts of the world. As scientific and industrial researches were scattered over various departments, a mechanism for coordinating them was found in the creation of a scientific consultative committee at a high level. The colonial bias against Indians in science and technology had to be watered down. Some Indian scientists were made fellows of the Royal Society during the War.

The War led to a number of salutary changes in India. It caused a large expansion of industry and thereby created a great demand for technicians of all grades. The Central Labour Department opened up as many as 300 centres for technical training and by 1945 as many as 80,000 technicians were trained and most of them were absorbed in the army.[16] Under the Bevin-boys' scheme some 800 technicians were trained in UK. On return many of them were employed in important war jobs and also in supervisory work in civil industries. As they became acquainted with the working of trade unionism in UK, they formed a nucleus of genuine trade union leadership in India. Moreover, the War changed the attitude towards technical education in India which now came to be recognized as a branch of education. It was now no longer a special training for industrial employment but an integral part of the educational system. The War propelled the unprecedented demand for technical education in India which became a wider and more liberal form of training than it had been in the past. It now included the study of design and distribution as well as the actual processes of manufacture. It covered the scientific principles underlying the processes of manufacture as well as the processes themselves. It also linked up the science of production and business organization with the art of design and salesmanship. It also formed a link between education and industry and at the same time received a separate consideration as a form of mental training. Moreover, the technical education included commercial education as well as art-in-industry and agricultural education. This indicated a change of outlook from colonial to national and marked a new era in the history of technical education in India.

To meet the impending requirement of technical personnel in the country a comprehensive system of technical education at all stages was called for. The formation of the Association of Principals of Technical Institutions (India) had been welcomed as an important step in the direction of coordinating technical institutions on an all-India basis. Subsequently, a committee on higher technical education under the chairmanship of Shri N.R. Sarkar was appointed to advise on the matter. It recommended the setting up of four Indian Institutes of Technology on the pattern of MIT of USA to meet the impending need of the country for technical personnel. It also recommended creation of All India Council for Technical Education to coordinate and guide the technical education in the country. Thus, during the War there was definite shift in the policy of the Government. For the first time it initiated a policy with a long-term objective which was to usher in an era of great social change. An earnest effort was made to organize and standardize technical education on an all India basis and a beginning was made to promote it as a means of progress in the country. A comprehensive and planned system of agricultural education from school to university was also outlined. The establishment of Delhi Polytechnic in 1941 was a landmark in the history of technical education in India. It was to help the industrial India in a big way. It was the first of its kind and later on similar institutions were set up in other parts of the country. In order to remove the dearth of technical and research personnel the Government agreed to provide scholarships in India and abroad immediately. Accordingly, about 600 students with high science qualifications were selected in 1945–46 to undergo advance training in UK and USA in various subjects.[17] The Government readily accepted the recommendations of the N.R. Sarkar Committee on higher technical education and took steps to establish four institutes of technology on the pattern of MIT of USA to ensure adequate supply of high grade technical personnel for post-War industrial development of the country. The rush for technical education began. A scheme for training of engineers and technocrats in business as well as in industrial administration was also undertaken.

The mineral policy of the Government had to be changed to suit the needs of the country. A large cadre of mining and metallurgical technicians was needed to speed up industrialization in the country. To meet the situation the expansion of the Geological Survey of India was undertaken seriously. The Central Technical Power Board was also constituted to act as a central agency for preparation of multi-purpose hydro-electric and thermal power schemes. War had focused the attention of the Government on development of electrical power in India. Its potentialities for economic development had been well recognized. Even before the end of the War a number of irrigational and hydro-electric schemes were prepared.

Before the Second World War agriculture was the Cinderella of the Indian economy. The Colonial Government in India did not pay adequate attention to its improvement. It contented itself with maintaining law and order and left the people alone to shape their economic destinies. It confined itself to the duty of preventing deaths from starvation and concerned itself with the supply of minimum quantities of foodgrains needed to sustain the population at a low level of nutrition. In normal times, protective works were undertaken to increase the resistance of the people against famines. In the nineteenth century the famine policy was developed to prevent the occurrence of famines. No attempt was made to increase the material prosperity of the people in the real sense of the term. But in the early years of the twentieth century a forward policy in the matter of agricultural research and improvement was formulated. In 1903 the Imperial Agricultural Research Institute was established at Pusa in Bihar and subsequently six agricultural colleges were established at Coimbatore, Poona, Nagpur, Sabour, Kanpur and Lyallpur. But the progress of research in agriculture was very tardy. Between 1921 and 1937 the outlook of the colonial administration was undergoing a change. It now began to realize that some positive steps had to be taken to improve the condition of the people. Consequently, the Royal Commission on Agriculture was constituted in 1926 to suggest ways and means to improve agriculture in India. Its recommendations proved a landmark in the social and economic history of India. In pursuance of its recommendations the Imperial Council of Agricultural Research was set up in 1929 in Delhi. It opened up a new era in the history of agricultural research in India and within less than twenty years its vitalising influence was felt in every branch of agriculture in India. It had become since then a model for application of science in agriculture. It could justly claim its credit for great success in connection with the production and utilization of new varieties of sugarcane. The old indigenous varieties had been largely supplanted by newer ones which doubled its production. During the Second World War the ICAR took up the challenge of the 'freedom from want' on war-footing and undertook agricultural research on problems of immediate economic importance to the cultivator both on cash and food-crops. Exigencies of the War and the Bengal famine brought home to the Government the necessity of paying greater attention to agricultural production and research than had been done before. Hence, the genetic improvement of major food-crops received special attention. The War focused attention on the absolute necessity of a national agricultural policy as a basis for every other action. A well considered policy in reference to food production was, therefore, an integral part of successful War efforts.

The UN Conference on Food and Agriculture at Hot Springs (Virginia, USA) focused on primary responsibility of each nation to see that its own people got the food needed for life and health. Never before had food and agriculture such recognition in the world. Never before had it been so widely established that better diets and improved agriculture were so fundamental to the well-being of all people. Governments represented at the Hot Springs Conference undertook to implement its resolutions to their best. As India was represented at the Conference, she was morally bound to implement its resolutions. But their implementation in India necessitated considerable planning in Indian agriculture both by nutrition and agricultural experts. It envisaged change in social outlook and habit. As the food of a considerable proportion of Indian population was lacking in protein, vitamins and minerals, these deficiencies could be met partly by consuming more vegetables, fruit and milk. They could be best met by consuming eggs, meat and fish in addition. This meant a change in the dietary habit of the people. It was a slow process but the War accelerated it. The soldiers returning home after the War with new ideas induced the people to adopt new dietary habits. Previously, nutrition experts did not come sufficiently into the picture because nutrition science was a new one. But during the War nutrition experts were in great demand. To meet the requirements of a wholesome diet, animal husbandry combined with agriculture was recommended as the best form of farming for a country like India. The need for increased production of vegetables, fruits, milk, eggs and fish was also emphasized for improving nutritive value of food in India. War forced the Government to look at these problems afresh and to adopt a new agricultural policy in India. There was a big gap between what appeared on the experimental farms and what happened on the cultivator's field. A great wealth of scientific knowledge was gathering dust in the research journals, but not enough was done to publicize this knowledge so as to lead to its application to agriculture. Educating the peasant was the dire need of the time. This implied rural reconstruction and called for a social change in the countryside. To meet the challenge of freedom from want the ICAR had expanded considerably during the War in the area of genetic improvement, hybridization and multiplication and distribution of improved seeds. As a matter of fact the agricultural scientists in India had to telescope researches of two centuries into two decades. The ICAR had been initiating and guiding research in most of the problems which confronted the agriculturists in India during the War. Research in agriculture and animal husbandry went hand in hand and were complementary to each other. Developing cattle not only helped to grow more cereals but also helped in producing more protective foods like milk, milk products and poultry.

As a matter of fact social and economic prosperity of India was intimately bound up with the health of Indian agriculture. The establishment of a rural dairy industry was a prime necessity for accelerating breeding of more economic livestock, for increasing crop production and for making a better 'land use'. Plant breeding needed special attention. Food chemists and nutrition experts were to be associated with plant breeders for producing grains of higher nutrition value. Adequate extension staff was needed to multiply the seed, to provide the cultivator with this seed and to make him grow this. A sound balance between food, fodder, fertility and cash crop was needed for permanent agricultural prosperity in the country. Ultimately, the Colonial Government in India had to change its old bureaucratic outlook and accepted its first and foremost duty to provide adequate quantity of good and nourishing food for all the people living in the country. Lord Wavell placed agriculture at the top in the post-War planning for development. The Famine Inquiry Commission defined the broad lines of an agricultural and food policy designed to prevent any future threat of famine and to improve the diet of the people. A new food production policy was needed to achieve self-sufficiency in cereals, the basic food of the country. To balance cereals it was regarded essential to increase the production of pulses, fish, vegetables, fruits, milk and eggs. Among the 'protected' group of foods, prominent place was given to production of fish and the Central Government was to undertake the responsibility of stimulating and coordinating the development of fishing industry. Transport, marketing facilities, method of preserving and processing of fish was to be investigated to increase its production. Moreover, nutrition research in all its branches was to receive sufficient attention and support as part of the programme of improvement of the health of the nation. Consequent upon the development of new outlook the people now began to think in a different way. They were now becoming conscious of the quality of food. They were now anxious to know what they should eat and why. The Government, therefore began to pay more and more attention to the science of nutrition. It was planning use of science in food industries to secure better food for India.[18]

During the War the demand for fresh vegetables of all kinds increased considerably for the army as well as for civil population. The War had dislocated the supply of seeds of European vegetables from UK, USA and other foreign countries. Hence arrangements were made to produce seeds of European varieties of vegetables from the "mother seed" available in the country. Climatically suitable areas like Kashmir and Baluchistan were selected for the purpose. Dr William Burns had already indicated the possibility of vegetable seed industry in India as a national asset after the War.[19] Moreover, arrangements were made to persuade rural areas to grow and consume more vegetables. As the War created a great demand for fruit and vegetables the problem of storage and transport had to be tackled. A scheme of research on fruit and vegetable preservation was carried out at Lyallpur in Punjab. The Central Institute of Fruit Technology was established there. Consequently, the Government had to recognize the importance of processed food in the economy of the country. The development made during the War in this respect had to be maintained and improved in the interest of preservation of foodstuffs, general nutrition and industrialization of the country. Canning of fruits had to be started on a large scale in NWF province for the army. The new industry of dehydration had also been greatly developed in India as a result of the War. Vegetable dehydration had travelled far along the path of progress from Canada to India. Peaches and other fruits were dehydrated. Jams and marmalades were prepared locally for army canteens and messes. To meet the most serious deficiencies of tropical diets the food-yeast manufacturing industry was started in India. It could be added to any liquid food like soup, milk or mixed with flour for bread. It could also be added to the diet of children, aged and those suffering from vitamin B deficiency.

One of the army's most important innovation for preservation of foodstuffs had been expansion of cold storage facilities in India. The army had built 2000 ton cold storage installations at Calcutta, Bombay and Madras and about 30 smaller units scattered all over India. Even before the War there had been cold storage facilities at the port towns, but they were generally not availed of except at Karachi. The people had not yet realized the advantages of cold storages for storing cheap and perishable commodities such as potatoes. But after the War a widespread use of cold storage facilities appeared to be the only way of regulating supplies and prices. The Government came forward to encourage construction of cold storages in rural areas to facilitate collection of milk. To meet the needs of the army, processing of food was started in India but in post-War period it formed an integral part of general production and planning. Food processing was put on the industrial map of India. Consequently, as soon as the War ended the Government undertook the planning and development of about 40 food industries. Thus, by the end of the War the Colonial

Government in India had to change its old outlook regarding its functions in relation to economic life of the people. War focused the attention of the Government on agricultural development which occupied a prominent place in post-War reconstruction of India. Hence in 1946 a comprehensive document embodying the agricultural and food policy in India was prepared. It embodied all that had happened in agriculture between 1926 and 1946 and also the outline of the course of action to be adopted for achieving the objectives in full.

During the War the inadequacy of social services was glaringly exposed. This made the Colonial Government change its outlook in the matter. Among the social services Lord Wavell gave priority to communications, public health and education in that order and the Government took some measures to improve them as far as possible even during the War. Many of the roads and even some railway lines had been constructed mainly with the purpose of bringing raw materials like cotton, linseed etc. to the ports for export to UK. But the railways had revolutionized agriculture by making possible growing of money crops which swelled the volume of exportable staple. On the other hand road communication in India was in a very bad shape due to long years of neglect. There was a glaring disparity between India and advanced countries of the world in this matter. In the USA, 75 per cent of all traffic was carried on roads and the position was the same in other advanced countries of the world. But in India roads did not carry even 10 per cent of the total traffic. This greatly affected the agrarian development of the country. Now it began to be felt that development of roads in India was essential for economic, social and cultural development of the rural areas. The road system of India was so inadequate that not even the metropolitan cities were connected completely with good modernized roads. But War brought into special prominence the necessity of an integrated road system in India. The Indian Road Congress took the initiative of planning for post-War road development by referring the matter to the special Conference of Chief Engineers of provinces and states held in December 1943 at Nagpur. This Conference produced the 'Nagpur Report' which marked the real beginning of road planning and development on all India basis. The War forced the Government to think of road development in India on scientific lines. The need for a national highway system was strongly felt. It became the dire necessity of the time. The village and district roads had been handed over to the local bodies in 1920 and since then they had deteriorated with increasing traffic of more money crops, more people and more travel arising from security and general awakening. In this competitive world every means of communication to market was as essential to the primary producer in the village as to the great manufacturer in the town. Hence, the need for improving the village and district roads was greatly felt during the War. Sir Kenneth Mitchell, the Controller of Road Transport, was strongly of the view that no village with a population of 1000 and more should be more than half a mile from a public road. It was realized during the War that the financing of post-War development and overtaking of years of neglect would be quite beyond the existing and potential resources of local bodies. Hence they should be relieved of this responsibility and the provincial governments should take them over. It was strongly felt that the province could only be a suitable area for road management and the district management was no longer necessary. War had revealed many weaknesses or missing links, particularly in the all-India highway. In order to rectify them it was thought essential to plan for a national highway system.

The Nagpur plan envisaged linking up of the remotest parts of India with a well planned road system. It was estimated that India would need 4,00,000 miles road, half of it all weather surfaced roads in order to bring all villages reasonably close to a planned road system. The estimated cost of executing such a plan would be Rs 450 crores. The system of national highway would serve as a framework within which to fit a network of provincial, district and village roads. In this scheme of national highways were to be included certain tracts of open communication through large undeveloped tracts which were not the particular concern of any province or state. To execute and coordinate such a plan the setting up of a Road Board was needed. This bold and imaginative road development plan envisaged two great new roads and improved highways radiating from Bombay. One was to run from Bombay to Khyber pass via Ahmedabad, Karachi and Peshawar and the second from Bombay to Cape Camorin hugging western coast. Moreover, there was to be one highway from Bombay to Madras and Vizagapatam. In addition there were plans for three new highways from Calcutta. A road into Assam was to link up the military road built in India and the Lushai hills and ultimately link with the Burma road to China. Another road was to connect Calcutta with Chittagong and join with the new military road to the Arakan and ultimately to Akyab. Delhi, being the capital of India, was to be one of the most important focal points with five national highways radiating from it. Thus, India was to have a mammoth network of highways stretching from north to south and east to west connecting India between Persia in the west and China in the east. This bold plan of national highways really marked the beginning of social changes of deep significance for the country.

Lord Wavell emphasized that the first step in all schemes for the social progress of India was improvements not only on the main roads but the minor district and village roads as well. It was expected that after the War motor vehicles would play a far greater part in transportation. There were likely to be many vehicles and many drivers available almost at once from the military organization after the end of the War. The development of motor transport in rural areas was likely to be of great advantage and benefit to the rural population as well as to the trade, industry and general prosperity of the country as a whole. To achieve this social change, development of roads and road transport was essential. It offered an opportunity to Indian agriculture and business to make greater use of mechanical transport to improve their prospects. Hence it was essential even during the War to plan for a system of national highways to serve as a framework within which to fit in a network of provincial, district and rural roads. This was to bring a great social change in the country. The development of health services, extension of educational facilities, opening of schools, improved postal system and extension of travelling cinema will follow. As a matter of fact the improvement in communications fell within the sphere of both economic development and social progress. Hence the National highway plan had given adequate attention to this aspect. The objective of the plan was that no village should be in future more than five miles from an all-weather road and more than 100 miles from a national highway. In fact at the end of the War India was on the threshold of a transport revolution. In the army there were about more than two lakh motor drivers-cum-mechanics in 1945 and a good number of them were later demobilized. On demobilization they gave a spurt to the transport industry in India. Many army vehicles were released for disposal and many drivers and mechanics were available almost at once after the War. India witnessed a big social change resulting from the unprecedented expansion of road transport after the War. The demand for city bus service as well as for mofussil areas increased considerably. Motor-transport became an important sector of the national economy.

It had been a scientific war and in some respects a radio war. Both sides used it for propaganda as well as for educating the people. In India radio transmission had just begun before the War but during the War its expansion became a dire necessity for the Government. In 1945 there were about 2.5 lakh listening sets in a population of 400 million. It was quite inadequate. Over 40,000 radio sets were imported from USA. The department of Information and Broadcasting was created during the War. The War had given enormous impetus to the development of internal services as well as external services covering the whole of Asia and beyond in 24 languages. The War proved a boon to the newspaper industry. People in general became news-hungry and eagerly awaited the arrival of newspapers both in urban and rural areas. Circulation of both English and vernacular papers increased considerably during the War and their income from advertisement soared high to make most of them self-sufficient. In 1937, there were 32 dailies and 22 weeklies in English in India but in 1947, their number increased to 51 dailies and 258 weeklies in English. The number of Indian language newspapers increased considerably and some covered even the rural area. The circulation and influence of the newspaper increased considerably throughout India as a result of the War. This brought about a great social and political consciousness in the country. Broadcasting had become very popular and a rival to the press.

During the War much progress had been registered in public health in Western countries but the condition in India was shameful. An average of two million women died annually from causes associated with pregnancy and child-bearing. 100 million people suffered from this disease annually. Thus, malaria, cholera and tuberculosis were causing havoc among the rural population of India and the Government had not taken adequate steps to eradicate them completely. It was during the War that the attention of the Government was drawn towards their eradication. The diet of the Indian population as a whole was seriously deficient both in quantity and quality. About 80 per cent of the food consumed by the people consisted of cereals. Of the other items of diet such as vegetable, fruit, milk, meat, fish and eggs – the quantities then produced were quite inadequate. The people viewed this state of affairs with apathy. Measures designed to change this outlook were essential if a definite improvement in public health was to be achieved. The development of civic consciousness was essential if an improvement of environmental hygiene was to be effected.

In the midst of the War the Health Survey and Development Committee with Sir Joseph Bhore as chairman was appointed. It was to make a broad survey of existing health conditions and health organizations in British India and to make recommendations for the future development of health services in the country. As the post-War development plan was in the offing, the Government thought it necessary to appoint such a committee in the health field. The ferment of ideas arising out of the War had resulted in an increasing awareness on the part of the governments and people of the need for measures which would ensure social security; health protection was being recognized as an essential part of social security. The idea that the state should assume full responsibility for all measures, curative and preventive necessary for safeguarding the health of the nation, was developing as a logical sequence. The Bhore Committee had been greatly influenced by this ferment of ideas arising out of the War. The modern trend was towards the provision by the state of as complete a health service as possible and inclusion within its scope of the largest possible proportion of the community. The need for ensuring this distribution of benefits to all irrespective of their ability to pay, had also received recognition. The Bhore Committee had taken the countryside as the focal point of their recommendations, because it was the tiller of the soil on which the economic structure of the country eventually rested. Hence, the essential aim of the committee was to ensure the health of the masses through effective working of health centres to be established in rural area. The emergence of 'social medicine' had widened the conception of disease by inclusion of social, economic and environmental factors which contributed a lot to the spread of sickness. As such, the 'social medicine' was beginning to develop its own methods of study of community health problem. This wider outlook brought into the sphere of 'social medicine' many workers besides the doctor. They included the public health nurse, the hospital social workers, the nutritionists, the public health engineers and the statisticians. The problem of nutrition came to the forefront and needed full attention. A food policy based on nutrition science became essential. The UN Conference on Food and Agriculture (May 1943) had accepted the principle that governments were responsible for introducing general and specific measures for improving the diet of the people. Nutritional advice should be requisitioned in connection with crop-planning, production of new varieties of seed and numerous other matters. Emphasis on nutrition became the hallmark of the new health policy. In the reorientation of medical studies, greater emphasis was laid on nutrition. A doctor should be a 'social physician' protecting the people and guiding them to a healthier and happier life. He should place prevention of disease in the forefront of his programme. Medical social workers were to be recruited in the field of medical service. They should be called upon to use their professional skill and knowledge in efforts to effect desirable changes in the relationship of the patient and his physical and human environment. They should be called upon to help in analysing the social and emotional aspect of the patient. Moreover, all big hospitals were required to employ a trained dietician with high qualifications. Special courses on dietics were to be arranged for selected nursing sisters. A training in nutrition was considered desirable for them. All children should be taught simple facts about food and diet as part of health education.

The Bhore Committee had drawn up a comprehensive health plan to provide a complete health service for the country. The plan had two parts: one a ten-year short term plan to meet the immediate health needs of the country, the other a long term plan covering a period of forty years designed to provide for the people a complete health service on modern lines. A programme of housing, improved water supply and better sanitation, measures to improve nutritional standards, elimination of unemployment and a living wage for all workers were recommended for ensuring good health to the people. Each district with a population of 3 million was to have 150 primary units for providing both curative and preventive medical attention. Each primary unit normally was to serve a population of 10,000 to 20,000. For every group of 30 primary units there was to be a secondary unit providing medical facilities of a high order. Lastly, three to five secondary units were to form a district health unit, where a hospital of the highest standard would be developed.

It was estimated that such a plan would cost a non-recurring expenditure of Rs 362 crores. The Ministry of Health at the Centre as well as in the provinces and health administration in local areas were to be constituted. It was suggested that social medicine like suitable housing, sanitary surroundings, safe drinking water, improvement of nutritional standards and health awareness should be undertaken. One hospital bed for a population of 1000 should be provided at the end of ten years. A Ministry of Housing as well as Town and Rural Planning should be constituted in each province. New industries should be dispersed in rural areas so that local people might benefit from them. The system of establishing factories in towns should be discouraged. Improvement trusts in all big cities of the country should be established to deal with slum clearance and re-housing problems. Every improvement trust should employ a town planning expert attached to the ministry of health.

It was further suggested that an India-wide housing programme should be undertaken giving priority to the needs of the lower income group of population. A water supply programme providing safe drinking water to the entire population within a period of 35 years was projected. Provision should be made for establishing sewage system in all towns with a population of 50,000 and over within ten years. The output of doctors of 4000 to 5000 a year should be the target in the first ten years. There should be one standard of training of medical graduates all over the country and the training of Licentiates was to be discontinued within ten years. The medical curriculum it was suggested should be reorganized and in every medical college there should be a department of preventive and social medicine. Ultimately the number of doctors had to be increased five times, nurses a hundred times, mid-wives 20 times and dentists about 90 times. The committee further recommended the establishment of All India Medical Institute at a central place to bring together in one place all educational facilities of the very highest order for training of important types of health personnel and to promote research of the highest order in all branches of medical science and also to inspire all persons undergoing training with the highest ideals of the profession. The Central Government was to be responsible for its establishment and maintenance. It was to have a medical college as well as a nursing college.

Any programme of social reconstruction could not afford to ignore the implications of population problem. This needed continuous study and measures had been taken to control the population growth effectively. The use of contraceptives for birth control was to be encouraged and the Government had to undertake the responsibility of supplying contraceptives free of cost. These recommendations implied social changes of great significance for the country. They gave a new direction to the public health measures and town planning in the country. They called for opening of a large number of medical colleges to meet the needs of the country. For the first time the state was to assume the responsibility of maintaining national health.

During the War medical science made a rapid headway. Prior to its outbreak blood transfusion service hardly existed in India. The Government led the way by establishing a unit for manufacture of blood serum at the All India Institute of Hygiene and Public Health, Calcutta. The provinces and states soon followed suit. Blood transfusion may well be regarded as one of the most noteworthy medical advances in the treatment of wounded soldiers that this War had produced. The Army blood transfusion service had been started with modern equipment. Modern medicine had become so complex that specialization had become essential. This had been fully recognized in the Army Medical Services in India. The total number of specialists in the AMS ran into four figures so that army patients in all regions were assured of expert attention of all kind. Facilities for physiotherapy and rehabilitation had been provided considerably. Facilities for occupational therapy proved of immense value to all patients. There grew up modern clinical pathology service started by specialists and skilled technicians. The military hospitals in India set a standard of excellence to be emulated by others. During the War the number of specialists in psychiatry increased ten times. The foundation of a modern psychiatry service was laid by the end of the War, it was not only intellectually but also popularly accepted. The military medical services had undergone a radical reorganization and development by the intensive application of modern science to medical problems.

During the War milk supply in urban areas posed a great problem. It was strongly felt that distribution of milk in a city or town should be entrusted to a properly constituted milk marketing organization and special legislation should be enacted for this work. At first the scheme was to be tried in metropolitan cities. Mr R.A. Pepperall was entrusted the task of making a rapid survey of the problems involved in the supply of milk to Indian cities, particularly of procurement, transport, processing, quality and price control. He described the prevailing efficiency of the dairy industry throughout India as 'probably the lowest in the whole world.' This was due to the total apathy of the general public in a matter which affected their health and pocket too. Hence, it was recommended that every province should have a milk authority with a paid director and at Centre there should be a coordinated milk policy as part of an all India food policy. Cattle from city stables should be dislodged and colonized in more natural environment. Berseem should be grown more extensively in irrigated areas. Village areas should be utilized for cultivating and feeding green fodder in preference to grazing and a total ban should be imposed on export of oil seeds and cakes from India. Manufacture of milk products should be confined to remote rural areas. Manufacture of butter in India should be discouraged; instead it should be imported from British Dominions. Modern dairies should be established in cities and dairy farms. To implement these suggestions schemes were drawn up in provinces and dairy development officers were appointed. The ICAR and IVRI as well as various provincial Governments took up measures to tackle the problem of milk supply seriously. The dislodging of cattle from city stables and colonizing them in more natural environment became the accepted policy of the Government. Big cities like Bombay, Calcutta and Madras tried to implement this policy immediately. Manufacture of milk products in rural areas became the accepted policy of the Governments. A twenty-one point programme for increasing the overall supply of milk to the country had been adopted. It dealt with the problem of procurement, processing, transport and sale of milk. Thus, India was undergoing the process of social change on the eve of independence.

The inauguration of provincial autonomy under the Act of 1935 was a turning point of the deepest significance. For the first time the provinces were now supposed to be independent units in charge of well defined functions. It aroused high hopes and aspirations among the Indian people. There was a stirring particularly in the education field with the formation of Congress ministries in seven provinces. Under the inspiration of Gandhiji they accepted the programme of basic education. Even in Bengal a process of social change of deep significance began. For generations the Hindu middle class kept its finger in every social, cultural and political pie of the province. But now with the inauguration of the provincial autonomy the emerging Muslim middle class began to arrive on the political scene with vengeance. The process of unscrewing of the Hindu hold on public life by the Muslim middle class had begun. The strongholds of the Hindu middle class fell one after another to the Muslim middle class. To remove the educational backwardness of the Muslims was an important programme of the Fazlul-Huq ministry in Bengal. He did some valuable work in this respect and accelerated the rise of Muslim middle class in Bengal. Education, reduction of rural indebtedness and land reforms were the three main planks of social reconstruction under the provincial autonomy almost all over British India. Some of the provincial ministers were bold enough to introduce mother-tongue as medium of instruction in schools and colleges. This greatly speeded up the expansion of education.

In November 1938 John Sargent was appointed educational adviser of the Government of India and was asked to tackle the long deferred issue of providing India with a comprehensive and up-to-date system of public instruction. He held the office for about a decade with great distinction. He played a great part in forming India's first integrated and comprehensive plan of national education. He succeeded in keeping alive the freshness of a democratic and liberal outlook. According to him the educational system in India required overhauling from top to bottom. He wanted to employ education as an instrument of social change in India. The education caravan moved very slowly in India. He undertook to mechanize it and to direct it from a central dynamo. He undertook to break up the inertia of the Government regarding the educational policy. He made the CABE a tool for implementing his educational ideas. He was perhaps the first British educationist to conceive of a national system of education in India. The CABE prepared a scheme of national education for India under John Sargent's guidance. It was popularly known as the 'Sargent Plan'. It was the first of the Central Government's post-War development scheme to be made public in January 1944. It envisaged India's educational needs from nursery to university and beyond. It indicated in broad outline the minimum educational requirements of India and showed how long it would take to satisfy them and at what cost. One of the main planks of the Sargent Plan was to provide universal, compulsory and free education for all boys and girls between the age group of 6 and 14 in order to ensure literacy and the minimum preparation for citizenship. Secondly, provision was to be made for those who would show capacity for further study. No boys and girls were to be deprived of further education by poverty. Thirdly, provision was to be made for university education including post-graduate and research for selected students. Fourthly, the higher stages of technical education was to be organized and administered on an all India basis. With this end in view an All India Council for Technical Education was to be established. Commerce, agriculture and art-in industry were to be included in technical education. Adult education was to be provided for those who were denied adequate opportunities in their earlier years. There was a proposal to make literate all persons below the age of 40 in a period of 25 years. The concept of adult education was widened. Literacy was not the end of it but only the beginning leading to further education. The Plan involved a massive programme of training of school teachers. Over two million additional teachers would be required for a national system of education and they were to be trained. Special schools for handicapped children were to be set up. An efficient educational administrative system was to be developed to implement the Plan successfully. Provincial Governments were to resume all educational powers from local bodies because they proved inefficient beyond doubt. At all stages of education the training of mind as well as training of character had been emphasized in the Plan.

The scheme was to cost, when in full operation about Rs 313 crores per annum. The Plan was to be completed in 40 years. The Bombay Plan had also covered the provision of compulsory primary and middle education for all as well as the liquidation of illiteracy. This was the cry of the hour. John Sargent thought that this should be done in the world's interests as well as in India's at an early date. He even suggested that India should take loans to implement the Plan. If money could be raised in war-time in any quantity, the same should be done in peace time for a nobler cause. The Plan had a wide favourable reaction all over India. All shades of public opinion were ready to cooperate in this task. India could not afford to wait indefinitely for its solution. There could be no half-way house between what was and what ought to be done. The period of War was just the time when such measures ought to receive the most serious attention. British practical interests and their history demanded that they should do all in their power to help India in implementing the Sargent Plan. There was even stirring of spirit in the Imperial secretariat in New Delhi. The colonial bureaucrats began to look at the problem in a sympathetic way. Education and public health ultimately were remunerative and tended to react beneficially on the economic stamina and productivity of the country.

The reorganization of the Delhi University during the War was an important event in the history of education in India. John Sargent piloted an amendment to the Delhi University Act in 1943 in the Central legislature and the three-year degree course was launched which later became the general pattern for the whole of India. Consequently, the higher secondary education was also reorganized. The reorganization of the Delhi University acquired an all India significance. Sir Maurice Gwyer, the Vice-Chancellor of the Delhi University, contemplated to make Delhi an all India centre for culture and learning and a main link between India and the outside world. To implement this ideal first rate post-graduate departments in Arts and Science in the Delhi University were created. Consequently, good students from all over India began to be attracted to Delhi for study and research.

During the Second World War the enthusiasm for English education for boys was immense so much so that the demand was greatly in excess of supply. The rush for government jobs was even more pronounced than before and the university graduates and even matriculates had very little difficulty in finding suitable jobs. The educated unemployed had practically vanished on account of opportunities for employment in the

War. The War gave impetus to the establishment of new colleges and schools all over the country. The caravan of education was on the move in India. It picked up speed quickly. The demand for science teaching and technical education increased considerably during the War.

During the War the British Government in India came round to realize that the indigenous crafts and artistic skills should be preserved and encouraged. Steps were taken to implement it. This coincided with the demands of the nationalists who were demanding the revival of cottage industries all over the country. This change in outlook of the Government was really interesting and fruitful.

Emergence of the Art-in-industry into a viable position during the War proved a blessing in disguise for the country. It had its impact on industrial design in India. Advertising agencies did commendable work in utilizing the artistic talents in the country in the preparation of layout of packages and other materials. This was followed by designing of products. The establishment of the National Institute of Design at Ahmedabad was the climax of the Art-in-industry movement in India.

Thus, the Second World War was really a great catalyst for social changes in India. It brought India at the doorstep of modernity. It put the country firmly on road to industrialisation. Exigencies of war led to the growth of unprecedented entrepreneurship as well as emergence of Indian capitalism as a powerful influence in the country's affairs. It opened up great opportunities for industrial, agricultural and scientific development in India. To meet the situation the colonial government took bold steps to create proper infrastructure. For the first time the government initiated a policy with a long term objective which was to usher in an era of great social change. Science and technical education was given top priority. This greatly revolutionised the outlook of people. So far, agriculture had been a neglected sector of Indian economy. But war necessitated adoption of a new agricultural and food policy which envisaged change in social outlook and habits. The government too had to change its old bureaucratic outlook and accepted it to be its first and foremost duty to provide adequate quantities of good and nousishing food to all people living in the country. The people were now becoming conscious of the quality of food. They new became anxious to know what they should eat and why. They now began to pay more and more attention to the science of nutrition. The application of science to agriculture bred new social outlook among tradition-bound peasantry. Genetic improvements of sugar cane, rice, wheat and maize created unprecedented prosperity in the country side. This called for a lot of social adjustments.

The War brought into prominence the necessity of an integrated road system in India. It was considered essential for social, economic and cultural development of the country. 'The Nagpur Report' marked the beginning of road planning and development on all India basis. The need for a national highway system was strongly felt during the War. It was the first post-War Recoustruction plan to be implemented. It brought social and economic changes of great importance.

The War led the government to accept that the state should assume full responsibility for safe guarding the health of the nation. It should provide as complete a health service as possible and should include within its scope the largest possible proportion of the community. The Bhore committee had drawn up a comprehensive plan to provide a complete health service in the country which envisaged far-reaching social changes. The essential aim was to ensure fair distribution of medical benefits to all irrespective of their ability to pay. It was, indeed, a noble idea. Thus, at the end of War, India found itself in the midst of new modern ideas concerning important aspects of national life.

Notes

1. C.N. Vakil, *Poverty and Planning*, Allied, New Delhi, p. 51.
2. Ibid.
3. Najma Heptullah, *India's Progress in Science and Technology*, Oxford, New Delhi, 1986, p. 20.
4. *Progs. Council of States*, 31 March 1942, p. 515.
5. Ibid., 28 September 1942, p. 196.
6. *Indian Information*, 1 September 1941, p. 193.
7. Ibid., 15 January 1943, p. 79.

8. Levkovsky, *Capitalism in India,* Delhi, 1972, p. 333.
9. Ibid.
10. Ibid., p. 355.
11. Ibid., p. 362.
12. Ghanshyam Shah (ed.), *Capitalistic Development in India,* Bombay, 1990, p. 85.
13. D.G. Tendulkar, *Biography of M.K. Gandhi,* Vol. VII, p. 5.
14. Rusi J. Daruwala, *The Bombay Chamber of Commerce,* Bombay, 1986, p. 117.
15. Ram Niwas Jaju, *G.D. Birla,* Vikas, 1985, p. 130.
16. *Indian Information,* 15 September 1945, p. 253.
17. Ibid., 1 November 1945, p. 495.
18. Ibid., 15 December 1945, p. 670.
19. Ibid., 15 June 1943, p. 470.

Bibliography

1. Proceedings of Central Legislatures
   (i) Central Legislative Assembly (1940–46).
   (ii) Council of State (1940–46).

2. Reports of Commissions and Committees
   (i) Abridged Report of Royal Commission on Agriculture 1926–28.
   (ii) Report of the Indian Road Development Committee 1927–28.
   (iii) Health Survey and Development Committee, 1946.
   (iv) Land Revenue Commission of Bengal, 1944.
   (v) Report on Post-War Educational Development, 1944.
   (vi) Report on Vocational Education in India, 1937.
   (vii) Progress of India: Decennial Review, 1947.
   (viii) Report of the Technical Education Committee, 1946.
   (ix) Report of the Agricultural Education Committee, 1944.
   (x) Report on the Measures of Rehabilitation and Reconstruction by Government of India in the Naga Hills and Manipur State in 1944–45.
   (xi) Planning for the Future of Bombay's Countryside, 1945.

3. Journals and Magazines
   Asiatic Review 1939–50
   Bombay Chronicle Weekly 1940–46
   Commerce, 1940–48
   Capital 1940–45
   Indian Information 1940–50
   Indian Farming 1940–47

Indian Economic and Social Review
Indian Association of Social Science Institutions Quarterly
Indian Social Reformer 1936–46
Indian Economic Journal 1926–27
Indian Annual Register 1940–46
Sunday Times of India
Seminar

4. SECONDARY BOOKS

Acharya, K.T., *The Food Industries of British India*, Oxford, Delhi, 1994.

Ali, Hashim Ameer, *The Environs of Tagore*, Indian Statistical Institute, Calcutta, 1960.

Ambedkar, B.R., *Writings and Speeches*, Vols. I to X, Government of Maharashtra, Bombay, 1990.

ASOSO, YUNUO, *The Rising Nagas*, Delhi, 1974.

Atal, Yogesh, *Daulat Darbar*, New Delhi, 1980.

Bagchi, A.K., *Private Investment in India (1900–1939)*, Cambridge, 1972.

Bardoloi, Gopinath, *A Fateful Hour in Discovery of Assam*, Gauhati, 1954.

Bedi, B.P.L., *Harvest from Desert*, Lahore, 1940.

Begum, Jahanara, *The Last Decade of Undivided Bengal*, Minerva, Calcutta, 1944.

Bhattacharjea, J.B., *Cachar under British in N.E. India*, Delhi, 1977.

Bose, M.L., *A Social History of Assam*, New Delhi, Concept, 1989.

Briggs, A., *Social History of England*, London, 1983.

Chandra, Bipan, *The Epic Struggle*, Orient Longman, 1992.

Chatterjee, Suhas, *Making of Mizoram*, Delhi, 1994.

Chattopadhyaya, Kamala Devi, *Inner Recesses Outer Spaces*, Memoirs, Delhi, 1987.

Clow, A., *The Future Government of Assam—Tribal People*, Shillong, 1945.

Cohen, P. Stephen, *The Indian Army*, Oxford, Delhi, 1992.

Constantine, R., *Manipur, Maid of the Mountains*, New Delhi, 1981.

Dalal, Sir A., *Memoirs*, Bombay, 1980.

Das, D.P., *The Untouchable Story*, Allied, New Delhi, 1985.

Dena, Lal, ed., *History of Modern Manipur*, New Delhi, 1991.
Dutta, B.C., *Mutiny of the Innocents*, Bombay, 1971.
Elwin, Verrier, *The Tribal World of Verrier Elwin*, Oxford, 1964.
——, *Nagaland*, Shillong, 1961.
——, *The Philosophy of NEFA*, Shillong, 1957.
Fisher, Louis, *A Week with Gandhi*, Bombay, 1944.
Fisher, B. Fred, *India's Silent Revolution*, New York, Macmillan, 1919.
Gandhi, Raj Mohan, *Patel—A Life*, Ahmedabad, 1990.
Gary, R. Hess, *Sam Higgonbottom of Allahabad*, Virginia, 1987.
George, T.J.S., *Pothan Joseph's India*, Sanchar, New Delhi, 1992.
Gore, M.S., *Ambedkar's Social and Political Thought*, New Delhi, 1993.
Guha, A., *Planter's Raj to Swaraj*, ICHR, New Delhi.
Hena, Abu, *Reactions and Reconcilement*, Dacca, 1969.
Heptullah, Najma, *India's Progress in Science and Technology*, Oxford, New Delhi, 1986.
Hopkins, Harry, *The New Outlook*, London, 1963.
Howard, Jane, *Margaret Mead—A Life*, Harwell Press, UK, 1983.
Howkes, J.G., ed., *Conservation and Agriculture*, UK, 1978.
Jaipal, Rakhi, *Memoirs of a Half Life*, Allied, 1985.
Jaju, Ram Niwas, *G.D. Birla*, Vikas, Delhi, 1985.
Jamila, Brijbhusan, *Kamala Devi Chattopadhyay*, New Delhi, 1976.
Kabir, Humayun, *Progress of Education in India (1947–52)*, Government of India Publication, Delhi.
Kadam, K.N. ed., *Dr B.R. Ambedkar, The Emancipator*, Popular, Bombay, 1993.
Kaul, T.N., *Remembrances*, New Delhi, 1982.
Khan, Tamizuddin, *The Test of Time*, Dacca, 1989.
Knight, Sir Henry, *Food Administration in India*, Stanford, California, 1954.
Kripalani, M.K., *A Pot-Pourri*, Oxford, 1970.
Kuber, W.N., *Ambedkar, A Critical Study*, PPH, New Delhi, 1991.
Kulkarni, V.B., *M.R. Jayakar*, Publication Division, 1976.
Kumar, Deepak, ed., *Science and Empire*, Delhi, NISTADS, 1991.
——, *Science and the Raj*, Oxford, Delhi, 1995.

Kuppuswamy, *Communication and Social Development in India*, Sterling, Delhi, 1976.

Lahiri, Pradip Kumar, *Bengali Muslim Thought (1918–1947)*, Bagchi, Calcutta, 1981.

Levkovsky (A.I.), *Capitalism in India*, Delhi, 1972 (reprinted).

Maitra, Kiran Shankar, *Nagaland, The Darling of the North-East*, New Delhi, 1991.

Mankekar, D.R., *On the Sleepy Slope in Nagaland*, Bombay, 1967.

Mann, Harold, *Land and Labour in a Deccan Village*, 1917.

——, *Village Betterment in New India and Pakistan*, Bombay, 1948.

Markot, Ramunny, *The World of Nagas*, New Delhi, 1988.

Masani, Zareer, *Indian Tales of the Raj*, Bombay, 1985.

Mason, Philip, *A Matter of Honour*, London, 1974.

Mead, Margaret, *Blackberry Winter*, New York, 1972.

Medhi, Bishnu Ram, *Towards a Welfare State*, Shillong, 1969.

Misra, B.B., *Middle Class*, Oxford, 1961.

Mitra, Asok, *Towards Independence, 1940–47*, Popular, Bombay, 1991.

——, *The New India 1948–55*, Popular, Bombay, 1992.

Mukherjee, Sushil, *The Story of the Calcutta Theatre*, Calcutta, 1982.

Nanda, B.R., *In Gandhi's Footsteps*, Oxford, 1990.

Pant, G.B., *Speeches and Statements*, New Delhi, Radiant Publisher, 1940.

Parthasarathy, Rangaswami, *Journalism in India*, Sterling, Delhi, 1989.

Prasad, R.N., *Government and Politics in Mizoram*, New Delhi, 1987.

Rajshekhariah, A.M., *B.R. Ambedkar, The Quest for Justice*, New Delhi, 1989.

Randhawa, M.S., *A History of Indian Agriculture in India*, Vols. I to IV, ICAR, New Delhi, 1983.

Rawntree, John, *Memoirs of a Forest Officer*, UK, 1981.

Ray, Rajak K., *Entrepreneurship and Industry in India 1800–1947*, Oxford, Delhi, 1992.

Ray, Renuka, *My Remembrances*, Allied, 1982.

Reid, Robert, *History of the Frontier Areas Bordering of Assam*, Shillong, 1942.

——, *Years of Change in Bengal and Assam*, London, 1966.

Roebuck, Janet, *The Making of Modern English Society*, London, 1973.

Royale, Trevor, *The Last Days of the Raj*, London, 1989.

Roychoudhary, Prafulla, *The North-East, Roots of Insurgency*. Firma KL, Calcutta, 1986.

Roy, Jyotirmoy, *History of Manipur*, Calcutta, 1973.

Rustomji, Nari, *Enchanted Frontiers*, Oxford, 1974.

——, *Imperilled Frontiers*, Oxford, 1983.

Sahare, M.L., *Dr B.R. Ambedkar*, NCERT, New Delhi, 1987.

Sanajaoba, Naroem, *Manipur—Past and Present*, Mittal, Delhi, 1986.

Sangwan, Satpal, *Science, Technology and Colonisation*, Anamika, Delhi, 1991.

Shahnawaz, Jahan Ara, *Father and Daughter*, Lahore, 1971.

Shiva Raman, B., *Bitter Sweet, Governance in Transition*, New Delhi, 1984.

Singh, Bhawani, *Politics of Alienation in Assam*, Ajanta, New Delhi, 1984.

Singh, Jagjit Singh, *Memoirs of a Mathematician Manque*, Vikas, Delhi, 1980.

Singh, Tarlok, *Poverty and Social Change*, Oxford, 1946.

Srampickal, Jacob, *Voice to the Voiceless*, Manohar, Delhi, 1994.

Srinivas, M.N., *The Dominant Caste and Other Essays*, Oxford, 1987.

Stein, Burton, ed., *The Making of Agrarian Policy in British India 1770–1890*, Oxford, Delhi, 1992.

Subramaniam, C., *India of My Dreams*, Orient Longman, 1973.

Subramaniam, V., *The Social Background of India's Administrators*, Publications Division, New Delhi, 1970.

——, *The Managerial Class in India*, AIMA, New Delhi, 1973.

Tandon, Prakash, *Punjab Saga (1857–1987)*.

——, *Return to Punjab*, Vikas, New Delhi, 1987.

Tendulkar, D.G., *Mahatma Gandhi*, Vols. I to VIII, Publications Division, Delhi, 1980.

Thapar, Raj, *All These Years*, New Delhi, 1991.

Timberg, Thomas A., *The Marawaris: From Traders to Industrials*, Delhi, 1978.

Thomas, P.J., *Development of Industries for War Supplies*, Government of India, 1944.

Thompson, F.M., ed., *Cambridge Social History of Britain (1750 to 1950)*, Vol. II, 1990.

Tyabji, Badruddin, *Memoirs of An Egoist*, New Delhi, 1982.

Tyne Ven, H. Claude, *India in Turmoil*, Delhi, 1985, reprint.

Tyson, Geoffrey, *The Bengal Chambers of Commerce and Industry*, Calcutta, 1955.

Vakil, C.N., *Poverty and Planning*, Allied, 1963.

Wolsey, E. Roland, *Journalism in Modern India*, Asia, Bombay, 1964.

Young, G.M., *Portrait of An Age*, London, 1952.

Index

Other Books from

Pragati Publications

Imperial Retreat S.B. SINGH Rs 210

An Economic History of Modern India (2nd edn)
GIRISH MISHRA Rs 395

Communalism and Indian Politics MEENA GAUTAM Rs 230

Growth of Muslim Politics in India Y.B. MATHUR Rs 250

Indian Nationalism and the Early Congress
JOHN R. MCLANE Rs 1295

Indigo and the Raj (Peasant Protests in Bihar, 1780–1917)
PRABHAT KUMAR SHUKLA Rs 250

Karkhanas under the Mughals, from Akbar to Aurangzeb
(A Study in Economic Development)
TRIPTA VERMA Rs 245

Quit India Movement Y.B. MATHUR Rs 250

Social and Cultural Vision of India A.K. BISWAS Rs 395

Society and Culture in Rajasthan, c. AD 700–900
SHANTA RANI SHARMA Rs 425

Sociology and Economics of Casteism in India
GIRISH MISHRA & BRAJ KUMAR PANDEY Rs 595

The Art of Gupta India (Empire and Province)
JOANNA GOTTFRIED WILLIAMS Rs 1600

Tarikh-i-Akbari MOHAMMAD ARIF QANDHARI (Annotated English Translation with Introduction by TASNEEM AHMAD, Foreword by IFRAN HABIB) Rs 350

Three Basics of Sikh Religious Thought SATNAM KAUR Rs 495

Changing Perspectives of the Welfare State (The Issue of Privatization) ASHA GUPTA Rs 245

Comparative Economic Development GIRISH MISHRA Rs 295

Contemporary Political Theory K.K. MISRA Rs 250

Economic Systems (3rd edn) GIRISH MISHRA Rs 395

Federalism and Political Development (Developed and Developing Areas) P.K. SHARMA Rs 200

Foundations of Indian Polity CHITTA RANJAN ROY Rs 280

Marxism and Liberalism K.K. MISRA Rs 200

Regionalism and National Identity—Canada and India (Interdisciplinary Perspectives) M.P. SINGH & CHANDRA MOHAN Rs 245

The Politics of Bhutan (Retrospect and Prospect) PARMANAND Rs 250

Towards Purity of Morals R.K. GUPTA Rs 200

Transformations of Transcendental Philosophy R. SUNDARA RAJAN Rs 395

Understanding Vagueness AMITA CHATTERJEE Rs 295

Attention: Readers/Authors

This includes all recent titles in the field of History, Political Science and Philosophy.

We welcome your comments which will be valuable to us to improve the quality of publications.

Invitation to authors: If you are working on a manuscript now or planning to write one in near future – maybe a textbook or a monograph – we shall be glad to receive your proposal for its publication.

If you want to receive our publication information sheet regularly please send your name and address indicating your areas of interest.